THE TRIVIUM

The Liberal Arts of Logic, Grammar, and Rhetoric

T0160540

THE TRIVIUM

THE LIBERAL ARTS OF LOGIC, GRAMMAR, AND RHETORIC

UNDERSTANDING THE NATURE AND FUNCTION OF LANGUAGE

BY SISTER MIRIAM JOSEPH, C.S.C., Ph.D.

EDITED BY MARGUERITE McGLINN

PAUL DRY BOOKS
Philadelphia 2002

First Paul Dry Books Edition, 2002

Paul Dry Books, Inc.
Philadelphia, Pennsylvania
www.pauldrybooks.com

Text type: Electra
Display type: Fenice and Antique Olive
Composed by Northeastern Graphic Services, Inc.
Designed by Adrianne Onderdonk Dudden

Photograph of Sister Miriam Joseph courtesy of the Saint Mary's College Archives

15   16   17   18   19
Printed in the United States of America

Library of Congress Cataloging-in-Publication Data

Miriam Joseph, Sister, 1898–
    The trivium : the liberal arts of logic, grammar, and rhetoric :
    understanding the nature and function of language / by Sister Miriam Joseph ;
    edited by Marguerite McGlinn.
        p. cm.
    ISBN 0-9679675-0-3 (pbk. : alk. paper)
    ISBN 1-58988-013-7 (cloth : alk. paper)
    I. English language—Rhetoric. 2. English language—Grammar.
    3. Reading comprehension. 4. Language and logic. 5. Critical thinking.
    I. McGlinn, Marguerite. II. Title.

PE1408 .M568 2002
808'.042—dc21

2001058498

Contents

Editor's Introduction

"In true liberal education...the essential activity of the student is to relate the facts learned into a unified, organic whole, to assimilate them as...the rose assimilates food from the soil and increases in size, vitality, and beauty."

The Trivium: The Liberal Arts of Logic, Grammar, and Rhetoric

What is language? How does it work? What makes good language? Coleridge defined prose as "words in their best order" and poetry as "the best words in the best order." Plain but apt, his definitions provide a standard, but where can a reader and a writer find the tools to achieve this standard? My search drew me to Sister Miriam Joseph's book, *The Trivium*. I knew that the skills I had learned as a liberal arts student, taught as a high school English teacher, and use as a writer and editor derived from the medieval and Renaissance approach to grammar, logic, and rhetoric, the three "language arts" of the liberal arts known as the trivium. However, a study of the original trivium showed me that the hodgepodge of grammar rules, literary terms, and syllogistic formulas offered as "language arts" differs from the original conception of the trivium that offered tools to perfect the mind.

Sister Miriam Joseph rescued that integrated approach to unlocking the power of the mind and presented it for many years to her students at Saint Mary's College in South Bend, Indiana. She learned about the trivium from Mortimer J. Adler, who inspired her and other professors at Saint Mary's to study the trivium themselves and then to teach it to their students. In Sister Miriam Joseph's preface to the 1947 edition of *The Trivium*, she wrote, "This work owes its inception...to Professor Mortimer J. Adler of the University of Chicago, whose inspiration and instruction gave it initial impulse." She went on to acknowledge her debt to Aristotle, John Milton, and Jacques Maritain. William Shakespeare, Thomas Aquinas, and Thomas More also make frequent appearances in *The Trivium*. This is good company indeed.

The Trivium teaches us that language evolves from the very nature of being human. Because we are rational, we think; because we are social, we interact with other people; because we are corporeal, we use a physical medium. We invent symbols to express the range of practical, theoretical, and poetical experiences that make up our existence. Words allow us to leave a legacy of our experience to delight and to educate those who follow us. Because we use language, we engage in a dialogue with the past and the future.

How does *The Trivium* help us use language to engage in such a dialogue with the past and the future and to negotiate our own lives? Aristotle's theories of language and literature underlie this work. His ten categories of being provide a central focus. Words are categorized by their relationship to being and to each other. When a speaker or writer uses a word, thus assigning it a particular meaning, it becomes a term and enters the realm of logic. Aristotle's categories enable us to translate the linguistic symbol into a logical entity ready to take its place in a proposition. From propositions, the reader moves to syllogisms, enthymemes, sorites, formal fallacies, and material fallacies.

The Trivium explains that logic is the art of deduction. As thinking beings, we know something and from that knowledge can deduce new knowledge. Where does the initial knowledge come from? The section on induction answers that question as it explores the process by which we derive general principles from individual instances.

Examples from the literary canon and Shakespeare, in particular, illuminate the explanations of grammar and logic. Sister Miriam Joseph, who was also a Shakespearean scholar, actually wrote about Shakespeare as a master of the trivium. For example, he often used litotes, the figure of speech based on the obversion of a proposition. *The Tempest* shows one instance of this. Sebastian, expressing his concern over the fate of Ferdinand, the king's son, says, "I have no hope that he's undrowned." Shakespeare makes the rhetorical decision to use obversion to dramatize that Sebastian faces a reality he cannot describe in direct speech.

Rhetoric concerns the choices a speaker or writer makes from the options grammar and logic offer. Sister Miriam Joseph reviews the history of rhetoric and presents Aristotle's perspective on the means of persuasion. She includes poetics—communication through the narrative created by the author—in addition to rhetoric or direct communication. Here, the reader will find Aristotle's six elements of poetics. The section on plot is extensive and includes a detailed analysis of structure a variety of interpretations as a living language is. A dead language is more likely to be understood in exactly the same way in all times and places.

According to the mode of expression, a common language may be a system of either spoken symbols or of other signs. The spoken language is the original and fundamental system of symbols for which all other signs are merely substituted. The written language is the most important substitute and the only one ordinarily understood. Among other substitute signs are Braille, sign language, the semaphore code. Each of these substitutes merely renders into its own system of signs words of a common language.

THE NATURE OF LANGUAGE

It is the nature of language to communicate through symbols. Language is a system of symbols for expressing our thoughts, volitions, and emotions.

A word, like every other physical reality, is constituted of matter and form. A word is a symbol. Its matter is the sensible sign; its form is the meaning imposed upon it by convention. Matter and form are metaphysical concepts necessary to the philosophical understanding of any material whole, for together they constitute every such whole.[7] Matter is defined as the first intrinsic and purely potential principle of a corporeal essence; as such, it cannot actually exist without form, for it is not a body but a principle of a body, intrinsically constituting it. Form is the first intrinsic and actual principle of a corporeal essence.

ILLUSTRATION: Matter and form

In animals, the body is the matter and the soul is the form.

In water, the matter consists of hydrogen and oxygen; the form is the precise mode of their union in a molecule of water and may be expressed by the chemical formula H_2O.

The matter of words in spoken language is the sound. This aspect of language is treated in phonetics. The matter of words in written language is the mark or notation. It is treated in orthography or spelling. The form of words is their meaning, and it is treated in semantics.

Language: a system of symbols for expressing our thoughts, volitions, and emotions

Matter of Words		Science
spoken language	sound	phonetics, study of sound
written language	mark	orthography, study of spelling
Form of Words	meaning	semantics, study of meaning

2-1 *Matter and Form in Language*

Matter of Language

Voice is the sound uttered by an animal. The voice of irrational animals has meaning from nature, from the tone of the utterance. The human voice alone is symbolic, having a meaning imposed upon it by convention.

Human beings have articulate voice by which they add to their simple voice modifications that are produced by the organs of speech: tongue, palate, teeth, lips. The capacity of the articulate voice to produce such modifications in almost limitless variety makes possible the many symbols needed to communicate the wide range of human thought.

The alphabet[8] of the International Phonetic Association is a system of written symbols aiming at an accurate and uniform representation of the sounds of speech. It distinguishes twenty vowel sounds, six diphthongs, and twenty-seven consonant sounds. The English language lacks three of the vowel sounds (those present in German *grün* and *schön* and in French *seul*) and two of the consonant sounds (those present in German *ich* and Scottish *loch*).

Form of Language

The form of language is meaning. Words can symbolize both individuals and essences. In metaphysics or ontology, the science of being, one can distinguish the individual and the essence. The individual is any physical being that exists. Only the individual exists in the sense that every material being that exists or has existed is an individual, is itself and not another, and is, therefore, in its individuality unique. Every man, woman, tree, stone, or grain of sand is an individual. Bucephalus, the horse which belonged to Alexander the Great, was an individual horse.

Essence is that which makes a being what it is and without which it would not be the kind of being it is. Essence is that in an individual which makes it like others in its class,[9] whereas its individuality is that which makes it different from others in its class.

Inasmuch as every individual belongs to a class, which in turn belongs to a wider class, we distinguish these classes as species and genus.

A species is a class made up of individuals that have in common the same specific essence or nature.

ILLUSTRATION: Species and class

Man is the species or class to which William Shakespeare, Albert Einstein, Jane Austen, Queen Victoria, and every other man and woman belong because the essence or nature of man is common to all of them.

Horse is the species or class to which Bucephalus and every other horse belong because the essence or nature of horse is common to all horses.

A genus is a wider class made up of two or more different species that have in common the same generic essence or nature.

ILLUSTRATION: Genus

Animal is the genus or class to which man, rabbit, horse, oyster, and every other species of animal belong because the essence or nature of animal is the same in all of them.

Flower is the genus to which rose, violet, tulip, and every species of flower belong because the essence or nature of flower is the same in all of them.

An individual animal or flower belongs to a genus only by being a member of a species within that genus. The abstract character of genus is such that one cannot draw a picture, for example, of animal but only of a particular kind or species of animal such as a horse or a dog. Yet, even species is abstract, for one cannot photograph the species horse or dog; one can photograph only an individual horse or dog since every horse or dog that exists is an individual.

In every individual is the specific essence or class nature which it has in common with every other member of its species and also the generic essence or class nature which it has in common with every member of the genus to which its species belongs. The generic essence is merely the specific essence with the more definite characteristics of the latter omitted. In addition to the essence which makes it like other members of its species and its genus, the individual has individuating characteristics which make it different from every other individual in its species or its genus.

An aggregate or group of individuals must be clearly distinguished from a species or a genus. An aggregate is merely a particular group of individuals, such as the trees in Central Park, the inhabitants of California, the Philadelphia Orchestra, the items on a desk, the furniture in a house.

A species or a genus always signifies a class nature or essence and includes all the individuals of every place and time having that nature or essence. For example, man is a species and includes all men and women of every place and time—past, present, and future. Tree is a genus and includes every tree. On the other hand, an aggregate is a particular group of individuals that may or may not have the same essence or class nature; but in either case, the aggregate does not include all the members that have that nature.

ILLUSTRATION: Aggregate

The women of the nineteenth century constitute an aggregate of individuals belonging to the same species, but they are only a part of the species, namely, those who existed at a particular time.

The things in a room constitute an aggregate of individuals belonging to different species, such as chair, desk, table, book, heat vent, window, etc., but they are only a small part of each species.

An individual is one. An aggregate is simply a group consisting of two or more individuals.

Essence is what makes a being what it is.

Species is a class made up of individuals that have in common the same specific essence.

Genus is a wider class made up of two or more different species.

Aggregate is a group consisting of two or more individuals.

2-2 *Essence Terms*

Language and Its Symbols

Language employs four important kinds of symbols to represent reality: two to symbolize the individual, two to symbolize the essence which is common to all the individual members of a class.

Language can symbolize an individual or an aggregate by either a proper name or a particular or empirical description. A particular or empirical description is a common name to which is joined a definitive which limits its application to a particular individual or group. Empirical means founded on experience. Since only individuals exist, our experience is directly concerned with them. Throughout this book the word *empirical* is used with reference to our knowledge of individuals as such.

ILLUSTRATION: Language used to symbolize empirical information

A proper name, such as Eleanor Roosevelt, the Mississippi River, Halloween, London, the United States Senate, the Rotarians, the Mediterranean Sea, can symbolize the individual or an aggregate.

A particular or empirical description, such as the present store manager, this computer, the woman who made the flag, the furniture in this house, the microbe now dividing in the petri dish, can symbolize the individual or an aggregate.

If language could not symbolize the individual, one could not designate particular persons, places, or times. This would be extremely inconvenient. For example, people could not direct emergency vehicles to their houses.

On the other hand, if language could symbolize only the individual, people would be in a worse plight. Every word would be a proper name, and it would therefore be necessary to give a different proper name to every object spoken of—not only to people and places but to everything—to every tree, blade of grass, chair, fork, potato, coat, shoe, pencil, etc.

No one would understand except those who had shared through simultaneous sense experience acquaintance with the identical individual objects described. Hence, the language of every town, even of every home, would be different and would be unintelligible to outsiders. The reader may have had a similar experience when three or four friends were reminiscing about an earlier time not known to the reader. The outsider would take little or no interest in the conversation because even though the words could be understood, the proper names of the absentees sprinkled plentifully through the conversation would have no meaning. But if every word were a proper name, unless the listener had personal experience of the very objects being spoken of, he would be not only bored but completely baffled by the conversation.

Words, being all proper names, would become meaningless at the time of the destruction of the objects they symbolized. They could not even be explained the way proper names are now explained by means of common names (for example, William Caxton, 1422?–1491, first

English printer; translator), for there would be no common names. Therefore, there could be no history, no literature. What authors wrote would be as dead as their voices in their graves.

General or universal ideas could not be expressed in language. Therefore, there could be no books on science or philosophy.

Language can symbolize essence by either of two kinds of symbols, both of which are applicable to all the members of a class. A common name, such as child, tree, chair, square, hour, can symbolize essence. Most of the words listed in the dictionary are common names. Obviously, then, the bulk of language is made up of common names; they symbolize either species or genus.[10] For example, *jump* names a species of movement; whereas *move* means the genus of jump, fly, creep, walk.

A general or universal description such as a rational animal, an equilateral triangle, an organ of sight can symbolize essence. The definitions given in the dictionary are general descriptions of the single-word entries. They clarify the meanings of the common names. A general description is itself made up wholly of common names.

Words that represent no reality are not symbols; they are only empty words devoid of meaning. A proper name or an empirical description must symbolize an individual or an aggregate existing in fact (past or present) or in fiction (wherein are characters, places, etc. created by the imagination). Otherwise, it is devoid of meaning, as are the present King of France or the Emperor of Iowa. The following, however, are truly symbols: Hamlet, Sidney Carton, Rapunzel, Nathan Hale, Queen Elizabeth I. So also are all the symbols given above as examples of an individual or an aggregate.

A common name or a general description must represent an essence or class nature which is intrinsically possible although it need not actually exist. Otherwise, it is devoid of meaning as are a square circle or a triangular square. The following, however, are truly symbols because they express something conceivable: a mermaid, a purple cow, an inhabitant of another planet, a regular polygon with one hundred sides, an elephant, a rose. So also are the symbols given above as examples of the essence, or class nature, of either a species or a genus.

Language that symbolizes an individual or aggregate

proper name

particular or empirical description

Language that symbolizes essence

common name

general or universal description

2-3 *Four Kinds of Language Symbols*

Creating Symbols from Reality

Words are symbols of ideas about reality. How does one derive ideas from reality and how does one classify them? Generating a universal idea or concept involves several steps, a process more fully treated in the study of psychology.

GENERATION OF A CONCEPT

First the external senses—sight, hearing, touch, smell, taste—operate on an object present before us and produce a percept. The internal senses, primarily the imagination, produce a phantasm or mental image of the individual object perceived, and this phantasm is retained and can be reproduced at will in the absence of the object.

ILLUSTRATION: Percept and phantasm

A **percept** is like a portrait being painted by the artist while she looks at the model.

A **phantasm** is like that same portrait possessed and looked at whenever one wishes for years afterward although the person painted is absent or even dead.

There are four internal senses: the imagination, the sensuous memory, the common or central or synthesizing sense, and instinct.

The intellect through abstraction produces the concept. The imagination is the meeting ground between the senses and the intellect. From the phantasms in the imagination, the intellect abstracts that which is common and necessary to all the phantasms of similar objects (for example, trees or chairs); this is the essence (that which makes a tree a tree or that which makes a chair a chair). The intellectual apprehension of this essence is the general or universal concept (of a tree or a chair).

A general concept is a universal idea existing only in the mind but having its foundation outside the mind in the essence which exists in the individual and makes it the kind of thing it is. Therefore, a concept is not arbitrary although the word is. Truth has an objective norm in the real.

Percept: the image created by the external senses upon encountering reality

Phantasm: the mental image created by the internal sense, primarily the imagination

Concept: the abstraction created by the intellect through recognition of the essence

2-4 *Generating a Concept*

A general concept is universal because it is the knowledge of the essence present equally in every member of the class, regardless of time, place, or individual differences. For example, the concept "chair" is the knowledge of the essence "chair," which must be in every chair at all times and in all places, regardless of size, weight, color, material, and other individual differences.

The real object (a tree or a chair) and likewise the corresponding percept and phantasm, is individual, material, limited to a particular place and time; the concept is universal, immaterial, not limited to a particular place and time.

Only human beings have the power of intellectual abstraction;[11] therefore, only human beings can form a general or universal concept. Irrational animals have the external and internal senses, which are sometimes keener than those of humans. But because they lack the rational powers (intellect, intellectual memory, and free will), they are incapable of progress or of culture. Despite their remarkable instinct, their productions, intricate though they may be, remain the same through the centuries, for example: beaver dams, bird nests, anthills, beehives.

ANALOGY: intellectual abstraction

Flowers contain honey. Butterflies, ants, bees, mosquitoes, and other insects may light upon the flower, but only bees can abstract the honey, for only bees have the power to do so. As the bee abstracts honey from the flowers and ignores everything else in them, so the intellect abstracts from the phantasms of similar objects the essence of that which is common and necessary to them and ignores everything else, namely, the individual differences.

There is nothing in the intellect that was not first in the senses except the intellect itself. Human intellectual powers need material to work upon. This comes from nature through the senses. Nature provides the materials, and the human intellect conceives and constructs works of civilization which harness nature and increase its value and its services to the human race.

ANALOGY: Raw material for intellect

There is nothing in fine cotton, lace, organdy, or heavy muslin that was not in the raw cotton from which they were made. To produce these, the manufacturer requires raw material obtained from nature by cotton planters. Likewise, the intellect requires for thought the raw material obtained from nature through the senses.

Abstract, or intellectual, knowledge is clearer although less vivid than concrete or sense knowledge. For example, circles and squares of various sizes and colors can be perceived by the senses and can, consequently, be perceived by a pony as well as by a man. A pony in a circus act might be trained to respond in various ways to colored disks and squares.

Only a human being, however, can derive from these various circles and squares the definition of a circle and of a square. A person can also know by abstraction the properties of these figures, such as the relation of the circumferences of a circle to its radius, which he expresses in the abstract formula $C = 2\pi R$. Such abstract knowledge is clearer although it is less vivid than the sense apprehension of the colored figures, which the pony can share with a human being.

Thomas More,[12] in his defense of the uses of statues and pictures, contrasts them with words as a means of instruction.[13] He points out that words are symbols of phantasms and concepts, as has been explained above:

> Images are necessary books for the uneducated and good books for the learned, too. For all words be but images representing the things that the writer or speaker conceives in his mind, just as the figure of the thing framed with imagination, and so conceived in the mind, is but an image representing the very thing itself that a man thinks of.
>
> As for example, if I tell you a tale of my good friend, the imagination that I have of him in my mind is not himself but an image that represents him. And when I name him, his name is neither himself nor yet the figure of him in my imagination, but only an image representing to you the imagination of my mind. If I be too far from you to tell it to you, then is the writing not the name itself but an image representing the

name. And yet all these names spoken, and all these words written, be no natural signs or images but only made by consent and agreement of men, to betoken and signify such thing, whereas images painted, graven, or carved, may be so well wrought, and so near to the quick and the truth that they shall naturally, and much more effectually represent the thing than shall the name either spoken or written. For he that never heard the name of my friend, shall if ever he saw him be brought in a rightful remembrance of him by his image.

—The Confutation of Tyndale's Answers[14]

TEN CATEGORIES OF BEING

Once the human intellect creates symbols from reality, those symbols or words can be manipulated and catalogued to increase our understanding of reality. Aristotle's ten categories of being classify words in relationship to our knowledge of being. These metaphysical categories have their exact counterpart in the ten categories or *praedicamenta*[15] of logic, which classify our concepts, our knowledge of being.

Every being exists either in itself or in another. If it exists in itself, it is a substance. If it exists in another, it is an accident. We distinguish nine categories of accident; these, with substance, constitute the ten categories of being.

1   Substance is that which exists in itself, for example, man.

2   Quantity is a determination of the matter of substance, giving it parts distinct from parts, for example, tall.

3   Quality is a determination of the nature or form of a substance, for example: dark, handsome, intelligent, athletic, chivalrous.

4   Relation is the reference which a substance or accident bears to another, for example: friend, near.

5   Action is the exercise of the faculties or power of a substance so as to produce an effect in something else or in itself, for example: clicking a camera, standing up, smiling.

6   Passion is the reception by a substance of an effect produced by some agent, for example: being invited to return, being drafted.

7   *When* is position in relation to the course of extrinsic events which measure the duration of a substance, for example, Sunday afternoon.

8   *Where* is position in relation to bodies which surround a substance and measure and determine its place, for example: on a bench, beside the lake.

9   Posture is the relative position which the parts of a substance have toward each other, for example: sitting, leaning forward.

10   Habiliment consists of clothing, ornaments, or weapons with which human beings by their art complement their nature in order to conserve their own being or that of the community (the other self), for example, in gray tweeds.

The categories can be organized into three subcategories by what they predicate[16] about the subject.

1   The predicate is the subject itself. If the predicate is that which is the subject itself and does not exist in the subject, the predicate is a substance. (Suzanne is a human being.)

2   The predicate exists in the subject. If the predicate exists in the subject absolutely as flowing from matter, the predicate is a quantity. (Suzanne is tall.) If the predicate exists in the subject absolutely as flowing from form, the predicate is a quality. (Suzanne is intelligent.) If the predicate exists in the subject relatively with respect to another, the predicate is in the category relation. (Suzanne is Mary's daughter.)

3   The predicate exists in something extrinsic to the subject. If the predicate exists in something extrinsic to the subject and is partially extrinsic as a principle of action in the subject, the predicate is an action. (Suzanne analyzed the data.) If the predicate exists in something extrinsic to the subject and is a terminus of action in the subject, the predicate is a passion. (Suzanne was injured.) If the predicate exists in something extrinsic to the subject and is wholly extrinsic as a measure of the subject according to time, the predicate is in the category *when*. (Suzanne was late.) If the predicate exists in something extrinsic to the subject and is wholly extrinsic as a measure of the subject according to place, the predicate is in the category *where*. (Suzanne is here.) If the predicate exists in something extrinsic to the subject and is wholly extrinsic as a measure of the subject according to the order of parts, the predicate is in the category posture. (Suzanne is standing.) If the predicate exists in something extrinsic to the subject and is merely adjacent

to the subject, the predicate is in the category habiliment. (Suzanne is in evening dress.)

LANGUAGE AND REALITY

Seven important definitions emerge from a consideration of language and reality.

1   The essence is that which makes a being what it is and without which it would not be the kind of being it is.

2   Nature is essence viewed as the source of activity.

3   The individual is constituted of essence existent in quantified matter plus other accidents. Essence is that which makes the individual like other members of its class. Quantified matter is that which makes the individual different from other individuals in its class because matter, extended by reason of its quantity, must be this or that matter, which by limiting the form individuates it. Accidents are those notes (shapes, color, weight, size, etc.) by which we perceive the difference between the individuals of a class. The individuals within a species (for example, all human beings) are essentially the same. But they are not merely accidentally different; they are individually different. Even if individuals were as alike as the matches in a box of matches or the pins in a paper of pins, they would be nonetheless individually different because the matter in one is not the matter in the other but is a different quantity or part even though of the same kind and amount.

4   A percept is the sense-apprehension of an individual reality (in its presence).

5   A phantasm is the mental image of an individual reality (in its absence).

6   A general concept is the intellectual apprehension of essence.

7   An empirical concept is the indirect intellectual apprehension of an individual. The intellect can know individual objects only indirectly in the phantasms because individuals are material, with one exception, the intellect itself; because it is a spiritual individual, the intellect can know itself directly and reflexively. (See Saint Thomas Aquinas, *Summa Theologica*, Part I, Question 86, Articles 1 and 3.)[17]

In a natural object the following are similar but distinct: substance, essence, nature, form, species. The knowledge of these is the concept, which is expressed fully in the definition and symbolized by the common name.

Since man cannot create substance but can merely fashion substances that are furnished by nature, an artificial object such as a chair has two essences: the essence of its matter (wood, iron, marble, etc.) and the essence of its form (chair). The essence of the form is expressed in the definition (of chair).

Frequently, a common name symbolizes a concept that is not simple nor equivalent to the essence of the natural species, like human being, but is a composite, like lawyer or athlete, including in its definition certain accidents which determine not natural species but classes that differ only accidentally. A composite concept may be called a construct.

Lawyer and athlete are constructs, for their definition adds to the simple concept human being certain accidents such as knowledge of law or physical agility, which are essential to the definition of lawyer or of athlete although not essential to the definition of a construct. For example, a particular lawyer may be tall, blond, irritable, generous, etc., but these accidents are not more essential to being a lawyer than they are to being a human being.

A construct may be analyzed into its components by showing in what categories its essential meanings lie.

ILLUSTRATION: Analysis of constructs

Carpenter

Substance—human being

Quality—skill in building with wood

Legislator

Substance—human being

Action—making laws

Relation—to an electorate

Blizzard

Substance—water

Quality—cold

Passion—vaporized, frozen into snow, blown about by a high wind

In the English language a construct is usually symbolized by a single word which does not make explicit the composite character of the construct. In an agglutinated language like German, a construct is more commonly symbolized by a compound word which does make explicit its composite character, for example, *Abwehrflammenwerfer* (defensive flame-thrower). Also, the English word *tank* in German is *Raupenschlepperpanzerkampfwagen* (a caterpillarlike, self-moving, armored war wagon). This has been shortened to *panzer*, a term familiar through films and books.

Logical and Psychological Dimensions of Language

Language has logical and psychological meanings which may be illustrated through a closer look at the words *house* and *home*.

If *house* is represented as <u>a b</u>, then *home* may be represented as <u>a b x</u>. Objectively, the definition (the logical dimension) of *house* and *home* are similar and may be represented by the lines ab; but subjectively, *home* is a much richer word, for to its logical content is added an emotional content (the psychological dimension) associated with the word and represented by the line bx. The fact that *house* has practically no psychological dimension while *home* has much accounts for the different effects produced by the following lines, which are equivalent in the logical dimensions.

ILLUSTRATION: Psychological dimension of language

House, house, loved, loved house!
There's no place like my house! There's no place like my house!

"Home, Home, sweet, sweet Home!
There's no place like Home! There's no place like Home!"
   —John Howard Payne, "Clari, the Maid of Milan"

LOGICAL DIMENSIONS OF LANGUAGE

The logical or intellectual dimension of a word is its thought content, which may be expressed in its definition, given in the dictionary. In rhetoric this is called the denotation of the word.

ANALOGY: Logical and psychological dimensions of language

The logical dimension of language may be compared to the incandescent electrified wire in a transparent bulb; the wire is obvious and its limits are clearly defined. The psychological dimension may be compared to a frosted bulb, in which all the light, it is true, comes from the incandescent wire within, but the light is softened and diffused by the bulb, which gives it a more beautiful and psychologically warmer glow.

Language with a purely logical dimension is desirable in legal documents and in scientific and philosophical treatises, where clarity, precision, and singleness of meaning are requisite. Consequently, synonyms, which usually vary in shades of meaning, ought to be avoided, and the same word should be employed throughout to convey the same meaning; or if it is used with a different meaning, that fact should be made clear. Abstract words are usually clearer and more precise than concrete words, for abstract knowledge is clearer, although less vivid, than sense knowledge. Yet to communicate abstract knowledge, one should employ concrete illustrations from which the reader or listener can make the abstraction for himself since by so doing he grasps the abstract ideas much better than if the writer or speaker gave them to him ready-made.

PSYCHOLOGICAL DIMENSIONS OF LANGUAGE

The psychological dimension of language is in its emotional content—the related images, nuances, and emotion spontaneously associated with words. In rhetoric this is called the connotation of the word. Propagandists often abuse the connotative value of words.

Language with a rich psychological dimension is desirable in poetry and other literature, where humor, pathos, grandeur, and sublimity are communicated.

In literary composition, one should employ words that are concrete rather than abstract, that are rich in imagery and idiomatic. Synonyms should be used in order to avoid monotony of sound and to convey subtle shades of meaning that vary in both the logical and the psychological dimension.

A sensitive awareness of the subtleties of language, particularly in its psychological dimension, enables one to recognize good style in the speech and writing of others and to cultivate good style in one's own composition, both oral and written.

The substance of a given composition may be translated almost perfectly from one language to another in the logical dimension. Translation is seldom satisfactory, however, in the psychological dimension.

That is why poetry in translation is usually less pleasing than in the original.

Sound and the Psychological Dimension
Various characteristics of words affect the psychological dimension of language.

The mere sound of a word may produce a pleasing effect which another word of the same meaning lacks. In "Silver" by Walter de la Mare, the poet's substitution of words like *shoon* for *shoes* and *casements* for *windows* are examples of the poet's use of sound to create a psychological effect.

ILLUSTRATION: The psychological value of sound

SILVER

Slowly, silently, now the moon
Walks the night in her silver shoon;
This way, and that, she peers, and sees
Silver fruit upon silver trees;
One by one the casements catch
Her beams beneath the silvery thatch;
Couched in his kennel, like a log,
With paws of silver sleeps the dog;
From their shadowy cote the white breasts peep
Of doves in a silver-feathered sleep;
A harvest mouse goes scampering by,
With silver claws and a silver eye;
And moveless fish in the water gleam,
By silver reeds in a silver stream.
                                        —Walter de la Mare

Pedantic Style
A pedantic or pompous style is psychologically displeasing. Compare these sentence pairs, identical in logical meaning.

ILLUSTRATION: Pedantic style

Behold! The inhabitants have all retired to their domiciles.
Look! The people have all gone home.

The vaulted dome of heaven is cerulean.
The sky is blue.

Idiom and Emotional Effect

The emotional effect of a word, often a by-product of its historical development, belongs to the idiom of language and would often be lost in translation. The following examples show that sentences alike in logical dimension can be quite different in psychological dimension.

ILLUSTRATION: Idiom

A young man tells a young woman, "Time stands still when I look into your eyes."

Another tells her, "You have a face that would stop a clock."

A young man tells a woman, "You are a vision." Another, "You are a sight."

At a meeting of the United Nations, an American produced bewilderment among the translators by speaking of a proposal as a "pork barrel floating on a pink cloud." A fellow American might understand this as "an impractical plan to be financed by public funds designed to gain local political patronage."

Ms. Smith and Ms. Baker had dinner together. Asked by Mr. Schofield, "What kind of meat did you have for dinner?" Ms. Smith replied, "I had roast pork." Ms. Baker replied, "I had roast swine meat."

We find Ms. Baker's answer revolting because *swine* has been regarded as a word unfit for polite discourse in English, certainly unfit to name meat, ever since the Norman Conquest in 1066. After that, the conquered and deposed Anglo-Saxons tended the live animal and called it *swine*, but the aristocratic Normans to whom it was served at the banquet table called it *pork*, a word derived from the Latin through the French, and in those languages applied to the live animal as well as to the meat. The associations built into the word *swine* in the history of the language are felt by modern English-speaking people who do not even know the occasion of the emotional response which they, nonetheless, experience.

Allusion

An allusion is a passing reference to phrases or longer passages which the writer takes for granted will be familiar to the reader. Sometimes the writer changes the phrases somewhat, but whether the same or modified, they depend for their effect on reminding the reader of the original; for instance, *With Malice Toward Some* is a title deliberately intended to remind the reader of the phrase in Lincoln's Second Inaugural Address, "with malice toward none."

An allusion depends for much of its effect on the psychological dimension of language, for it enriches the passage in which it occurs with emotional overtones and associated ideas derived from the context in which it originally appeared. The following examples show the importance of allusion.

ILLUSTRATION: Allusion

Most of the paper is as blank as Modred's shield.
—Rudyard Kipling, "The Man Who Would Be King"

Bores make cowards of us all.
—E. V. Lucas, "Bores"

Friend, on this scaffold Thomas More lies dead
Who would not cut the Body from the Head.
—J. V. Cunningham, "Friends, on this scaffold . . ."

For those whose literary background is inadequate and who therefore are unfamiliar with the source of the allusion, a work such as the concordance to the Bible or to Shakespeare, both frequent sources of allusion, will prove helpful. A dictionary of people and places mentioned in Greek and Latin literature will explain classical allusions.

The writers who make allusions expect, of course, that their readers will be familiar at first hand with the literature to which they refer. One of the rewards of literary study is the possession of a heritage of poetry and story which causes many names and phrases to echo with rich reverberations down the centuries. The language of allusion often provides a sort of shorthand which links and communicates in a few words experiences shared by people facing similar situations in all periods of human history.

Combination of Words

The psychological dimension of words is especially affected by their combinations.

Some combinations, particularly of adjectives and nouns and of nouns and verbs, are "just right," for example, the following combinations in Milton: "dappled dawn," "checkered shade," "leaden-stepping hours," "disproportioned sin jarred against nature's chime." It is fitting to speak of azure light or the azure sky or an azure evening gown, but not of an azure apron because *azure* and *apron* clash in the psychological dimension. The combination is disharmonious. It is certainly not "just right."

Certain combinations of words and thoughts produce a vivid con-
centration of meaning rich in the psychological dimension.

ILLUSTRATION: Combination of words

I have stained the image of God in my soul.
— Catherine of Siena, *Dialogue*

What passing bells for those who die as cattle?
Only the monstrous anger of the guns.
Only the stuttering rifles' rapid rattle
Can patter out their hasty orisons.
— Wilfred Owens, "Anthem for Doomed Youth"

. . . inland among stones
The surface of a slate-grey lake is lit
By the earthed lightning of a flock of swans,
Their feathers roughed and ruffling, white on white,
Their fully grown headstrong-looking head
Tucked or cresting or busy underwater.
— Seamus Heaney, "Postscript" to *The Spirit Level*

The flesh-smell of hatred.
— Eavan Boland, "The Death of Reason"

Logical and Poetic Understanding
What is false when taken literally in the purely logical dimension
may be true when understood imaginatively or figuratively in the psychological dimension.

ILLUSTRATION: Poetic use of language

Song

Go and catch a falling star,
  Get with child a mandrake root,
Tell me where all past years are,
  Or who cleft the devil's foot,
Teach me to hear mermaids singing,
  Or to keep off envy's stinging,
        And find
        What wind
Serves to advance an honest mind.

If thou be borne to strange sights,
  Things invisible to see
Ride ten thousand days and nights,

Till age snow white hairs on thee,
Thou, when thou return'st wilt tell me
  All strange wonders that befell thee,
        And swear
        Nowhere
Lives a woman true, and fair.

If thou findst one, let me know,
  Such a pilgrimage were sweet—
Yet do not, I would not go,
  Though at next door we might meet;
Though she were true, when you met her,
  And last, till you write your letter,
        Yet she
        Will be
False, ere I come, to two, or three.
                                    —John Donne

This poem understood literally, in its logical dimension, is false and even ridiculous. But understood imaginatively, as it is meant to be since it is metaphorical, the poem has emotional truth. The very sound and movement of the words and the symmetry—the parallel grammatical and logical structure—of the three stanzas contribute to the pleasing effect.

The Ambiguity of Language

Since a word is a symbol, an arbitrary sign whose meaning is imposed on it, not by nature, not by resemblance, but by convention, it is by its very nature subject to ambiguity; for, obviously, more than one meaning may be imposed on a given symbol. In a living language, the common people from time to time under changing conditions impose new meanings on the same word, and therefore words are more subject to ambiguity than are the symbols of mathematics, chemistry, or music, whose meaning is imposed on them by experts.

The ambiguity of a word may arise from: (1) the various meanings imposed on it in the course of time, constituting the history of the word; (2) the nature of a symbol, from which arise the three impositions of a word and the two intentions of a term; (3) the nature of the phantasm for which the word is originally a substitute (see Chapter Two, Generation of a Concept).

AMBIGUITY ARISING FROM THE HISTORY OF WORDS

The symbol or word acquires various meanings during the course of time. The fact that one sound or word can have many meanings can create ambiguity because it might not be known which meaning is symbolized. Such words are homonyms, ambiguous to the ear, and they may or may not differ in spelling when written. The ambiguous sound may be within the same language, or it may be in different languages.

ILLUSTRATION: Ambiguity in sound

The ambiguous sound may be within the same language.

road, rode; right, wright, rite, write;
sound "that which is heard" and *sound* "a body of water"

The ambiguous sound may be in different languages.

pax (Latin, "peace") and *pox* (English, "eruption")
hell (German, "bright," and English, "abode of wicked spirits")
nix (Latin, "snow"; English slang, "nothing") and *nicks* (English, "notches")
bright (English, "shining") and *breit* (German, "broad")
bower (English, "a leafy shelter") and *Bauer* (German, "farmer")

Note that the above pairs of words would be spelled alike if written in the alphabet of the International Phonetic Association whereby one can write such directions as "Spell [tu] three ways" without giving away the answer: "two, too, to."

A given notation is ambiguous when it symbolizes different meanings, whether in the same or in different languages. Some homonyms lose their ambiguity when they are written, for example, *road, rode, bright, breit*. Some retain it, for example, *sound, hell*. Some words, unambiguous when spoken, become ambiguous when written, for example, *tear* "rend," and *tear* "a drop from the lachrymal gland."

The dictionary records the meanings that have been imposed on a given notation in the history of the language. The dictionary does not legislate but merely records good usage. A work like Fowler's *A Dictionary of Modern English Usage* concentrates particularly on present usage. The *Oxford English Dictionary* undertakes to give the dates, if possible, when new meanings were imposed on a word and to cite passages illustrating that particular use.

An instance of a new imposition is that on *swastika*, both the word and the graphic symbol. After the revolution of 1918 in Germany, the swastika, which was an ancient symbol of good luck, was adopted by the Nazi Party.

Still another instance is the imposition of the meaning "treasonous group, working from within" on *fifth column*. In 1936, during the Spanish civil war, General Emilio Mola declared that he would capture

Madrid since in addition to his four columns of troops outside the city, he had a fifth column of sympathizers within the city.

The relationship between the various meanings that have been imposed on a given notation may be equivocal, having nothing in common—for example, *sound* "a body of water" and *sound* "that which is heard"—or analogical, having something in common—for example, *march* "a regular measured step" and *march* "a musical composition to accompany marching."

AMBIGUITY ARISING FROM IMPOSITION AND INTENTION

Ambiguity is caused by the very nature of a symbol, from which arise the three impositions of a word and the two intentions of a term.

The ultimate purpose of words and terms is to convey to another one's ideas about reality. But between the reality as it exists and as one apprehends it and expresses it are a number of intermediate steps: the creation of the phantasm, the creation of the percept, and the creation of the concept.

If one uses a word or a term to refer directly to a reality not itself, to what we know, it is used predicatively (that is, said of another, or referring to another, to the reality which it symbolizes). This is the ordinary use of a word or a term, and it is then used in first imposition and in first intention. If, however, one uses a word or a term to refer to itself as an instrument in any one of the intermediate steps by which we know or by which we symbolize what we know, it is used reflexively (that is, referring to itself, as a concept, a sound, a mark, a noun, etc.). This is the peculiar use of a word or a term in an imposition or an intention different from the ordinary use, as may be seen in the following examples.

ILLUSTRATION: Imposition and intention

Jane married a man. (Here the word *man* refers to another, a real man who exists; therefore, *man* is here used in first imposition and first intention.)

Man is a monosyllable. (Here the word *man* refers to itself as a mere sound. One can know *man* is a monosyllable without even knowing its meaning; therefore *man* is here used in zero imposition. It is false to say, "A man is a monosyllable," because when the article is added the word man refers to a real man, not to a mere sound. Jane did not marry a monosyllable.)

Man has three letters. (Here *man* refers to itself as a mere notation or mark. One can see that *man*, when written or printed, has three letters without knowing its meaning; therefore *man* is here used in zero imposition. It is false to say, "A man has three letters," because, with the article, *man* refers to a real man, not a mere notation. Jane did not marry three letters.)

Man is a noun. *Man* is the direct object of *married*. (Here *man*—and *married* also—refers to itself as a word, a sign with meaning. One cannot classify a word grammatically as a part of speech or as subject, object, or the like, without knowing its meaning; *man* is here used precisely as a word, as a sign with meaning, and is said to be used in second imposition. It is false to say, "A man is a noun" or "A man is the direct object of married," because, with the article, *man* refers to a real man, not to a word. Jane did not marry a noun or a direct object.)

Man is a concept. Man is a term. Man is a species. (Here the term man refers to itself as an idea in the mind, or an idea communicated, or a class nature—all of which are logical abstractions; man is a term used here in second intention to refer to itself, not to a real man. It is false to say, "A man is a concept"—or a term or a species—because, *with the article, man* refers to a real man, a physical entity, not a logical entity. Jane did not marry a concept or a term or a species.)

Man is a substance. (Here the word or term *man* refers to another, a real man, who is a substance. The categories are primarily metaphysical classifications of real being; man is here used in first intention and in first imposition. It is true to say, "A man is a substance." Jane did marry a substance.)

Since a word is a symbol, that is, a sensible sign with meaning, it may be used in any one of three impositions. **First imposition** is the ordinary predicative use of a word with reference only to its meaning, the reality which it symbolizes (its reference to another, for example, a real child, dog, tree) without adverting to the word itself as a sensible sign. The word is then used like a window or like eyeglasses through which we see objects but of which we are unaware.

Zero imposition is the reflexive use of a word with reference only to itself as a sensible sign (a sound or a notation) without adverting to its meaning, which need not even be known. When a word is used in zero imposition, it is like a window or like eyeglasses at which we look instead of through which we look to see something else. This is not the ordinary use of words or windows or eyeglasses. Phonetics is concerned with the word as a sound, for it deals with its correct pronunciation, with the likeness of terminal sounds in words that rhyme, etc. Spelling, or orthography, is concerned with the word as a notation.

ILLUSTRATION: Zero imposition

Exquisite is often mispronounced.
Ally is accented on the second syllable.
Hamora has three syllables.
Do not mispronounce *fire*; it is not a dissyllable.
You use too many *and's* in your writing.
Erase *much* and substitute *many*.
Similes has seven letters, not eight.

Zero imposition is the basis of a certain type of conundrum.

Nebuchadnezzar, King of the Jews!
Spell that with four letters and I'll tell you the news.

Which word in the English language is most often pronounced incorrectly?
Answer: incorrectly.

Second imposition is the reflexive use of a word; it refers to itself precisely as a word, with reference both to the sensible sign and to the meaning. This use of the word is confined to grammar; a word cannot be classified in grammar if its meaning is not known. Grammar is therefore the science of second impositions.

Jump is a verb.
Hamora is a noun, genitive plural (Old English).
On the hill is a phrase.
Cake is the direct object of *is eating*.

Any word, phrase, or clause, no matter what part of speech it is in ordinary usage, becomes a noun when used in second imposition or in zero imposition because then it names itself. Words in zero or in second imposition should be italicized, and they form their plural by adding the apostrophe and *s*, for example: *and's, 2's, p's,* and *q's*.

Words of the science of grammar and words of the sciences of phonetics and spelling, like all other words, can be used in each of the three impositions.

Coldly is an adverb. (*Coldly* is in second imposition; *adverb* is in first imposition because it refers to another word, to *coldly*, not to itself.)

Adverb is a noun. (*Adverb* is in second imposition.)

An adverb is not a noun. (*Adverb* is in first imposition, and *noun* is in first imposition because both refer to other words, not to themselves.)

Adverb has two syllables. (*Adverb* is in zero imposition; *syllables* is in first imposition because it refers to another word, to *adverb*, not to itself.)

Syllables is a plural noun. (*Syllables* is in second imposition; *noun* is in first imposition.)

Write *syllables* on the board. (*Syllables* is in zero imposition, referring to itself as a mere notation.)

First Imposition: a word used to refer directly to reality.

Zero Imposition: a word used reflexively with reference to itself as a sensible sign.

Phonetics (pronunciation)

Orthography (spelling)

Second Imposition: a word used reflexively with reference to the sensible sign and to the meaning. Grammar is the science of second imposition.

2-5   *Imposition of Words*

Since a term is a word, or symbol, conveying a particular meaning, it may be used in either of two intentions. **First intention** is the ordinary predicative use of a term to refer to a reality. This is its reference to another, to a reality (an individual or an essence). A term used in first intention corresponds exactly to a word used in first imposition. The term is then used like eyeglasses through which we see objects and of which we are unaware. **Second intention** is the reflexive use of a term to refer to itself as a term or a concept, that by which we know, not what we know.[18]

ILLUSTRATION: Second intention

Chair is a concept. Chair is a term. Chair is a species of furniture. (We cannot sit on a concept or a term or a species or any merely logical entity. We can sit on a real chair, which is a physical entity.) The term is here used like eyeglasses at which we look instead of through which we see something else.

The use of a term in second intention is confined to logic; therefore, logic is the science of second intentions, just as grammar is the science of second impositions. The terms peculiar to the science of logic, like other terms, may be used in each of the two intentions.

ILLUSTRATION: Logic terms used in first and second intention

Square is a concept. (Square is in second intention because it refers to itself as a concept; concept is in first intention because it refers to square, not to itself.)

A square is a concept. (Square is in first intention; concept is in first intention. Neither refers to itself, and the statement is false.)

A concept should be clear. (Concept is a term used in first intention because it refers predicatively to other concepts, not reflexively to itself.)

A horse cannot form a concept. (Concept is in first intention.)

Concept is a term. (Concept is in second intention, referring to itself as a term.)

First Intention: a word used to refer to a reality

Second Intention: a word used reflexively to refer to itself as a term or a concept. Logic is the science of second intentions.

2-6   *Intention of Words*

AMBIGUITY ARISING FROM THE NATURE OF THE PHANTASM
The phantasm is a mental image of an object or objects outside the mind (the designation, or extension,[19] of the term); from this image the intellect abstracts the concept (the meaning, or intension, of the term) within the mind. Because of this threefold character of the phantasm, for which the word is originally a substitute, the word is subject to three kinds of ambiguity:

1   Ambiguity can arise from the image the word evokes. The word *dog* spontaneously evokes a different image in, for instance, a Swiss mountaineer, an Arctic explorer, a British hunter, an Illinois farmer. The power of words thus to evoke images affects the psychological dimension of language and is especially important in literary composition.

Ambiguity can arise from a word's extension or designation—the object or the objects to which the term can be applied, its external reference. The primary purpose of a proper name is to designate a particular individual or aggregate; yet a proper name is sometimes ambiguous in designation because the same name has been given to more than one individual or aggregate within the same species, for example, William Shakespeare, dramatic poet, 1564–1616, and William Shakespeare, a carpenter.

To make proper names unambiguous is a special problem in drawing up legal documents such as wills, deeds, contracts. If a man were to leave half of his estate to Tom Jones, many claimants would appear, unless the heir were designated with less ambiguity so as to exclude every person except the Tom Jones whom the testator had in mind.

Telephone books add addresses, empirical descriptions, to proper names in an effort to make them unambiguous in their reference. The identification cards of criminals are attempts to make a proper name unambiguous by supplementing it with an empirical description, a photograph, and fingerprints, which are regarded as unique in the truest sense of the word, because no two are exactly alike.

An empirical description is less ambiguous in designation than a proper name, for example, the first president of this country.

2   Ambiguity can arise because a common name, such as man, ship, house, hill, is meant to be applicable to every object of the class named and therefore to be general, or universal, in its designation. For example: the full extension, or designation, of ocean is five; of friend, with reference to you, is the number of your friends; of mountain, tree, book, is the total number of objects past, present, or future to which the term can be applied.

3   Ambiguity can arise because both common and proper names acquire many meanings; in other words, the intension[20] or meaning or concept can be many. The primary purpose of a common name is to be precise in meaning, or intension; yet a common name is often ambiguous in intension because a number of meanings have been imposed on it. For example, *sound* may mean "that which is heard" or "a body of water." Each of these explanations of sound is called a general, or universal, description. The general description is less ambiguous in meaning than is the common name.

A definition is a perfect general description. The dictionary lists the various meanings that constitute the intensional ambiguity of words. The words defined are common names; the definitions are general, or universal, descriptions. A common name is used primarily in intension (although it has extension) in contrast to a proper name, which is used primarily in extension (although it has intension).

A proper name, like George Washington, although used primarily to designate an individual, must designate an individual of some particular species, for example, a man, a bridge, a ship, a hotel, a university, because every individual is a member of some class.

Inasmuch as the individual designated may be one of various different species, a proper name may be ambiguous in intension. For example, Bryn Mawr may designate a college or a town in Pennsylvania.

Madeira may designate a group of islands in the Atlantic Ocean near Morocco, a river in Brazil, or a fortified wine.

DELIBERATE AMBIGUITY

Although ambiguity is a fault to be carefully guarded against in purely intellectual communications, it is sometimes deliberately sought in aesthetic or literary communication.

Irony is the use of words to convey a meaning just the contrary of the one normally conveyed by the words. (It is a form of deliberate ambiguity in intension.)

A pun is the use of a word simultaneously in two or more meanings. (It too is a form of deliberate ambiguity in intension.) The pun is commonly regarded in our time as a trivial form of humor. It was, however, held in esteem by Aristotle, Cicero, and Renaissance rhetoricians (who classified puns among four different figures of speech). It was used by Plato, the Greek dramatists, and Renaissance preachers and writers, often in a serious way.

ILLUSTRATION: Deliberate ambiguity

Death is most fit before you do
Deeds that would make death fit for you.
   —Anaxandrides in Aristotle's *Rhetoric*

. . . having both the key
Of officer and office, set all hearts in the state
To what tune pleased his ear.
                    —*The Tempest* 1.2.83–85[21]

Vex not his ghost. O, let him pass! He hates him
That would upon the rack of this tough world
Stretch him out longer.
                    —*King Lear* 5.3.313–316

If he do bleed,
I'll gild the faces of the grooms withal,
For it must seem their guilt.
                    —*Macbeth* 2.2.52–54

Now is it Rome indeed, and room enough
When there is in it but one only man!
                    —*Julius Caesar* 1.2.156–7

Falstaff. My honest lads, I will tell you what I am about.
Pistol. Two yards, and more.

Falstaff. No quips now, Pistol! Indeed I am in the waist two yards about; but I am now about no waste; I am about thrift.

—*The Merry Wives of Windsor* 1.3.39–43

William Somer, King Henry VIII's fool, seeing that the king lacked money, said: "You have so many Frauditors, so many Conveyors, and so many Deceivers to get up your money, that they get all to themselves" [playing on Auditors, Surveyors, and Receivers].

—Thomas Wilson, The Arte of Rhetorique (1553)

Metaphor is the use of a word or a phrase to evoke simultaneously two images, one literal and the other figurative. (It is deliberate ambiguity of images.)

The metaphor is of great value in poetry and in all imaginative writing, including the best scientific and philosophical writing. Aristotle regarded the metaphor as a compressed proportion, a statement of equality between two ratios. The full proportion may be represented thus: $a:b::c:d$. The compressed proportion is *a is c.*

ILLUSTRATION: Metaphor as a compressed proportion

O Wild West Wind, thou breath of Autumn's being. (*a is c*)
  —Percy Bysshe Shelley, "Ode to the West Wind"

The West Wind (a) is to Autumn (b) as breath (c) is to a human being (d). ($a:b::c:d$).

Love . . . is the star to every wandering bark. (*a is c*).
  —William Shakespeare, "Sonnet 116"

Love (a) guides a wandering soul (b) as a star (c) guides a wandering bark (d). (*$a:b::c:d$*).

The moon is a boat. (*a is c*)
The moon (a) moves through the sky (b) as a boat (c) sails over the sea (d). (*$a:b::c:d$*).

A dead metaphor is one which at one time evoked two images but which now fails to do so, usually because the one-time figurative meaning has completely supplanted what was once the literal meaning. In the quote, "Your sorrows are the tribulations of your soul," *tribulation* is a dead metaphor. At one time *tribulum* meant threshing flail. The full proportion then was: Your sorrows are to your soul as a threshing flail is to wheat (*$a:b::c:d$*). This metaphor, first used by an early Christian writer, was so good that *tribulation* came to mean sorrow and lost its original meaning, threshing. Its metaphorical use has become its ordinary use. We do not recognize the one-time metaphor. *Tribulation* now evokes only one image; the sentence is, therefore, a dead metaphor.

Man-of-war is a dead metaphor. Originally it had the force of the following proportion: A ship is to a sea battle as a warrior is to a land battle (*a:b::c:d*). Therefore, a battleship is a *man of war* (*a is c*). The figurative meaning has become the literal meaning, for *man-of-war* now means only a battleship. *Candidate* "clothed in white" and *skyscraper* are other dead metaphors that have lost their original meaning.

In the series of meanings attached to a word like *spring*, one can observe how new meanings, derived from the fundamental one by figurative use later became ordinary meanings having lost their figurative quality. The dictionary lists the following meanings for *spring*: (1) To leap, bound (2) To shoot, up, out, or forth; to issue as a plant from seed, a stream from its source, etc. (3) An issue of water from the earth (4) An elastic device that recovers its original shape when released after being distorted (5) A season when plants begin to grow (6) Time of growth and progress. (Although the dictionary lists this as an ordinary meaning of *spring*, to say "Youth is the spring of life" is still felt, at least mildly, as a metaphor.)

Irony: the use of words to convey a meaning just the contrary of the one normally conveyed by the words

Pun: the use of a word simultaneously in two or more meanings

Metaphor: the use of a word or phrase to simultaneously evoke two images

---

2-7   *Deliberate Ambiguity*

THE TRIVIUM

After the preceding considerations, the reader can better understand the comparative scope of the three arts of the trivium: logic, grammar, and rhetoric, which were discussed in the preceding chapter.

One can distinguish the powers of the mind: cognition, appetition, and emotion. Cognition includes the lower or sensuous cognition, which produces percepts, and the higher or rational cognition, which produces concepts. Appetition includes the lower or sense appetites, which seek primarily food, clothing and shelter, and the higher or rational appetite, the will, which seeks the good, and unity, truth, and beauty under the aspect of good.

Emotion is a pleasurable or painful tone which may accompany the exercise of both sensuous and rational powers. Pleasure is the concomitant of the healthy and normal exercise of any of our powers. Pain is the concomitant of either the excessive or the inadequate or inhibited exercise of any of our powers.

Logic is concerned only with operations of the intellect, with rational cognition, not with volition nor with the emotions.

Grammar gives expression to all states of mind or soul—cognitive, volitive, emotional—in sentences that are statements, questions, wishes, prayers, commands, exclamations. In this sense, grammar has a wider scope than logic; and so does rhetoric, which communicates all these to other minds.

Rhetoric judges which one of a number of equivalent grammatical symbols for one idea is best for communication in the given circumstance, for example, steed, horse; silver, argent. Grammar deals only with the sentence, with one thought; logic and rhetoric deal with extended discourse, with relations and combinations of thoughts.

Logic is addressed only to the intellect; rhetoric, including poetry, is addressed not only to the intellect but also to the imagination and the affections in order to communicate the pleasant, the comic, the pathetic, the sublime.

Logic may function without rhetoric or poetry; but these without logic are shallow. Grammar is requisite to all.

If the imperfections of a common language, especially its ambiguity, are realized, we can more readily understand the value of rules of grammar, logic, and rhetoric as means of interpretation. For example, the rules of grammar direct us to the correct reading of these lines from Gray, which are often misread. What is the subject of the first sentence? What is the predicate?[22]

> The boast of heraldry, the pomp of power,
> And all that beauty, all that wealth e'er gave
> Awaits alike the inevitable hour:—
> The paths of glory lead but to the grave.
> —Thomas Gray, "Elegy Written in a Country Churchyard"

It is true that the correct use of grammar, rhetoric, and logic (often based on implicit knowledge only) is most important. Habits of daily thought and expression at home and in school measure our practical, personal mastery over language. Nevertheless, formal knowledge of grammar, rhetoric, and logic (explicit knowledge) is valuable also, for we should know why certain reasonings and expressions are correct or effective, and others just the opposite, and should be able to apply the rules in speaking, writing, listening, and reading.

Being is either the being of the whole individual or of the essence which is common to the individuals of either a species or a genus.

The **phantasm** is (1) a mental image of (2) an object outside the mind (its extensional reference); from this image the intellect abstracts (3) the concept within the mind (its intensional reference).

A **symbol** is an arbitrary sensible sign having meaning imposed on it by convention. (A concept is not arbitrary.)

Language has a logical and a psychological dimension.

Matter and **form** constitute a composite whole.

2-8 *Key Ideas in Chapter Two*

3 GENERAL GRAMMAR

GENERAL GRAMMAR AND SPECIAL GRAMMARS

General grammar[1] is concerned with the relation of words to ideas and to realities, whereas a special grammar, such as English or Latin or French or Spanish grammar, is concerned principally with the relation of words to words, as, for example, with the agreement of subject and verb in person and number or the agreement of adjective and noun in number, gender, and case.

General grammar is more philosophical than the special grammars because it is more directly related to logic and to metaphysics or ontology. Consequently, it differs somewhat from the special grammars in point of view and in resulting classification both in the part-of-speech analysis and in the syntactical[2] analysis.

PARTS OF SPEECH IN GENERAL GRAMMAR

From the point of view of general grammar, the essential distinction between words is that between categorematic words and syncategorematic words.

Categorematic words are those which symbolize some form of being and which may accordingly be classified in the ten categories of being—substance and the nine accidents.[3] Categorematic words are therefore of two great classes: (1) substantives, which primarily symbolize substance, and (2) attributives, which symbolize accidents.[4] From this point of view, verbs and adjectives are properly classified together as attributives, as accidents existing in substance because action as well as quality or quantity must exist in substance. These distinctions are an outstanding illustration of the difference in point of view between general grammar and the special grammars.

Syncategorematic words are those which have meaning only along with other words, for, taken by themselves, they cannot be classified in the categories. They do not symbolize being. Rather, they are mere grammatical cement by means of which we relate in a sentence the categorematic words which do symbolize being. For that reason, they are sometimes called form words. Syncategorematic words are of two classes: (1) definitives, which point out substances, and (2) connectives, which join either words or sentences or subject and predicate.

ANALOGIES: Difference between categorematic and syncategorematic symbols

In music the notes are categorematic symbols, while marks of time, of phrasing, of staccato or legato, etc. are syncategorematic symbols of operation. In mathematics, the numbers, figures, angles, etc. are categorematic symbols, while +, −, ×, %, =, etc. are syncategorematic symbols of operation indicating how the categorematic symbols are related.

Accordingly, in general grammar we distinguish four fundamental parts of speech: substantives, attributives, definitives, and connectives.

We may subdivide these, however, and distinguish nine true parts of speech; and, if we add the interjection, which for reasons stated below cannot be regarded precisely as a part of speech, we list ten, as follows: nouns, pronouns, verbs, adjectives, adverbs, definitives, prepositions, conjunctions, the pure copula, and interjections.

Categorematic Words (words significant by themselves)

Substantives

Nouns

Pronouns

Attributives

Primary—attributes of substances
Verbs (and verbals)
Adjectives

Secondary—attributes of attributes: Adverbs

Syncategorematic Words (words significant only along with other words)

Definitives, associated to one word
Articles
Pronomials

Connectives, associated to many words
Prepositions—connect words
Conjunctions—connect sentences (either expressed or implied)

The pure copula, which connects subject and predicate

3-1   *Categories of Parts of Speech*

Interjections are named with the parts of speech only because it is desirable that there be a name for every class of words. Interjections are not, however, true parts of speech for two reasons. They cannot be assimilated into the structure of a sentence and therefore have no grammatical import. They express emotion, not thought,[5] and therefore have no logical import.

CATEGOREMATIC PARTS OF SPEECH

Substantives: Nouns and Pronouns

According to the kind of reality it refers to, a substantive symbolizes either a concrete substance or an abstraction. A concrete substance is an object as it exists in itself, whether natural or artificial. Tree, stone, and horse are examples of natural substance, and chair, glass, and clock are examples of artificial substance.

An abstraction is an accident[6] conceived by the mind, for the sake of emphasis, as if it existed by itself apart from the concrete substance in which alone it can really exist; for instance, smoothness, quantity, shape, or prudence actually exist as part of substance. An abstraction is also substance regarded in its essence, for the sake of emphasis apart from its concrete existence; for instance, humanity, corporeity, womanhood, chairness, treeness actually exist as part of substance.

Abstract substantives symbolize ideas in every one of the ten categories, for example: animality, length, whiteness, similarity, motion, sensitivity, futurity, ubiquity, erectness, accouteredness. In fact, the very names of seven[7] of the nine categories of accident are examples of abstract substantives.

The human ability thus to distinguish, to select, to abstract one aspect of reality and to make it the object of thought has been the indispensable means whereby the limited human mind has been able to advance in the search for truth. Each of the various sciences and branches of philosophy abstracts from reality a selected aspect; for instance, mathematics deals only with quantity; physics, with motion; metaphysics, with being. The human power to abstract and to study a selected aspect of reality is the measure of intellectual progress which contrasts strikingly with the utter absence of such progress among irrational animals despite their wonderful instincts, which are often superior to the instincts of man. As human civilization advances, the proportion of abstract substantives in the language increases.[8]

According to its logical classification, a substantive symbolizes either an individual, a species, or a genus.

ILLUSTRATION: Logical classification of a substantive

Individual	Species	Genus
Eleanor Roosevelt	man	animal
Excalibur	sword	weapon
Atlantic	ocean	body of water

GRAMMATICAL CHARACTERISTICS OF SUBSTANTIVES

Number

A substantive naming a species or a genus has number; that is, it may be either singular or plural because it may designate either one or more than one of the individuals that constitute the species or the genus. Such a substantive is either a common name or a general description.[9]

Strictly speaking, a substantive naming an individual has no number because an individual is unique and cannot be pluralized in respect to that which makes it individual but only in respect to that which makes it a member of its species or its genus. A substantive that names an individual is either a proper name or an empirical description.

Gender

A substantive may be masculine, feminine, neuter, or common. The nouns in modern English have natural gender; the nouns in French, Latin, German, and many other languages have grammatical gender.

Person

This is a characteristic much more important to pronouns than to nouns. It has its natural origin in conversation, for first person is the speaker; second person is the one spoken to; and third person, the one spoken of.

A pronoun agrees in person, as well as in number and gender, with its antecedent, the noun to which it refers; its case, however, is determined by its use in its own clause.[10]

The relative pronoun simultaneously performs three functions: (1) It stands for a noun. (2) It connects clauses. (3) It subordinates one clause to another.

Case

Case shows the relationship of a noun or a pronoun to other words in the sentence. Four cases of substantives are distinguished in general grammar, for these are the relationships necessary in every language, although not in every sentence.

Four Cases of Substantives

Nominative is the case of the subject. It is the only case necessary to every sentence.

Genitive is the case which names the possessor.

Dative is the case which names the term[11] to which the action proceeds.

Accusative is the case which names the object which receives the action.

3-2   *Case*

The special grammar of a particular language may distinguish fewer or more cases than these four, the number usually depending on inflectional forms, rather than on the underlying relationships of ideas and words. Thus, modern English grammar distinguishes only three cases: nominative, genitive, and accusative. It is obvious, however, that the uses of the dative case[12] are present in the English language as clearly as in the Latin language; moreover, the dative case and the instrumental, which is analogous to the ablative in Latin, had inflectional forms and distinctive uses in the Old English period of our language (before 1150 A.D.).

Cases of nouns may be expressed by word order, prepositions, or case endings.

ILLUSTRATION: Case

Word order   John killed the snake. The snake killed John.

Prepositions   Mother is in the garden. The decision of the umpire was applauded.

Case endings   Father's, him, my, *puero, noctis*.[13]

THE TEN GRAMMATICAL FUNCTIONS OF SUBSTANTIVES

Substantives can act as subject, subjective complement, direct object of a verb or verbal, indirect object of a verb or verbal, objective complement, object of a preposition, possessive modifier, nominative absolute, nominative of direct address, or an appositive of any of these.

ILLUSTRATION: Grammatical functions of substantives

Cobb whacked the ball into the outfield and gave the spectators a thrill by making a home run, thereby tying the score.
Cobb is the subject. *Ball* is the direct object of *whacked*; *thrill* is the direct object of *gave*; *home run* is the direct object of the gerund[14] *making*; *score* is the direct object of the participle *tying*.[15] *Spectators* is the indirect object of *gave*. *Outfield* is the object of the preposition *into*; *making*, a gerund, is the object of the preposition *by*.

Jane, my uncle's law partner considers that man to be a scoundrel.[16]
Jane is the nominative of direct address. *Uncle's* is a possessive modifier of *partner*. *Scoundrel* is a subjective complement, or predicate noun, for it completes the copula[17] *to be* and refers to the subject *man*; it agrees in case with *man*, which is here accusative because it is the subject of an infinitive[18] in indirect discourse.[19]

The class elected John president.
President is an objective complement, for it completes the verb *elected* and refers to *John*, the direct object of *elected*. (*Elected* is one of a group of words including *choose, name, painted* which take two accusatives to complete their meaning.) The sentence is really a condensed combination of two sentences: The class elected John. John is president. In the second of these two sentences, *president* is a subjective complement, for it completes the copula *is* and refers to the subject *John*; its relation to *John* is the same as in the combined statement above, but there it is called an objective complement because it refers to the object of the verb.

The audience insistently applauding, Lawrence Tibbett, noted baritone, graciously consented to sing the song "Edward" again.
Audience is the nominative absolute, for the phrase of which it is a part has no grammatical relation to any word in the rest of the sentence. In Latin, the absolute construction is expressed by the ablative case; in English, by the nominative. *Song* is the direct object of the infinitive *to sing*. *Baritone* is in apposition with the subject *Lawrence Tibbett*. "*Edward*" is in apposition with the direct object *song*.

Attributives

Attributives are words which express the accidents that exist in substance. Primary attributives include verbs, verbals, and adjectives.

VERBS AND THEIR FUNCTIONS

There are four functions of a verb. A verb expresses an attribute along with the notion of time. A verb indicates tense. A verb expresses mode or mood. A verb asserts.

Expressing an attribute along with the notion of time is the essential function of a verb and constitutes its definition. Aristotle, in the *Organon*, defines a verb as that which, in addition to its proper meaning, carries with it the notion of time. It is by this characteristic of carrying with it the notion of time or change that he distinguishes it from the adjective and from every other part of speech.

To understand this definition, it is necessary to understand what is meant by time. Time is the measure of change. The year measures a change, the movement of the earth around the sun. The day measures a change, the movement of the earth turning on its axis. The hour measures an artificial movement such as that of sand from the upper to the lower half of an hourglass or of the minute hand around a clock.

Since action is change, and change involves time, a verb, which expresses action, necessarily involves time. The particular action expressed varies from verb to verb, as in *jump, speak, sing, swim.* Each of these has its own proper meaning, but since change is common to all of them, every verb carries with it the notion of time. The verb *exist*, when predicated of contingent beings, involves having been moved from potency to actuality and continuance in that actuality. Therefore it involves duration or time.

Thus, time is a concomitant of the meaning of verbs, not their principal meaning. When we wish to make time the principal meaning, we do so by means of abstract nouns like *year, day, hour* or by means of adverbs like *yearly, daily, hourly, instantly, gradually.*

Tense is the relation between the time of the act spoken of and the time of speaking of it. If I speak of an action while it occurs, I use present tense (The bird flies); if after it occurs, past tense (The bird flew); if before it occurs, future tense (The bird will fly). In addition to these, there are the present perfect, past perfect, and future perfect tenses. In English grammar there are two forms for every tense: the simple (I think) and the progressive (I am thinking). In the present and past tenses there is a third form, the emphatic (I do think, I did think).

We must be careful not to confuse tense with time. Time is essential to the verb. Tense is not essential. It is a mere accidental variation. Aristotle likens the tenses of verbs to the cases of nouns.

In the statement of a general truth there is, strictly speaking, no tense at all. Examples are: Fire burns. Acids contain hydrogen. Man acquires knowledge by reasoning. Good ought to be done. Evil ought to be avoided. A triangle has three sides. Fishes live in water. Planets move around the sun.

Such general statements express a relation which, so far as our observation goes, does not cease to be nor come to be; it is continuous. Therefore, the relation between the time of the act spoken of and the time of speaking of it never varies. The use of the past or future tense would violate the truth of such general statements. Nor can one truly say that the present tense is used, for that has a temporal signification not here intended. Although the grammatical form of the present tense is used, the statements of general truths are really tenseless.

Mode or **mood** asserts the manner in which the subject and predicate[20] are related as certain, possible, conditional, etc.

1   *Indicative mood* asserts the relation as a matter of fact, with certainty. Examples are: The car raced past. He wished me success.

2   *Potential mood* asserts the relation as possible, or contingent. Examples are: A rose may be white. This acorn may become an oak tree. The brakes might have been defective.

3   *Interrogative mood* requests information, and it requires a response in words. For example: Who spoke? English idiom requires that either the progressive or the emphatic form be used in asking questions about matters of fact in the present or past tense active, unless the question has as its subject an interrogative pronoun, and then the simple form may be used. Examples are: Is she coming? Where did you find that? Who thinks so? The following are not idiomatic: Comes she? Where found you that?

4   *Volitive mood* seeks the gratification of volitions, and it requires a response, usually in deeds. It has direct reference to the future only. So true is this that the future indicative often has the force of command, as in the Decalogue:[21] Thou shalt not steal.

The tone of the volitive may be imperative or optative. Imperative relates to a command, issued usually to inferiors.[22] For example: John, close the door. Optative or hortatory[23] relates to a wish, expressed usually to equals or to superiors. Examples are: May you be successful. Would that I had the means to help them!

Here again, in distinguishing the moods of verbs, we see a difference in the points of view of general grammar and the special grammars. The special grammars, which are principally concerned with the relations of words to words, distinguish (in English, Latin, etc.) three moods marked by a difference in grammatical form: (1) the indicative mood, which expresses the relation as a matter of fact, whether in statement or question; (2) the subjunctive mood, which expresses the potential, the subjunctive, and the optative relations, and sometimes the interrogative, as in asking permissions; (3) the imperative mood, which expresses a command.

It is reasonable in English grammar, or in Latin or French or Spanish grammar, not to distinguish between the interrogative and the indicative moods but to treat them as one, because the same grammatical forms of the verb are ordinarily used for both question and answer. In general grammar, however, it is reasonable and even necessary to distinguish between these two moods because from the point of view of logic, to which general grammar is intimately related, these two moods differ essentially: the indicative mood expresses a statement which must either be true or false; the interrogative mood expresses a question which is incapable of being either true or false.

Only the indicative and the potential moods are capable of expressing either truth or falsity; the interrogative and the volitive moods are not. The potential mood asserts not a fact but a possibility, or contingency; therefore, its truth or falsity depends on conformity not to fact, as that of the indicative mood does, but to possibility, or contingency. For example, "It may rain tomorrow" is a true assertion of a possibility. Its truth is not dependent on whether it actually does or does not rain the day after the statement is made.

A verb asserts. This function is necessary to form a sentence, which must express a complete thought.

Classes of Verbs: Transitive and Intransitive

The transitive verb expresses action that begins in the subject (agent) and "goes across" (*trans + ire*) to the object (receiver). The object may be the same as the subject, for example: He cut himself. But it need not be the same, for example: He cut the cake. He rowed the boat. A transitive verb always requires a complement, that is, a word which completes the meaning of the predicate. Every transitive verb requires at least one complement, the direct object; some transitive verbs, like *give*, require both a direct and an indirect object; others, like *elect*, require two accusatives to complete their meaning, one the direct object, the other the objective complement.

The intransitive verb expresses action that begins and ends in the agent, the subject; consequently, the subject must be both agent and patient, for example: The bird flies. There are two classes of intransitive verbs: (1) Some express action complete in itself, for example, *blooms, withers*; (2) Some require a complement, a word to complete the meaning of the predicate, for example, *becomes*.[24] An intransitive verb which requires a complement is a copulative verb.[25]

COPULA: A SPECIAL CASE

A copula is a word that links an attributive or a substantive to the subject. Such an attributive (adjective or verbal) or substantive is variously named by grammarians the predicate adjective or predicate noun, the predicate complement, the attribute complement, the subjective complement (meaning that it completes the predicate and modifies the subject).

The pure copula *is* is not a verb because it does not express an attribute along with the notion of time. It is a syncategorematic word of operation, and it will be discussed with that category of words.

The intransitive verb *is*, which is a categorematic word and a synonym for the verb *exists* but which is not a copulative verb, must be distinguished from the copula *is*. Like other verbs, the verb *is* is capable of having an adverbial modifier, which it could not have unless the verb *is* expressed an attribute, for an adverb is an attribute of an attribute, as will be explained more fully.

ILLUSTRATION: Intransitive verb *to be*

John is. (John exists.)
John is in the garden. (John exists in the garden.)

A copulative verb is one which performs simultaneously the functions of a copula and of a verb. There are two classes of copulative verbs: the true copula and the pseudocopula.

The true copula, for instance, *becomes*, is a true copula and a true verb. For example: The green leaves become yellow. (1) *Becomes* is a true verb because it expresses an attribute along with the notion of time. It involves change. In fact, it expresses change itself. (2) *Becomes* is a true copula because it links an attributive or a substantive to the subject; it links the *before* and the *after* of change.

The pseudocopula is a true verb and expresses sense-perception, for example: looks, sounds, tastes, smells, feels. "The apple tastes sour."

Here *tastes* acts as a copula in linking *sour* to *apple*. The sentence represents good English idiom, even though it is illogical and literally false, for the apple cannot taste at all. In its primary meaning, the pseudocopula is a transitive verb. The sentence is a grammatical condensation of two sentences: I taste the apple. The apple is sour. Here *taste* is a transitive verb.

Attributives: Verbals

There are three classes[26] of verbals: the infinitive, the participle, the gerund. Like the verb, the verbal: (1) expresses an attribute along with the notion of time; (2) indicates tense.

Unlike the verb, the verbal: (1) does not assert; (2) does not express mood. Because the verbal does not assert, it is a frequent occasion of the fragmentary sentence error.[27]

The infinitive is an abstract substantive and can therefore perform all the grammatical functions of a substantive, for example: To think is to exercise the mind.[28]

The gerund is a verbal which, like the infinitive, may perform all the functions of a substantive. The gerund has the same form as the participle,[29] but it differs in function, for example: Thinking is exercising the mind.

The participle is a verbal functioning grammatically as an adjective, for it modifies a substantive, for example: John, thinking clearly, solved the problem.

Attributives: Adjectives

The essential difference between the adjective and the verb or verbal is that the verb or verbal expresses an attribute of substance along with the notion of time and hence involves change, whereas the adjective expresses an attribute simply.

Secondary Attributives: Adverbs

Secondary attributives function as attributes of attributes—namely, adverbs, for example: The man walks swiftly. Walking is an action existing in the man; hence it is an attribute of substance. Swiftness is a quality existing in the walking; hence *swiftly* expresses an attribute of an attribute of a substance. The reality spoken of is a swiftly walking man.

Substantives: nouns and pronouns

Attributives: verbs, verbals, and adjectives

Secondary Attributives: adverbs

3-3   *Categorematic Parts of Speech*

SYNCATEGOREMATIC PARTS OF SPEECH

Syncategorematic parts of speech refer to words which are only signifi-cant with other words. Definitives and connectives are syncategore-matic parts of speech.

Definitives

A definitive is a word which, when associated to a common name, is ca-pable of singling out an individual or a group of individuals from the whole class designated by the common name. This is the essential func-tion of the definitive. The definitive joined to a common name is called an empirical description. Definitives include articles and pronomials.

James Harris[30] notes that a definitive may designate individuals such as:

Known: the man
Definite: a certain man
Present and near: this man
Present and distant: that man
A definite multitude: a thousand men
An indefinite multitude: many men, some men
The ones of a multitude taken with distinction: each man
The ones of a multitude taken in order: the first man, the second

THE ARTICLE

The article never stands alone. It may be either indefinite or definite. An **indefinite article** singles out an individual but does not designate which one; it also signifies first acquaintance. For example: I saw a tall, red-haired, hook-nosed man downtown today.

The repetition of the article is often an aid to clarity. For example, the sentence, "He entertained a poet and philosopher," is unclear. Is the same person both a poet and philosopher or are there two people?

The sentence "He entertained a poet and a philosopher" is unambiguous in showing that two people were entertained.

The **definite article** singles out a particular individual. It may also signify preestablished acquaintance or eminence.

ILLUSTRATION: Use of the definitive article

Preestablished acquaintance: There goes the tall, red-haired, hook-nosed man I saw downtown yesterday.

Eminence: the poet; the philosopher; the Mrs. Jamieson

THE PRONOMIAL

The pronomial's primary function is to act as a definitive, that is, to limit a common name. Sometimes, however, it stands alone and thereby performs the functions of a pronoun. For example, in the phrase "this pencil," *this* is a definitive. In the sentence "This is a pencil," *this* is a pronoun.

Pronomials used as definitives may be employed to express antithesis, for example: This hat I like, but that one I dislike.

A modifier of a substantive, whether it be a word, a phrase, or a clause, is either definitive or attributive (adjectival) in function. The definitive modifier is essentially associated to the subject, whereas the attributive modifier is essentially a predicate.

For example, in the phrase "this apple," *this* is a definitive because *this* is associated to the subject; *this* does not predicate something about the subject. In the phrase "red apple," *red* is attributive because *red* could be predicated of the apple.

This essential and profound difference in function between the definitive and the adjective requires that they be sharply distinguished in general grammar. So great is the difference between them that the adjective is a categorematic word and the definitive is syncategorematic.

Here again we see that the point of view of general grammar differs radically from that of the special grammars. The latter, such as Latin, German, or French grammar, treat the definitive as an adjective since it has inflectional endings like those of the adjective and must likewise agree in number, gender, and case with the noun it modifies. The definitive is not one of the eight parts of speech distinguished in the special grammars, but in them it is classified as an adjective.

Rules for Punctuating the Definitive and the Attributive Modifier[31]

Since its function is to point out, the definitive modifier is restrictive,[32] and it is never separated by commas from the substantive it modifies, for example: The man who is standing nearest the window is a labor leader.

Since its function is to describe, the attributive modifier is nonrestrictive, and if it is a clause, it should be separated by commas from the substantive it modifies, for example: John Lewis, who is standing nearest the window, is a labor leader.

3-4 *Punctuating the Definitive and Attributive Modifier*

It is to be noted that the distinction between a definitive and an attributive modifier is functional. If a modifier describes in order to point out, it is a definitive, as in the first example above. If the individual is already designated by a proper name, the modifier, no longer needed to point out the individual, becomes attributive—descriptive, nonrestrictive, merely additive, as in the second example above.

It is important to distinguish between functional and part-of-speech analyses. For instance, a definitive modifier need not contain a single definitive. For example: The girl with red hair is my cousin. *With red hair* is a definitive modifier of *girl*, but not a single word in this phrase is a definitive.

Connectives

Connectives are syncategorematic parts of speech which associate words to other words. Connectives include prepositions, conjunctions, and the pure copula. Connectives are words analogous to cement, for they hold the categorematic parts of speech together in the unity of thought expressed in the sentence.

PREPOSITIONS

Prepositions join words. A preposition unites substantives, which do not naturally coalesce. In nature, accidents exist in substance, and in grammar, attributives and substantives naturally coalesce, for example, red rose. But substances do not unite with one another in nature,[33] nor do substances coalesce in grammar, hence the need of prepositions, the verbal cement for uniting substantives, for example, "the curtain on the window." *On* joins *curtain* and *window*.

If you add five apples, three tables, four chairs, and two dogs, what is the sum? The answer is five apples, three tables, four chairs, and two dogs. It is true that there are fourteen objects, or things, or substances, and under this most general aspect the sum may be stated as fourteen; but to so lump objects together is to ignore their specific nature. One can, however, say, Two dogs, chasing each other, knocked five apples off three tables under four chairs. The prepositions express a relation between these substances without robbing them of their specific nature.

Prepositions show the precise relation between substances. For example: The dog ran around the table, crept under the table, jumped over the table, lay beside the table, stood near the table.

The repetition of the preposition is often a means to secure clarity. Examples are (1) The invasion of the Angles and the Saxons (one invasion), (2) The invasion of the Danes and of the Normans (two invasions).

Relationships, especially those of place, may undergo transfer to intellectual relationships. Examples are: to come under authority; to rule over minds; to act through jealousy. Such relationships may also enter into compounds—overlook as compared to look over; understand as compared to stand under. Prepositions are often used to express the genitive (of the children) and dative (to the children) relationships of nouns.

Prepositions may lose the connective function and become adverbs; then, of course, they become categorematic words. Adverbs derived from prepositions convey a meaning more vague, less specific, than the corresponding prepositional phrase.

ILLUSTRATION: Same word as preposition and adverb

He walked around the house. He walked around.
They gazed up the shaft. They gazed up.

CONJUNCTIONS

Conjunctions join sentences. The sentences joined may be either explicit or implicit.

ILLUSTRATION: Conjunctions joining sentences

Explicit: The guests arrived, and dinner was served.
Implicit: The army and navy prepared for war.
Explicit: The army prepared for war, and the navy prepared for war.

Pure conjunctions are coordinating. They join independent clauses or sentences. They may conjoin or disjoin. For instance, *and* conjoins; that is, *and* joins both sentences and meaning. Conjunctions like *but, or, either . . . or, neither . . . nor* disjoin; that is, they join sentences but not meaning.

Rule for punctuation of coordinating clauses joined by a coordinating conjunction

Unless the coordinate clauses joined are very short, use a comma before the coordinating conjunction.

3-5 *Punctuating Coordinating Clauses*

Conjunctive adverbs may be coordinating. These conjoin independent clauses or sentences. Examples include *hence, consequently, therefore, then, nevertheless.* Conjunctive adverbs may be subordinating. These subjoin a dependent clause to an independent clause, forming a complex sentence. Examples include *while, where, when, although, unless, if.*

Rules for punctuation between clauses with a conjunctive adverb

Use a semicolon or a period between clauses or sentences conjoined by a conjunctive adverb, for example: It rained; therefore, we postponed the picnic. The violation of this rule results in the very serious error of the run-on sentence or comma splice, two sentences punctuated as if they were one.

Use either a comma or no punctuation where a dependent clause is subjoined to an independent clause by an adverbial conjunction, for example: Because it rained, we postponed the picnic. The violation of this rule results in the very serious error of the sentence fragment or half-sentence, punctuated as if it were a complete sentence.

3-6 *Punctuating Conjunctive Adverbs*

THE PURE COPULA

The pure copula connects subject and predicate. Because of its relation to logic, nothing else in general grammar is so necessary to understand as the nature and functions of the pure copula.

The pure copula *is* is a strictly syncategorematic word which asserts the relation between a subject and a predicate, both of which are categorematic. It is to be noted that in general grammar, as in logic, the pure copula is neither the predicate nor a part of the predicate, but is completely distinct from the predicate. The predicate itself is equivalent in the broad sense to a subjective complement which completes the pure copula.

Every simple declarative sentence is made up of subject, pure copula, and predicate. The pure copula and the subjective complement, or predicate, are either explicit or implicit.

If the sentence contains an explicit copula, it will, of course, also contain an explicit subjective complement, which may be either an adjective, a verbal, or a noun. Examples are: The grass is green. The rose is blooming. The horse is an animal.

If the sentence contains the simple verb form, the copula and the subjective complement are implicit in the verb and may be made explicit in English by changing the simple verb form to the progressive form. If the verb has modifiers, or if it is either a transitive or a copulative verb, the subjective complement is a construct of which the modifiers and the direct object or other complements form parts.

ILLUSTRATION: Simple verb form to progressive verb form

The sun shines.	The sun is shining.
The green leaves become yellow.	The green leaves are becoming yellow.
The wind bends the trees.	The wind is bending the trees.
The girl swam gracefully in the lake.	The girl was swimming gracefully in the lake.
He gives her a book.	He is giving her a book.

"The wind bends the trees" illustrates a construct.[34] *Bending the trees* is a construct because it is an attributive joined by the pure copula *is* to *wind*. The reality spoken of is a tree-bending wind.

In the progressive verb form, the pure copula *is* links the attributive (a participle, which is a verbal) to the subject. Consequently, it makes clear and explicit the precise nature and functions of both the pure copula and the verb (or verbal). In the simple verb form, these functions are not so clear.

Tense	Simple form	Progressive form
Pres. ind.	The bird flies.	The bird is flying.
Past	The bird flew.	The bird was flying.
Future	The bird will fly.	The bird will be flying.
Pres. perf.	The bird has flown.	The bird has been flying.
Past perf.	The bird had flown.	The bird had been flying.
Fut. perf.	The bird will have flown.	The bird will have been flying.
Pres. subj.	The bird may fly.	The bird may be flying.
Past subj.	The bird might fly.	The bird might be flying.

3-7 *Conversion of Simple Form to Progressive Form*

The progressive form makes clear that the pure copula *is*, undergoing inflection, performs three functions important in general grammar: (1) it asserts; (2) it expresses mood; (3) it indicates tense.

The verb, which in the progressive form is reduced to a verbal, a participle, performs its one, genuine, and essential function, which is to express an attribute along with the notion of time; flying involves change and hence involves time.

The bird's flying requires time, but tense is inconsequential to the act; tense indicates merely that the speaker chooses to make the remark either during, after, or before the act. Hence tense is not an essential characteristic of a verb.

The pure copula *is* is strictly syncategorematic; the only reality symbolized here is the flying bird. On the other hand, there is a different meaning in the following: The flying bird is. The flying bird was. In these two sentences *is* and *was* are verbs, meaning exists and existed; they are not copulas at all. The second sentence might imply that the bird was shot; in any case, it states that the bird has ceased to be.

The Intransitive Verb *To Be*

An intransitive verb meaning "to exist"   The orchestra is in the concert hall.

The Copulative Verb or True Copula

An intransitive verb which requires a complement   She became a violinist.

The Pseudocopula

A verb which expresses sense perception   The orchestra sounds good.

The Pure Copula

A nonverb which connects subject and predicate   The pianist is a woman.

3-8   *The Copula and the Verb* To Be

SYNTACTICAL ANALYSIS IN GENERAL GRAMMAR

Any simple sentence or complex sentence may be divided into the complete subject and the complete predicate. A compound sentence can be divided into simple sentences.

In the study of logic, the important analysis of a simple declarative sentence is that which divides it into complete subject, pure copula, and complete predicate, as explained above.

A less important but more detailed syntactical analysis is that which divides a sentence into a maximum of five functional units as follows:

1   Simple subject.

2   Simple predicate, including the complement or complements, if present. There are four kinds of complements: the subjective, the objective, the direct object, the indirect object.

3   A clause. This is a group of words which contains a subject and a predicate and which functions as either a substantive, an attributive, or a definitive.

4   A modifier of a modifier.

5   Connectives to join these parts or to join simple sentences so as to form a compound sentence.

Another type of syntactical analysis is one which shows that each functional unit must be classified materially as either:

1   A word.

2   A phrase. This is a group of words which does not contain a subject and a predicate, which functions as either a substantive, an attributive, or a definitive, and which can be classified as either a prepositional or a verbal phrase. For example, *on that day* and *into the house* are prepositional phrases. *To sing, to make excuses* are infinitive phrases. In the sentence, "Making excuses is the weakling's first thought," *making excuses* is

a gerund phrase. In the sentence, "John stood before his employer, making excuses," *making excuses* is a participial phrase.

3 A clause. This is a group of words which does contain a subject and a predicate and which functions as either a substantive, an attributive, or a definitive.

The difference between syntactical analysis and the analysis required for the study of logic can be illustrated through an analogy. Functionally, a building may be a hotel, a church, a school, a home, a factory, a jail, a garage, a barn. Materially, it may be of brick, stone, or wood.

FUNCTION OF GRAMMAR

The fundamental function of grammar is to establish laws for relating symbols so as to express thought. A sentence expresses a thought, a relation of ideas, in a declaration, a question, a command, a wish, a prayer, or an exclamation. Categorematic symbols are what are related; syncategorematic symbols are the means for relating them; the relation itself is the sentence.

The rules for relating symbols govern three grammatical operations: substituting equivalent symbols, combining symbols, and separating symbols.

Rules for Substituting Equivalent Symbols
EXPANSION

1 Every proper name is convertible into an empirical description, for example: Benjamin Franklin = the man who discovered that lightning is electricity = the inventor of the lightning rod = the diplomatic representative of the Continental Congress to France during the Revolutionary War.

2 Every common name is convertible into a general description, for example: cat = a small, furry, sharp-clawed, whiskered animal that mews.

3 A word can be expanded into a phrase, a group of words, for example: horseshoe = a shoe for a horse; bookseller = a seller of books. Not every compound word, however, can be thus expanded without a change of meaning. Consider: wallflower, moonshine, streetwalker, goldenrod, sheepskin, greenhorn, greenback.

4   A phrase can be expanded into a sentence or a group of sentences, for example: this clock = This object is a clock. Cloudy sky = Sky is cloudy. The cheerful, wounded soldier = The soldier is cheerful. The soldier is wounded. Compare in meaning a large hot dog; a large, hot dog; a juicy hot dog; an angry, hot dog.

CONTRACTION

1   Theoretically, every empirical description is convertible into a proper name. Actually we have not invented proper names for every existent object.

2   Theoretically, every general description is convertible into a common name, for example: a rushing, roaring, violent stream = torrent; walked with long and measured steps = strode; walked slowly and aimlessly = sauntered.

3   A sentence may be contracted into a phrase, for example: The man has a red beard = the man with a red beard = the red-bearded man.

4   A phrase may be contracted into a word, for example: man who sells = salesman; light of day = daylight; herder of sheep = shepherd. Contraction of some phrases creates a change in both the logical and the psychological dimensions, for example: man fearing God, God-fearing man; man of God, godly man.

Contraction and expansion are devices determining style and its effects. Contraction should characterize language addressed to adults; expansion, that addressed to children.

Rules for Combining Symbols

There are five means of combining symbols: form words, inflections, word order, stress, intonation.

1   *Form words* are syncategorematic words of operation: the pure copula, verbal auxiliaries,[35] conjunctions, prepositions, definitives. Form words are the most important means of relating words in a sentence. They are indispensable to every language.

2   *Inflections* have the same grammatical functions as form words. For example, *puero* expresses the dative relation by means of an inflectional ending; *to the boy* expresses the dative relation by means of form words.

3   *Word order* is very important in a comparatively uninflected language like English or Chinese. Probably the reliance of English on word order has given rise to some of its illogical idioms, such as the so-called retained object.[36]

The following sentence illustrates active voice: She gave me a pencil. (*Pencil* is the direct object.) In true passive voice the direct object of the action is the subject. For example: A pencil was given to me by her. (*Pencil* is the subject.)

"I was given a pencil by her" illustrates pseudopassive voice. *Pencil* is a retained object. Reliance on word order probably occasioned the development in English of the pseudopassive voice with the so-called retained object. True passive voice, with the word order of pseudopassive voice is illustrated by the following sentence, "To me was given a pencil by her." Here *pencil* appears in its true function as the subject, not as object, retained or otherwise, and *I* becomes *me* to express precisely its true function as the indirect object. Only the true passive voice, expressed in normal word order in the second sentence above and in abnormal word order in the fourth sentence, can be translated into a precise, logical language, such as Latin or French. Although it is illogical, the pseudopassive voice, like the pseudocopula, is correct, idiomatic English; it has been in use at least since the thirteenth century.

4   *Stress*, the relative force with which a sound is uttered, is a way of expressing the relations of words. It is of importance chiefly in spoken language. The following sentences require interpretation through the use of stress.

That that is is not that that is not.

He was my friend.

A tall dark man with a mustache who is he stole my purse.

Compare the effect of stress within words by accenting each of the following on the first and then on the second syllable: record, object, converse, project, compact, august, entrance.

5   *Intonation*, the controlled use of pitch, is another way of expressing the relations of words. It is of importance chiefly in spoken language. The following sentences require interpretation through intonation.

He's a fine fellow.

Oh she is dead.

Yet Brutus says he was ambitious
And Brutus is an honorable man.
          —*Julius Caesar* 3.2.86–87

Macbeth. . . . If we should fail?
Lady Macbeth. We fail!
But screw your courage to the sticking place
And we'll not fail.
                    —*Macbeth* 1.7.58–61

No language can dispense with form words. No language can rely exclusively on word order, stress, and intonation. English relies chiefly on word order and form words, and so does Chinese; hence English and Chinese are structurally, or morphologically, similar. Latin relies mainly on inflection. English is related to Latin genealogically because many English words are derived from Latin. Likewise, many English words are derived from Germanic,[37] and English is therefore related to German genealogically. It is also related to German morphologically because both languages employ form words extensively. English, German, Latin, Greek, and a number of other languages are all derived from the parent Indo-European language.

Oral Punctuation

Marks of punctuation do for written language what phrasing, stress, and some forms of intonation, such as raising the voice for a question, do for spoken language.

That oral punctuation does for reading what punctuation marks do for writing becomes evident if one tries to read pages unpunctuated. A passage read with grotesque phrasing, that is, with wrong methods of combining and separating, becomes almost nonsense.

Interpret:

There's a divinity that shapes our ends
Rough hew them how we will.[38]
                    —*Hamlet* 5.2.10–11

That that is is that that is not is not.[39]

He said that that that that that sentence contains is a definitive.[40]

The boy said his father was to blame.[41]

Since languages are imperfect because they are too rich in meaning, the grammatical problem is to interpret the written page. Spoken language is clarified by the speaker who punctuates it orally, who combines and separates the elements by phrasing, by stress, and by intonation. Difficulties in writing are identical with difficulties in reading. Students fail in expression, in speaking or writing, for the same reason that they fail in impression, in listening or reading; they do not understand or do not apply the rules of grammar which must guide both writer and reader, both speaker and listener.

4 TERMS AND THEIR GRAMMATICAL EQUIVALENTS: DEFINITION AND DIVISION

TERMS AND THEIR GRAMMATICAL EQUIVALENTS

Words are symbols created to represent reality. A term is a concept communicated through a symbol. Once words are used to communicate a concept of reality, they become terms.

Communication is dynamic; it is the conveying of an idea from one mind to another through a material medium, words or other symbols. If the listener or reader receives through language precisely the ideas put into it by the speaker or writer,[1] these two have "come to terms"— the idea has passed successfully, clearly, from the giver to the receiver, from one end or term of the line of communication to the other.[2]

A term differs from a concept only in this: a term is an idea in transit, hence is dynamic, an *ens communicationis*; the concept is an idea representing reality, an *ens mentis*. A concept is a potential term; it becomes an actual term when it is communicated through a symbol. Hence a term is the meaning, the form the logical content, of words (see Chapter Two, Nature of Language). Words are therefore the symbols, the means by which terms are conveyed from mind to mind.

ANALOGY: Reality and the symbols for reality

The coffee in the coffee pot can reach me only by means of a conveyor, such as a cup. An idea can get from one mind to another only by means of a conveyor, a symbol. The idea is analogous to the coffee; the symbol, to the cup. The word used as a conveyor for the idea becomes a term when the thought is communicated.

Not every word, however, can symbolize a logical term. Only categorematic words (substantives and attributives) can do so. Although a syncategorematic word (a preposition, a conjunction, a definitive) cannot symbolize a logical term, it can be grammatically a part of the complete symbol, which expresses a logical term. A complete symbol, which must be either a proper name, an empirical description, a common name, or a general description, is, therefore, the grammatical equivalent of a logical term. Whether the complete symbol is one word or a group of words, it expresses only one logical term.

A term is the element of logic, just as the word is the element of grammar and the letter is the element of spelling.

A term is always unambiguous, or univocal because a meaning is always one: it is itself and not another. The grammatical symbol which expresses a term may, however, be ambiguous, for the same symbol is capable of expressing different terms. The dictionary lists for every word a number of meanings. Whoever uses a word normally intends but one of its various meanings; that one meaning is the term symbolized by the word in that particular instance.

The same term, whether it signifies a particular individual or an essence, may be expressed through different symbols in the same or in different languages.

EXAMPLES: Term expressed in different symbols

Individual	Essence
The red-bearded man	An equilateral rectangle
The man with a red beard	A rectangular equilateral
The man who has a red beard	A rectangle with equal sides
L'homme qui a une barbe rouge	A square
Der Mann mit einem roten Barte	*Un carré*
El barbirroja	*Ein gleichseitiges Rechteck*
Dan Dravot (in Kipling's "The Man Who Would Be King")	*Un cuadrado*

Complete symbols that are logically equivalent in meaning, in designation, or in both, are substitutable for one another (see Chapter Three, Rules for Substituting Equivalent Symbols). Such equivalency makes possible translation from one language to another; it also makes possible a variety of styles within the same language and provides means to improve style.

Words in different languages are usually equivalent in their logical dimension but often are not equivalent in their psychological dimension. That is why poetry is difficult to translate satisfactorily. Synonyms within the same language are seldom exactly the same in meaning. The least ambiguous of all symbols is a general description, especially one so perfect as to be a definition.

CLASSIFICATION OF TERMS

Empirical and General Terms

The fundamental distinction between terms is that which classifies them according to the kind of reality signified as either an empirical term or a general term.

An empirical term designates an individual or an aggregate of individuals. It must be symbolized by either a proper name or an empirical description, for example: Christopher Columbus, the desk in this room.

A general term, also called a universal term, signifies essence (of either a species or a genus). It must be symbolized by a common name or a general description, for example: tree, a three-sided rectilinear plane figure.

To be able to distinguish between an empirical term and a general term is of the utmost importance.[3] In doing this, one cannot rely on grammatical tags; one must look through the words at the reality symbolized.

EXAMPLES: General and empirical terms

A bird has feathers.	(Bird is a general term.)
A bird flew past my window.	(Bird is an empirical term.)
The dance lasted until midnight.	(Dance is an empirical term.)
The dance is an art form.	(Dance is a general term.)

Contradictory Terms: Positive and Negative Terms

Terms are contradictory when one is positive and the other is the corresponding negative. A positive term is one that expresses what is present in reality. A negative term is one that expresses what is absent. Some examples are: voter, nonvoter; Christian, non-Christian; white, nonwhite; conscious, unconscious; complete, incomplete; varnished, unvarnished.

Some grammatically negative words symbolize logically positive terms. Examples are: infinite (the absence of limit connotes fullness of being), unkind (meaning positively cruel or harsh), and impatient (meaning positively peevish or irritable).

A privative term is a kind of negative term which expresses a deprivation, the absence from a reality of a characteristic which belongs to its nature and which ought to be present. Examples include lame, blind, dead, and headless. A dog may be blind; a stone cannot be blind, for sight does not belong to the nature of stone.

Concrete and Abstract Terms

A concrete term is one that represents realities as they actually are in the order of being. Examples are animal, fast, smooth, long, near, and warm.

An abstract term is one that represents either substance or accident mentally abstracted from concrete reality and regarded, for the sake of emphasis, as an object of thought; it is symbolized by an abstract substantive. Examples are animality, speed, smoothness, length, nearness, and warmth.

Recall that in Chapter Two the importance of abstract terms was stressed. There too it was noted that concrete terms are more vivid (to the senses); abstract terms are more clear (to the intellect).

Absolute and Relative Terms

An absolute term is one that can be understood by itself without reference to another term. Examples include man, tree, dog, field, red, and hard.

A relative term is one of two terms, each of which must be understood with reference to the other. Examples include husband, wife; parents, child; teacher, pupil; cause, effect; friend, friend; larger, smaller; longest, shortest.

Relative terms are correlatives and are always absolute in at least one of the categories.[4] They have meaning in at least two and often in three or more categories; one of these is always the category relation; another is usually action or passion, for this is most often the bond by which the two terms are related to each other. For example, teacher and pupil may be thus analyzed.

EXAMPLES: Relative terms and their categories

Teacher is a term having meaning in the following categories:

Substance: man
Quality: knowledge and the skill to impart it

Relation: to a pupil
Action: imparting knowledge

Pupil is a term having meaning in the following categories:

Substance: man
Quality: ignorance
Relation: to a teacher
Passion: receiving knowledge

Note that receiving knowledge cannot be purely passive although it is passive with reference to its correlative, imparting knowledge. Teaching and being taught must be cooperative.

Collective and Distributive Terms

A collective term is one that can be applied only to a group as a group but not to the members of the group taken singly. Examples are army, jury, crew, group, senate, family, team, flock, swarm, and herd. (Jane may be a member of the jury, but she cannot be a jury.) The rule of grammar requiring the agreement of subject and verb or copula, and also of pronoun and antecedent, makes it necessary to distinguish two uses of a noun symbolizing a collective term.

The *collective use* requires that the verb or copula and the pronouns be singular. For example: The audience shows its pleasure by demanding encore after encore.

The *distributive use* requires that the verb or copula and the pronouns be plural because the members of the group are thought of as acting individually rather than collectively. For example: The audience express uproarious approval by tossing their hats into the air and shouting with loud voices.

A distributive term is one that can be applied to individual members of a group taken singly. For example, man is applicable both to every individual man and to the species man.

Ten Categories of Being

The ten logical categories of terms constitute an important classification. They correspond exactly to the ten metaphysical categories of being, namely: substance, quantity, quality, relation, action, passion, *when*, *where*, posture, habiliment.

DIFFERENCE BETWEEN TERMS

According to the basis of the difference, terms may be either categorically, generically, specifically, or individually different.

Difference Based on Category, Genus, Species, Individual

1   Terms are categorically different if they are in different categories (see Chapter Two, Ten Categories of Being). Examples include apple, large, red, there, now, and chosen.

2   Terms are generically different if they belong to different genera within the same category. Examples include round, smooth, sour; stone, tree, animal.

3   Terms are specifically different if they belong to different species within the same genus. Examples include white, red, blue, yellow, gray, black; round, square, triangular; elm, oak, maple, pine; dog, elephant, horse; walk, creep, fly.

4   Terms are individually different if they designate individuals within the same species, for every individual is unique, is itself and not another. Examples include: this woman, that woman, my mother; the Hudson River, the Mississippi River, the Snake River.

Difference by Nature: Repugnant or Nonrepugnant

According to the nature of the difference, terms are either repugnant or not. Terms are repugnant when they are incompatible, that is, when they signify realities that are mutually exclusive, that cannot coexist in the same substance at the same time and in the same period.

1   Terms that are categorically different or generically different are not necessarily repugnant, for often they signify realities that can coexist in the same substance.[5]

2   The following terms are necessarily repugnant:

All terms that are individually different are repugnant. An individual cannot be itself and another at the same time.

All terms that are specifically different are repugnant, for example: elm, oak, maple; dog, horse; square, circle, triangle.

Contradictory terms are necessarily repugnant, for example, white, nonwhite.

Contrary terms, which are pairs of terms that are either species within the same genus (for example, black, white [color]; long, short [length]), or species in contrary genera (for example, truthfulness and lying, the one a species of virtue, the other of vice) are repugnant.

Contrary genera are repugnant, for example, good and evil.

Contrary terms represent extremes of difference. Not every term has a contrary. There are, for instance, no contraries in the following genera: animal, tree, flower, vehicle, shape. Some of the classifications of terms in this chapter are contrary terms which together constitute a genus; they are therefore specifically different and, consequently, repugnant, or incompatible. This is true of each of the following pairs: general and empirical terms; positive and negative terms; concrete and abstract terms; absolute and relative terms.

The members of each pair of contrary terms are repugnant and, therefore, mutually exclusive, but a given term may be simultaneously a member of more than one pair because the pairs themselves are not mutually exclusive. Thus a given term cannot be both general and empirical, or both positive and negative, etc. It can, however, be at one and the same time general, positive, abstract, and absolute; for example, *length* is all of these simultaneously. *My grandmother* is, at one and the same time, empirical, positive, concrete, and relative.

Of great importance is the distinction between contrary terms and contradictory terms. There is no middle ground between contradictory terms. For example, everything is either white or nonwhite; and everything is either a tree or a nontree. Every pair of contradictory terms thus performs a dichotomy, that is, cuts everything in two sharply, leaving no middle ground between.

There is a middle ground between contrary terms. For example, everything need not be either white or black; it may be gray, or red, or blue.[6]

Every term has its contradictory; not every term has a contrary. Contrary terms represent the greatest degree of difference. Contradictory terms represent a necessarily clean-cut difference.

THE EXTENSION AND INTENSION OF TERMS

Definitions: Extension and Intension

Every term has both extension and intension. The extension of a term is its designation: the total set of objects to which the term can be applied. This is its objective, extramental reference to reality. For example, the extension of *friend* is the set of people who are friends to an individual; the extension of *ocean* is all the oceans on earth; the extension of *tree* is all trees. One uses a term in its full extension when applying it to all the objects it designates. One need not know the number.

The intension of a term is its meaning, the sum of the essential characteristics that the term implies.[7] This is its conceptual or logical reference. To make explicit the intension, the meaning, of a term is to define it. For example, the intension of *friend* is the sum of the qualities which make a friend, such as loyalty, congeniality, mutual affection, unselfish devotedness, trustworthiness, fidelity. Likewise, the intension of *ocean* or of *tree* is made explicit in its definition.

The extension and intension of terms have their roots in the twofold reference of the phantasm, which is a mental image of the objects (extensional references) from which the intellect derives the concept (intensional reference).

Relationship Between Extension and Intension

There is a relation between the extension and the intension of terms as expressed in the following law.[8]

Relation Between Extension and Intension of Terms

As a term increases in intension, it decreases in extension.

As a term increases in extension, it decreases in intension.

4-1 *Extension and Intension of Terms*

The Tree of Porphyry illustrates the inverse relation between the extension and intension of terms in addition to the relation between these and definition and division. This is a progressive, essential, dichotomous division leading from the *summum genus* substance to the *infima species* man. It was devised by Porphyry (233–303 A.D.).[9]

The *summum genus* is the highest and largest genus; it cannot become a species, for there is no higher genus of which it can form a species or part. The *infima species* is the lowest and smallest species; it cannot become a genus by further division into essentially different species.

A division that proceeds from the *summum genus* to the *infima species* is, therefore, a complete series; it cannot be continued above or below these.

Tree of Porphyry

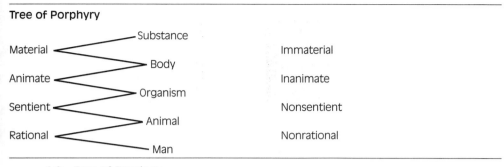

4-2 *Tree of Porphyry*

In considering the Tree of Porphyry, note that every term between the *summum genus* and the *infima species* can be either genus or species because for intermediate terms, genus and species are relative to the point of view: a term is a genus of those below it and a species of those above it. A term is the proximate genus of the term directly below it; for example, animal is the proximate genus of man; body is the proximate genus of organism. All terms above a given term, but not immediately above it, are remote genera of that term; for example: organism, body, and substance are remote genera of man, substance being the most remote.

Accordingly, the Tree of Porphyry illustrates the law of inverse relation of the extension and the intension of terms: as the intension of substance is increased (by adding the attributes material, animate, sentient, rational), its extension is decreased. Substance, the *summum genus*, has the greatest extension and the least intension. Man, the *infima species*, has the least extension and the greatest intension, that is, the greatest number of characteristic notes: man is a rational, sentient, animate, material substance.

DEFINITION

Definition makes explicit the intension or meaning of a term, the essence that it represents. A definition is symbolized by a general description, not by one word. A definition is a perfect general description. There are two kinds of definition constructed from a logical point of view: a logical definition and a distinctive definition.

Logical Definition

A logical definition expresses the essence of a species in terms of its proximate genus and its specific differentia. The pattern is species is proximate genus plus specific differentia. For example: Man is an animal possessing rationality.

Species is the term to be defined; the subject of a definition is, therefore, always species.

The specific differentia is that part of the essence which belongs only to a given species and which distinguishes it from every other species in the same genus. For example, rationality is that part of his essence which makes man different from every other species of animal.

Genus is that part of essence which is common to all the species that constitute the genus. For example, animality is that part of his essence which man shares with other species of his genus, such as horse, sparrow, oyster.

The Tree of Porphyry provides data for the logical definition of man, animal, organism, and body.

A logical definition cannot be constructed for every term because for some terms there is no proximate genus, or the specific differentia is not known. Such terms can be made clear, however, by a general description that is not a logical definition.

A logical definition cannot be constructed for the following: a *summum genus*, a transcendental concept, or the individual.

A *summum genus*, such as substance or any other of the ten categories, or a predicable cannot be defined logically. It might seem that being is the genus of substance and of the other categories, since the ten categories classify being. Being is not, however, understood in the same way of substance and of accident, nor of the different accidents; furthermore, being transcends the categories, and therefore it cannot be their genus.

A transcendental concept is a concept that cannot be classified because it extends through and beyond all categories. The transcendentals are being and its transcendental attributes: unity, truth, goodness, *res, aliquid*;[10] some philosophers include beauty.[11]

The individual, as an individual, cannot be defined, for its essence is that which it shares with other individuals of its species. That which makes the individual unique, different from other individuals in its species, serves for designation rather than for signification.

Hence only species can be defined. When a term such as animal is defined, it must be defined as species of its genus (organism), not as genus of its species (man, horse, etc.). For example, an animal is a sentient organism.

Distinctive Definition

A distinctive definition is definition by property. The pattern is as follows: species is genus (proximate or remote or even being) plus property. For example, man is a being (or animal or organism) capable of mirthfulness.

Property is not the essence, nor a part of the essence, but it is a necessary concomitant of the essence and follows from it. Thus, mirthfulness is not man's essence, nor a part of his essence, but it follows from his essence, that is, from both the genus and the differentia: because man is rational, he can see that something is funny; because he is an animal, he can laugh. A man possesses a capability for mirth, whether he exercises it or not. The laugh of a hyena is not mirthful; it is merely a cachinnation, a noise, hideous, not mirthful.

ILLUSTRATION: Relationship between concomitant and essence

On a sunny afternoon, my shadow is a concomitant of my body.

If I draw a convex line, it is concomitantly a concave line when viewed from the other side.

Taste is the concomitant of an animal's eating; it is not a concomitant of a tree's nutrition.

A distinctive definition by property is usually the best definition that science can achieve. In chemistry, an element such as hydrogen, chlorine, sodium, copper, zinc is defined by its specific properties such as natural physical status (gas, liquid, solid), atomic weight, specific gravity, and valence. In geometry, the propositions to be proved simply make explicit the properties of the triangle, the circle, the sphere, etc. It is to be noted that a species has but one specific differentia; it may have a number of specific properties.

Other Types of Definition

A **causal definition** is one that makes explicit the meaning or intension of a term by naming the cause which produced the reality which the term signifies. A causal definition may name any one of the four causes: efficient, material, formal, final.[12] For example, pneumonia is a disease caused by the pneumococcus (efficient cause). Water is H_2O (material cause, naming the constituents; formal cause, indicating how they are related).

A definition by matter and form is sometimes called a genetic definition. Such are all chemical formulas and chemical equations. Such also are all recipes. A definition by final cause is sometimes called a purposive definition.

A **descriptive definition** merely enumerates the characteristics by which the species can be recognized. For example: An elephant is a huge, thickset, nearly hairless mammalian quadruped with a long, muscular proboscis and two long tusks.

Definition by example provides data for definition rather than the definition itself. Sometimes the presentation of familiar examples will enable the mind to make from them an abstraction clearer to it than the ready-made abstraction presented in an actual definition would be. Examples are: An evergreen is a tree such as the cedar, pine, spruce, hemlock. A military genius is a man like Alexander the Great, Julius Caesar, Washington, Napoleon, Marshall Foch, George Patton, Jr. The only authentic and really enlightening definition of a neighbor is that by example, the parable of the Good Samaritan.

Grammatical and rhetorical definition or nominal definition introduces the problem of making clear which term is imposed upon a given symbol, a word, or a phrase,[13] rather than making explicit the meaning of a term. Consequently, the problem is the clarification of language, the getting rid of ambiguity, the "coming to terms" of reader and writer, of listener and speaker, both of whom must attach the same meaning to the given symbol.

1   Definition by etymology. A word is often understood more clearly from its derivation. Examples: *Infinite* is derived from Latin *in* (not) plus *finitus* (limited); *elect* is derived from Latin *e* (out) plus *lectus* (chosen).

Be aware that etymology is not a secure guide, for sometimes the present meaning does not agree with the etymological meaning. Etymologically, *hydrogen* means water-former, and *oxygen* means acid-former. But hydrogen is really the acid-former, and oxygen is the principal water-former in the sense that it constitutes nearly eight times as much of the weight of water as hydrogen does. Their names should therefore be interchanged, but this will not be done, for although oxygen is misnamed, the name had become permanently attached to the element before the error was discovered. This is only one striking instance which shows that etymology is not a safe guide to the current meaning of words, even though it is usually very helpful and illuminating. By a strange anomaly, goods transported in a car by rail are called a ship-ment, and goods transported in a ship are called a cargo.

2   Definition by synonyms. This pointedly illustrates the fact that grammar provides a choice of nearly equivalent symbols for the same term. Such symbols, however, differ somewhat either in the logical or in the psychological dimension or in both.

3   Arbitrary definition. There are certain words, very important words, about whose precise meaning there is not common agreement. The dictionary offers little practical help in defining such words.

Certain legal terms such as larceny, treason, and vagrant must be de-fined by law for the courts of each state. Such legal definitions may dif-fer greatly. Thus treason as defined by the Constitution of the United States is a term very different from treason as defined by law under Henry VIII or Elizabeth I of England or under the Czars of Russia.

Many commonly used terms, like liberty, patriotism, justice, reli-gion, courtesy, culture, and many literary terms, like classicism, ro-manticism, style, poetry, ought, for clarity, to be defined by each user of the word. A reader must be careful to discover just what meaning a writer is attaching to words as ambiguous as these; otherwise reader and writer cannot "come to terms." Debaters, in particular, must "come to terms"; otherwise they argue beside the point.

To define words of such broad and shifting meaning, one should say what is included in the term and what is excluded, dealing especially with disputable borderline instances, not merely with those obviously included or excluded.

EXAMPLES: Famous definitions

Charity is patient, is kind: charity envieth not, dealeth not perversely; is not puffed up; is not ambi-tious, seeketh not her own, is not provoked to anger, thinketh no evil; rejoiceth not in iniquity, but rejoiceth with the truth; beareth all things, believeth all things, hopeth all things, endureth all things. Charity never falleth away whether prophecies shall be made void or tongue shall cease, or knowl-edge shall be destroyed.

—Paul I Cor. 13:4–8

Literature is the best that has been thought and said in the world.

—Matthew Arnold, "Literature and Science"

A classic is a work that gives pleasure to the passionate few who are permanently and intensely in-terested in literature.

—Arnold Bennett, "Why a Classic Is a Classic"

Rules of Definition

A definition should be:

1 Convertible with the subject, the species, the term to be defined. For example: A man is a rational animal. A rational animal is a man. The term to be defined and its definition coincide perfectly both in intension and in extension; hence they are always convertible. Convertibility is the test of a definition. A statement is convertible if it is equally true with the subject and predicate interchanged.

2 Positive rather than negative. A violation of this rule is: A good man is one who does not harm his fellow men. (It is not very enlightening merely to tell what something is not.)

3 Clear, symbolized by words that are neither obscure, vague, ambiguous, nor figurative. A violation of this rule is Samuel Johnson's famous definition of a network: "Network is anything reticulated or decussated, at equal distances with interstices between the intersections."

4 Free from a word derived from the same root as the word to be defined. A violation of the rule is a definition like the following: Success is succeeding in whatever you undertake.

5 Symbolized by a parallel, not mixed, grammatical structure; for example: a gerund should be used to define a gerund; an infinitive, to define an infinitive. The following are violations: Pessimism is when a person looks on the dark side of everything. To cheat is defrauding or deceiving another.

DIVISION

Division is an extremely valuable tool of thought. In Plato's *Phaedrus*, Socrates says, "I am a great lover of these processes of division and generalization. . . . And if I find any man who is able to see unity and plurality in nature, him I follow, and walk in his step as if he were a god."

Logical division is the analysis of the extension of a term, whereas definition is the analysis of its intension. The *Summa Theologica* of Saint Thomas Aquinas illustrates how division deepens insight and manifests comprehensive order.

Logical Division Distinguished from Other Kinds of Division

Logical division is the division of a genus into its constituent species. For example, tree may be divided into its species—oak, elm, maple, poplar, etc. The test of logical division is that the logical whole (genus) can always be predicated of each of its parts (species). For example, tree can be predicated of each of its species. Oaks are trees. Elms are trees. No other whole can be predicated of its parts. Logical division never deals with the individual. It is always the division of a group (genus) into smaller groups (species), never of a species into its individual members. This last is enumeration, not division.

Quantitative division is the division of a singular extended whole, such as a line or a body, into its quantitative parts. For example, a pound of butter may be divided into servings.

Physical division is the division of a singular composite whole into its essential diversified parts. A composite may be divided into matter and form. For example: a human being may be divided into body and soul; a human body into head, hands, feet, heart, etc.

Virtual or functional division is the division of a potential or functional whole into its diversified virtual or functional parts.[14]

EXAMPLES: Virtual or functional division

"The human soul is wholly in the whole body and wholly in each part because it is the form or principle of operation; yet the whole soul is in each part of the body by totality of perfection and of essence but not by totality of power or function, for with regard to sight it is only in the eye, to hearing only in the ear, etc."[15]

A government is a functional whole exercising a single authority in different persons and places but not according to the same power in each.

Human society is a functional whole with functional parts (family, school, state, church, local community) that together educate the individual. The school is a functional whole of which the curriculum, general lectures, drama, concerts, athletics, campus organizations, etc. are functional parts. The curriculum is a functional whole directed toward wisdom of which the various subjects are parts, each making its own contribution.

A play or a story in which a unifying theme informs the whole expresses the theme more forcefully in certain scenes and characters than in others.

Metaphysical division is the distinction between substance and accidents or between accidents. For example, an orange (substance) is distinct from its accidents (color, size, shape, weight, taste, smoothness, coldness, etc.), and these are distinct from one another. A metaphysical division is a distinction, not a separation. It cannot be physically performed; for example, the shape of an orange cannot be actually separated from the orange, nor can its taste, size, and color be set separately before us, apart from the orange and apart from one another.

The distinctions perceived in metaphysical division are used as the bases of logical division; for example, we may divide fruits according to accidents, such as color, shape, size, sugar content, etc. Or we may divide them according to their essential nature into oranges, apples, bananas, cherries, etc.

Verbal division is the distinction which the dictionary makes between the meanings that have been imposed upon a word, that is, between the terms that a given notation can symbolize.

Elements of Logical Division

Logical division includes three elements: the logical whole, the basis of division, and the dividing members. The logical whole, which is to be divided, is the genus. The basis of division is the metaphysical aspect, the point of view from which division is made. The dividing members are the species resulting from the logical division.

Kinds of Logical Division

LOGICAL DIVISION ACCORDING TO THE CHARACTER OF THE BASIS OF DIVISION

According to the character of the basis of division, we distinguish among natural objects and among artificial objects.

Natural Objects

Among natural objects essential division aims to determine natural species, for example, the division of edible plants into carrots, lettuce, peas, beets, spinach, potatoes, etc.

Accidental division is based on accidents that do not determine natural species, for example: the division of edible plants according to color, shape, or nutritive value; the division of men according to color, nationality, religion, occupation, height, or weight.

Note that the *infima species*, such as man, resulting from natural essential division, can undergo further division only on an accidental basis.

Artificial Objects

Among artificial objects, essential division is based on the form imposed by man on matter. This is the division of an artificial genus into artificial species, for example: the division of silverware into knives, forks, spoons, ladles, etc.; the division of vehicles into wagons, trucks, cars, bicycles, etc.

Accidental division is based on accidents that do not determine artificial species, for example, the division of chairs according to size, color, weight, etc.

LOGICAL DIVISION ACCORDING TO THE MANNER OF APPLYING THE BASIS OF DIVISION

According to the manner of applying the basis of division, we distinguish positive division and dichotomy.

Positive Division

Positive division divides a genus into its constituent species, for example: the division of elements into hydrogen, oxygen, nitrogen, sulphur, carbon, silver, gold, etc.; the division of color into white, red, yellow, blue, gray, black, etc. This is the type of division science aims to accomplish.

Dichotomy

Dichotomy is division by contradictory terms, for example: the division of elements into gold and nongold; of color into red and nonred, or white and nonwhite.

In division by dichotomy, the negative term is unexplored in the sense that it may contain within itself either a number of positive species or only one. Thus, investigation reveals that nonwhite contains many positive species: red, yellow, blue, green, brown, gray, black, etc.; but noneven is a negative term which contains only one positive species, namely, odd.

Rules of Logical Division

1   A logical division must have one and only one basis.

2   The constituent species must be mutually exclusive (with no overlapping).

3   The division must be collectively exhaustive, or complete; that is, the constituent species must equal the genus.

No one species may equal the genus, for then there would be no division. This is the error present in an outline when a person attempts to divide by one subtopic. Such an attempt results in no division at all; there must be at least two species, at least two subtopics.

A shift in the basis of division is the error of applying simultaneously, but incompletely, two or more different bases of division, for example, the division of books into Latin, English, French, poetry, history, science, octavo, quarto, blue, red. A shift in the basis of division is the prime error in division, creating confusion and disorder. It makes it impossible to achieve what logical division aims at—a division that is collectively exhaustive (complete) and mutually exclusive (with no overlapping).

From a strictly logical point of view, although not from a scientific one, dichotomy is superior to positive division, because—since there is no middle ground between contradictory terms—dichotomy guarantees the realization of the aims of logical division as stated in the foregoing rules whereas positive division cannot do so with equal assurance.

The principle of contradiction—that a thing cannot both be and not be at the same time and in the same respect—is an axiom of thought, a law of reason, of greater certitude than any law of science. Dichotomy employs this principle.

Positive division is based on empirical knowledge, which often requires revision because further investigation proves earlier conclusions to have been incomplete, inadequate, misleading. For example, the early Greek observers classified the elements as four: earth, water, fire, and air. Modern chemistry[16] distinguishes more than one hundred elements and shows that not one of the four so long regarded as elements is really an element; for example, water is a compound and air is a mixture. We cannot be certain how many elements science will distinguish five hundred years from now. Because positive division relies on investigation, not on a principle of reason, it is inferior from a logical point of view.[17]

The Tree of Porphyry is a division by dichotomy. By no other means could we achieve a progressive, essential, exhaustive, and mutually exclusive division of all substance.

Subdivision and Codivision

Subdivision is a division subordinate to a preceding division; it may employ the same or a different basis of division and should result in a single, orderly system. An example is the Tree of Porphyry.

Codivision is a series of independent divisions of the same whole, each employing a different basis of division. For example, a codivision of books could be made by applying successively, and each time exhaustively, these four bases of division: subject, language, size, color of binding.

The earlier part of this chapter deals with the codivision of terms.[18] Each of the six classifications divides all terms according to one basis of division into species mutually exclusive and collectively exhaustive.

5 PROPOSITIONS AND THEIR GRAMMATICAL EXPRESSION

THE PROPOSITION: DEFINITION AND DISTINCTIONS

Proposition and Relation of Terms

The proposition asserts a relation of terms. It consists of subject, copula, and predicate. The terms (the subject and the predicate) constitute the matter of the proposition; the copula which relates them constitutes its form.[1]

Proposition: Modal and Categorical

MODAL PROPOSITION

A proposition may or may not assert the mode[2] of the relation of its terms. If it does, it is modal; if it does not, it is categorical, that is, asserted simply as a matter of fact.

A modal proposition explicitly asserts the relation of its terms as either necessary or contingent.

Necessary

If the proposition asserts a relationship that is necessary, the necessity may be metaphysical, physical, moral, or logical.

Metaphysical. The relation is metaphysically necessary if it could not be otherwise for the reason that it would be impossible, inconceivable, involving sheer contradiction.

Metaphysical necessity is such that not even God can make it otherwise. God is the source of order, not of disorder and confusion. To be unable to do what is contradictory is not a limitation of His Omnipotence; it is not an imperfection but a perfection. Thus God cannot make a square circle, nor can He make a stone so big that He could not lift it.

ILLUSTRATION: Propositions expressing relations metaphysically necessary

An equilateral triangle is necessarily equiangular.

The effect cannot be greater than its cause.

A being is necessarily itself and not another.

Things equal to the same thing are necessarily equal to each other.

Physical. Physical necessity rests on the laws of nature. God can suspend the laws of nature in contrast to metaphysical laws. Miracles such as the three young men in the fiery furnace (Daniel 3:46–50) and Christ walking on the Sea of Galilee (Matthew 14:29) demonstrate that abrogating physical necessity is the essence of a miracle.

ILLUSTRATION: Propositions expressing relations physically necessary

Fire necessarily burns.

Water necessarily boils at 100 degrees centigrade at sea level.

Mercury (Hg) is necessarily liquid at room temperature.

Moral. Moral necessity is a normative necessity referring to a free agent. Because of free will, humans can act counter to these laws. Even so, the laws remain, either expressing natural human tendencies, as in economic laws; or expressing the demands of order in society, as in civil laws; or, most important, expressing a duty binding on conscience, as in the moral law.

ILLUSTRATION: Propositions expressing relations morally necessary

The quality of the goods being equal, people necessarily tend to buy the goods priced lowest. This tendency can be counteracted to some extent by a contrary appeal to the free will, as, for instance, by a campaign to "Buy American."

Cars must stop when the traffic light is red.[3]

Good must be done and evil avoided.

Logical. For a consideration of the relations of necessity and contingency on strictly logical grounds, see the predicables: species, genus, differentia, definition, property, and accident. The predicables are fully explained later in this chapter.

Contingent

If a modal proposition does not assert the relations of its terms as necessary, then the relationship is contingent. Whatever is not necessary is contingent. A relation is contingent, or possible, that does not involve either necessity or metaphysical incompatibility; it may or may not exist in the natural order. It may also be contingent on future acts or events or on our knowledge.

EXAMPLES: Contingent propositions

A raven may be red.

A lion may be tame.

A triangle may be isosceles.

This water may contain typhoid germs.

Your mother may be writing you a letter now.

Amelia Jones may win the election.

CATEGORICAL PROPOSITION

A categorical proposition asserts the relation of its terms as they are actually related, without expressing the mode of their relation. If the mode is afterwards considered, it is, of course, found to be either necessary or contingent. Consequently, the copula in a categorical proposition is ambiguous in the sense that, if examined, the simple *is* means either *is necessarily (must be)* or *is contingently (may be)*.

Grammar Note

The indicative mood of the copula expresses the categorical relation.

The potential mood expresses the contingent relations.

5-1 *Mood of Categorical and Contingent Propositions*

Proposition: Simple or Compound

A proposition is either simple or compound.

A *simple proposition* is one that asserts the relation of two terms and only two.[4] A simple proposition is categorical if it asserts the relation as a matter of fact. Every categorical proposition is a simple proposition, but not every simple proposition is categorical. A simple proposition is modal if it explicitly asserts the relation as either necessary or contingent.

A *compound proposition* is one that relates at least three terms. A compound proposition may be either hypothetical or disjunctive. A hypothetical proposition asserts the dependence of one proposition on another. For example: If he does not study, he will fail (three terms). A disjunctive proposition asserts that of two or more suppositions, one is true. For example: A triangle is equilateral, isosceles, or scalene (four terms).

CHARACTERISTICS OF PROPOSITIONS

Propositions are characterized by reference to reality, quantity, quality, modality, and value. Each of these characteristics divides propositions into two classes.

Reference to Reality: General or Empirical

Reference to reality, the fundamental distinction between propositions, is determined by the reference of the subject.

A *general* proposition is one whose subject is a general term, referring to an essence, symbolized by a common name or a general description.

An *empirical* proposition is one whose subject is an empirical term, referring to an individual or an aggregate, symbolized by a proper name or an empirical description.

Quantity: Total or Partial

The *quantity* of a proposition is determined by the extension of the subject. A proposition is **total** if its subject is a term used in its full extension.

A general proposition does not have quantity in the concrete sense because its subject is essence, a class nature. The subject of a general proposition is, however, used in its full extension and is, in that sense, regarded as total. A categorical proposition, in which the subject is used in its full extension and is therefore total in quantity, may be worded in various ways.

Spinach is a vegetable.

A rabbit is an animal.

All birds have feathers. (This proposition is explicitly quantified by "All.")

To be a square is to be a rectangle.

When the general proposition is asserted as a necessary modal, it might be worded thus: A square must have four equal sides.

A singular empirical proposition, because its subject is one individual, is used in its full extension and is, in that sense, regarded as total. When the singular empirical proposition is asserted categorically, it might be worded thus: This man is a thief. When the singular empirical proposition is asserted as a necessary modal proposition, it might be worded thus: John is necessarily mortal.

Quantity, in the strict sense, is proper only to plural empirical propositions. A plural empirical proposition is total when the subject is a total aggregate of individuals.

All the members of this class are American citizens.

No chair in this room is a rocker.

These women are lawyers.

Twelve horses were entered in the race.

A proposition is **partial** if its subject is a term used in only part of its extension. In plural empirical propositions the partial extension of the subject is expressed by a limiting word such as "some" or an equivalent.

Some men are handsome.

Some roses are not red.

All violets are not purple. ("All are not" idiomatically means "Some are not.")

Not every day is rainy. (This means: Some days are not rainy.)

When a general proposition or a singular empirical proposition is contingent in modality the subject is used in only a part of its extension (as is proved by the test of conversion).[5]

EXAMPLES: Contingent propositions

A contingent general proposition: A rectangle may not be a square.

A contingent singular proposition: John may not be sad.

Quality: Affirmative or Negative

The quality of a proposition is determined by the copula, which joins or separates, composes or divides the terms. A proposition is affirmative if it asserts the inclusion of the subject (all of it or a part of it) in the predicate. A proposition is negative if it asserts the exclusion of the predicate (always all of it) from the subject.

Modality: Necessary or Contingent

The modality of a proposition is determined by the copula. Necessary and contingent relations have been explained and illustrated at the beginning of this chapter.

Value: True or False

The truth or falsity of an empirical proposition can be known only from investigation, from experience, from an appeal to the facts. In this sense it is synthetic, a putting together of facts.

"Every high school in America teaches calculus." To discover the truth or falsity of this proposition, one must either visit every high school in America or by other means get authentic information about every one of them.

The truth or falsity of a general proposition can be known from an analysis of the terms without an investigation of all the facts. In this sense it is analytic. Because it depends upon intellectual insight into a class nature or essence, our knowledge of its truth or falsity has greater certainty than that of an empirical proposition, which depends on the investigation of individual instances.

"A circle cannot be square." To discover the truth or falsity of this proposition, it is not necessary to find all the circles in the world and attempt to make them into squares. Intellectual insight reveals the incompatibility of the terms, once they are understood.

A proposition must be either true or false. Whatever is capable of being true or false must be a proposition or more than one, for this characteristic (truth or falsity) is a property of propositions.

A proposition is true if the relation it asserts is really as asserted; otherwise it is false. For example, a proposition which asserts a possibility is true if the relation is really possible, even though it is not actual: A raven may be red. It is, however, false to assert as a matter of fact: Some ravens are red.

Three Kinds of Truth

Metaphysical truth is the conformity of a thing to the idea of it in the mind of God primarily and in the minds of men secondarily. Every being has metaphysical truth.

Logical truth is the conformity of thought to reality; its opposite is falsity.

Moral truth is the conformity of expression to thought; its opposite is a lie.

5-2 *Three Kinds of Truth*

PROPOSITIONAL FORMS: A E I O FORMS

Since classical times, propositions have been classified according to quality and according to quantity or modality. All propositions are either negative or positive. All propositions are either categorical or modal. If a proposition is modal, it may be necessary or contingent. These distinctions have been presented in this chapter, and they form the basis of conceptualizing and manipulating propositions. Using quality and either quantity or modality as the basis, every proposition can be labeled A, E, I, or O. Hence we have either quantitative (also called categorical) or modal A E I O forms.

Display 5-3 summarizes the A E I O forms. In the formulas, S symbolizes the subject and P the predicate. Tot. is an abbreviation for total, and part., for partial. Affirm. is an abbreviation for affirmative, and neg., for negative. Nec. is an abbreviation for necessary, and cont., for contingent. For example, an A proposition is total (subject is used in its full extension) and affirmative (predicate is affirmed of the subject). Thinking of a proposition as one of the A E I O forms quickly becomes second nature in the study of logic.

Quantitative A E I O forms (The propositions are categorical)

A	Tot. affirm.	S a P	All S is P.	All lions are animals.
E	Tot. neg.	S e P	No S is P.	No lions are horses.
I	Part. affirm.	S i P	Some S is P.	Some lions are tame.
O	Part. neg.	S o P	Some S is not P.	Some lions are not tame.

Modal A E I O forms (The propositions are explicitly modal)

A	Nec. affirm.	S a P	S must be P.	A lion must be an animal.
E	Nec. neg.	S e P	S cannot be P.	A lion cannot be a horse.
I	Cont. affirm.	S i P	S may be P.	A lion may be tame.
O	Cont. neg.	S o P	S may not be P.	A lion may not be tame.

5-3 *Forms of Propositions*

The indefiniteness characteristic of I and O propositions may be expressed either by the indefinite *some* or by the contingent *may*. The quantity of a proposition is determined by its subject and hence by the matter, not by the form. The modality and the quality of a proposition are determined by the copula. Since the copula is the form of a proposition, the modal forms, determined altogether by the copula, more properly express propositional forms. Yet the quantitative forms are usually more convenient and are more frequently used, for we are inclined to use categorical propositions more often than modal ones.

The A E I O designations are a Latin mnemonic. A and I are the first two vowels in *affirmo*, I affirm, and thus designate the affirmative propositions. E and O are the vowels in *nego*, I deny, and thus designate the negative propositions.

THE DISTRIBUTION OF TERMS

Distribution is a characteristic of terms used in a proposition, not of a term standing alone. A term is distributed if it is used in its full extension. It is undistributed if it is used in less than its full extension.

The Formal Rules of Distribution

The quantity (or modality) of a proposition determines the distribution of its subject. The quality of a proposition determines the distribution of its predicate.

1   A total (or necessary) proposition distributes its subject.

2 A partial (or contingent) proposition has its subject undistributed.

3 A negative proposition distributes its predicate (because it excludes all of it from the subject).

4 An affirmative proposition has its predicate undistributed (because the predicate is normally a term wider in extension than the subject).

The predicate of an affirmative proposition is, however, distributed whenever the proposition is a definition, by virtue of the following reasoning: (1) a definition is always an A proposition (necessary affirmative) and therefore its subject is distributed through the form; (2) the predicate, being the definition of the subject (whether by genus and differentia or by property), has not only the same intension but the same extension as the subject, namely, full extension, and is therefore distributed (through the matter, the terms, although not through the form, the copula). The very fact that a definition is convertible proves that the predicate has the same extension as the subject, and therefore, since the subject is distributed, so is the predicate. Conversion is the test of distribution.

Applying the Rules to the A E I O Forms

Distribution is an important concept in logic. The formal rules of distribution can be reduced to formulas that apply to the A E I O forms. In considering the formula, note that d means distributed, and u, undistributed.

d　u

1 S a P　　Because it is total (or necessary), an A proposition distributes its subject; because it is affirmative, its predicate is undistributed. (All lions are animals.)

d　d

2 S e P　　Because it is total (or necessary), an E proposition distributes its subject; because it is negative, it distributes its predicate. (No lions are horses.)

u　u

3 S i P　　Because it is partial (or contingent), an I proposition has its subject undistributed; because it is affirmative, its predicate is undistributed. (Some lions are tame.)

u   d

4   S o P   Because it is partial (or contingent), an O proposition has its subject undistributed; because it is negative, it distributes its predicate. (Some lions are not tame.)

Note that knowing the distribution of terms is as indispensable to success in the study of logic as knowing the basic axioms is in the study of geometry. If you become bewildered, or seem to get lost in a fog, go back to this point, grasp it clearly, and then work your way through to the light.

The Relation and the Distribution of Terms: Euler's Circles

The relation and distribution of terms in A E I O forms may be graphically represented by Euler's circles.[6] Two terms, S and P, can be related in four ways.

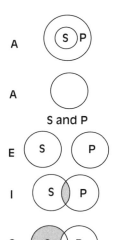

A

A

S and P

E

I

O

1   Total inclusion of S in P. S is distributed. If P exceeds S in extension, as it usually does, P is undistributed. If P exactly coincides with S in extension, as when one dime is placed on another, P is distributed through the matter, not through the form; this occurs only when P is the definition or the property of S.

2   Total exclusion of P from S. Both are distributed.

3   Inclusion of part of S in part of P. Neither is distributed.

4   Exclusion of all of P from part of S. Therefore, S is undistributed; P is distributed.

THE PREDICABLES

Classification by the Predicables

The predicables represent the ultimate classification of the relations a predicate may be affirmed to have to a subject, just as the categories represent the ultimate classification of being-as-it-is (the metaphysical categories) and of being-as-it-is-known (the logical categories).

The classification of predicates in the predicables in logic is analogous to the syntactical analysis of the sentence in grammar, just as the classification of terms in the categories in logic is analogous to the part-of-speech analysis in grammar.

The predicables are species, genus, differentia, definition, property, and accident. Although in the treatment of definition all these have been explained except accident, for convenience they are repeated here.

Species as a predicate expresses that which the individual members of a class have in common. When a species is the predicate of a categorical proposition, the subject is always an individual or an aggregate. *Infima species*, as a predicate, expresses the whole essence or intension of its subject, an individual member (or members) of the species. Two examples are: Socrates is a man. These animals are horses.

Genus is that part of the essence which is common to all its constituent species. Examples are: Man is an animal. A square is a rectangle.

The *differentia* is that part of the essence which belongs only to a given species and which distinguishes it from every other species in the same genus. Examples are: Man is rational. A square is equilateral.

Definition is constituted of the genus plus the differentia; it makes explicit the essence of the species which stands as its subject, and therefore it coincides perfectly with the subject in both intension and extension. Two examples are: Man is a rational animal. A square is an equilateral rectangle.

Property is not the essence nor a part of the essence, but it flows from the essence and is present wherever the essence is present, for it is a necessary concomitant of the essence. Therefore, it perfectly coincides with the subject in extension but not in intension. Examples are: Man is mirthful. A square is divisible by its diagonal into two equal isosceles right triangles.

Accident is a predicate contingently related to the subject, whereas all the other predicables are related necessarily to the subject. The contingency may be either explicit or implicit. Examples are: Man may be white. A square may be large. The grass is green.

The predicable accident must be carefully distinguished from the predicamental accident (any of the nine categories of accident).[7] The predicables and the categories (or *praedicamenta*) are codivisions of terms, each using a different principle of division, one depending altogether on the relations of terms, the other classifying terms independently.

Predicates Classified by Predicable and Category

Proposition	Predicable	Category
Man is rational.	Differentia	Accident (quality)
Man is mirthful.	Property	Accident (quality)
Man is an animal.	Genus	Substance
John is a man.	Species	Substance
John is a lawyer.	Accident	Substance (construct)
John is tall.	Accident	Accident (quantity)
Snow is white.	Accident	Accident (quality)

5-4 *Dual Classification of Predicates*

An inseparable accident, which is a contingent predicate, must not be confused with property, which is a necessary predicate. For example, a raven is always black, but blackness is not therefore a necessary predicate of raven. The contingent general proposition "A raven may be red" is therefore true as a possibility.

For years whiteness was considered an inseparable accident of swans, for no swans except white ones were known until black swans were discovered in Australia. Nevertheless, even before the discovery, white was correctly regarded as a contingent, not a necessary, predicate of swan.

The Number of the Predicables

There are five predicables which classify the predicates of a general (or universal) affirmative proposition, and a sixth, which appears only in an empirical affirmative proposition.

In his exposition of the predicables, wherein he shows that they analyze modality as either necessary or contingent, Aristotle distinguishes five. His analysis is applicable only to general affirmative propositions. Let S a P symbolize a general affirmative proposition. Then P is either convertible with S or it is not. If it is convertible, P is either the definition (signifying the essence) or a property. If it is not convertible, P is either one of the elements of the definition (genus or differentia) or it is not; if it is not one of the elements of the definition, it is an accident (*Topics*, 1.8).[8]

Aristotle also says emphatically (*Categories*, 2.5)[9] that all predication is primarily and essentially of first substance, that is, of an individual, the object of our experience, expressed by a singular empirical term as subject. A general or universal term can stand as a subject only because it can itself be predicated of singulars, that is, of individuals. Hence Aristotle includes a sixth predicable, species, which states the class nature of an individual and can therefore be predicated normally only of individuals. In its extensional relation to its subject, as revealed by the test of conversion, species resembles genus in not being convertible, for its extension is greater than that of the subject. For example: Socrates is a man.

The extensional relationships of the six predicables to the subject can be graphically represented by Euler's circles.

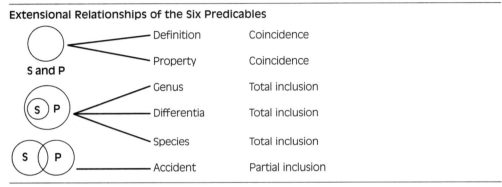

Extensional Relationships of the Six Predicables

S and P	Definition	Coincidence
	Property	Coincidence
S P	Genus	Total inclusion
	Differentia	Total inclusion
	Species	Total inclusion
S P	Accident	Partial inclusion

5-5 *Euler's Circles Showing Extensional Relationships of the Six Predicables*

Porphyry and the Scholastics listed five predicables, including species but omitting definition. It is true that species and definition are identical in both extension and intension, and that in order of being, on which Porphyry's classification is based, species, like definition, signifies the whole essence; moreover, the Scholastics exemplify the predicable species by a predicate which is definition. Yet species, as commonly understood, when used as a predicate cannot be identified with the predicable definition, since species is the subject, the one possible subject of the predicable definition, and species can be the predicate normally only of a singular empirical subject. Species as a predicate has more in common with genus than with definition because in both of these relations the subject is totally included in a wider predicate, as Euler's circles indicate.

Limits of Predication

In their narrow signification the six predicables do not represent an exhaustive analysis of predication, not even of necessary predication.

The first reason why the six predicables do not represent an exhaustive analysis of predication rests on the understanding that a predicate is affirmed necessarily of a subject if it is a property or the differentia of a remote genus of the subject; but it cannot be classified as either a property or the differentia of *that* subject. For example: A man necessarily has weight (is ponderable).

Weight is a property of body, and body is a remote genus of man; but weight is not, in the narrow sense, a property of man, for it is not a term convertible with man. Yet it is predicated necessarily of man. In terms of Aristotle's analysis, a property or the differentia of a remote genus of the subject would be a part of the definition, in the broad sense that it is included in its intension, but not in the narrow sense of being the differentia of *that* subject, or a property of *that* subject, as differentia and property are defined. (Property, as defined, is, of course, not a part of definition in the narrow sense, because it is not a part of the essence, although it flows from the essence.) The same is true of the Scholastic interpretation of species as a predicable.

Secondly, because the individual is a member of a species, one can predicate necessarily of an individual not only species but other necessary predicates which he has by virtue of his species. For example, John is necessarily a man, an animal, a rational animal, capable of mirth.

Animal is a genus of man but not of John. Rational animal is the definition of a man but not of John, for an individual cannot be defined. Mirthfulness is a property of man but not of John, for it is not convertible with John.

The predicables are, moreover, a classification of the predicates in affirmative propositions only, for the predicate in a negative proposition, always wholly excluded from the subject, obviously cannot be related to the subject as its species, genus, differentia, definition, property, or accident. Yet the predicate may be necessarily excluded from the subject. Some of the most important propositions in philosophy are necessary negative propositions. Two examples are: Contradictory judgments cannot both be true. A square is necessarily not a circle.

Predicates can, of course, also be classified in the categories or *praedicamenta*. When the predicate is in the same category as the subject, it states the species or the genus of the subject with greater or less determinateness.

EXAMPLES: Subject and predicate in the same categories of being

John is a man, an animal, an organism, a body, a substance.

A square is a figure, a shape, a quality.

Prudence is a habit, a virtue, a good, a quality.

The categories are direct metaphysical universals, called terms of first intention because they classify our concepts of being or reality. The predicables are reflex logical universals, called terms of second intention, because they are wholly mental in that they classify the relations which the mind perceives between our concepts of reality.

SENTENCES AND PROPOSITIONS

Grammatical symbols are required to express propositions.

Grammatical Symbols and Propositions

If a proposition is symbolized by a sentence, it must be a declarative sentence. A nondeclarative sentence (a command or prayer or wish or question or exclamation) cannot symbolize a proposition, for it is neither true nor false; it expresses volition, not cognition, and has therefore no status in logic, although it has thoroughly sound status in grammar.

Because every simple declarative sentence is made up either explicitly or implicitly of subject, copula, and subjective complement, it can symbolize perfectly the logical proposition made up of subject, copula, and predicate. Consequently, every declarative sentence symbolizes a proposition or a number of propositions, whether the copula and subjective complement are explicit or not.

A general proposition must be symbolized by a sentence whose subject is a common name or a general description. If the common name or the general description does not symbolize an essence that is possible, it does not express a term, for one cannot have a concept of an impossible essence.

A violation of this rule is: A square circle is a curvilinear figure.

This sentence does not symbolize a proposition because it does not express a relation of two terms; it has but one term. It takes a logical subject, for square circle expresses no meaning whatever, although square and circle understood separately are words that have meaning. This sentence is neither true nor false, for only a proposition is true or false.

An empirical categorical proposition must be symbolized by a sentence whose subject is a proper name or an empirical description. If the proper name or the empirical description does not symbolize an individual or an aggregate existent at present or in the past, in fact or in fiction, it does not express a term because one cannot experience what is nonexistent.

A violation of this rule is: Astronauts on Mars live in underground buildings. Because it does not express a relation of two terms, this sentence does not symbolize a proposition; therefore, it is neither true nor false.

The following two empirical modal propositions, however, are true as possibilities: Astronauts may live on Mars, and they may live in underground buildings.

The same proposition can be expressed by different but equivalent grammatical symbols in the same or in different languages.

EXAMPLES: Same proposition with language differences

The first man elected as executive head of the United States is noted for his skill as a military leader.

The first President of the United States is famed as a great general.

Le premier président des États-Unis est renommé comme un grand général.

Der erste Präsident der Vereinigten Staaten ist als ein grosser General berühmt.

El primer presidente de los Estados Unidos es renombrado como un gran general.

A sentence which symbolizes a proposition may be ambiguous. A proposition cannot be ambiguous because the meaning, the judgment, which the mind intends to express, must be one, that is, univocal. When the listener or reader obtains from and through language the identical proposition intended by the speaker or writer, he understands; they have "come to terms."

The purpose of translation is to express in the symbols of other languages the propositions embodied in the symbols of a given language.

Unless the propositional content of a scientific treatise obtainable in four different languages were univocal and common to all of them, there would be four treatises, not one. These books differ in language, that is, in the symbols used to embody one and the same logical content.

When a given composition is compared with its translation in another language, we recognize that there is something the same (the form, the logical content) and something different (the matter, the grammatical symbols). If the composition is a poem, the something different includes not only the difference of symbols but differences in the psychological dimension of language, its sensuous and emotional qualities such as sound, rhythm, tone, associated ideas and feelings, all having their roots in the particular language. To embody in different symbols only the logical content of a poem is to translate only a part of the complex whole that is the poem. Consequently, poetry is in its total effects practically untranslatable.

Differences of style in expressing a given logical content in the same language are occasioned by a difference of choice between symbols logically, but not psychologically, equivalent—between words, phrases, and clauses that vary in rhythm, structure, and emotional connotation. To improve style through revision is to substitute better equivalent symbols for those first chosen. The master art of rhetoric guides one in this choice.

Propositional Content and Grammatical Symbols

Propositional content can be symbolized through a simple declarative sentence, a complex declarative sentence, a compound declarative sentence, or even, in rare circumstances, a nonsentence.

SIMPLE DECLARATIVE SENTENCE

A simple declarative sentence may symbolize one simple proposition, two or more simple propositions, or a disjunctive proposition.

An example of a simple proposition is: That chair may be uncomfortable.

An example of two or more simple propositions is: This tall, handsome boy is exceptionally intelligent. There are four propositions:

This boy is tall.

This boy is handsome.

This boy is intelligent

His intelligence is exceptional.

Examples of disjunctive propositions are: A rectangle is either a square or an oblong. Either Mary or John or James will be valedictorian. Here it should be noticed that a simple sentence may have a compound subject or a compound predicate.

COMPLEX DECLARATIVE SENTENCE

A complex declarative sentence may symbolize one simple proposition, two or more simple propositions, a hypothetical proposition, or a syllogism.

An example of one simple proposition is: The yellow cat which was prowling around our garage yesterday was run over. The clause is definitive in function, for it points out a particular cat.

An example of two or more simple propositions is: Tall, gaunt Abraham Lincoln, who was the first Republican to become President of the United States and who issued the Emancipation Proclamation, was assassinated. (Five propositions.) The clauses are attributive in function, for they state attributes of an individual already clearly designated by a proper name.

Grammatical modification except by definitives is implicit logical predication. Hence if the modifier is not definitive in function, that is, if it is not necessary to the designation of the subject, it is an implicit predicate, and, in relation to the subject, it symbolizes another proposition; if it is definitive in function, it constitutes but one term with the subject and does not symbolize another proposition. For example: That tall man with brown eyes, brown hair, and a small mustache, standing near the microphone, is a Frenchman. (This symbolizes but one proposition, for the modifiers are definitive.) Charles de Gaulle, who is a tall Frenchman with brown eyes, brown hair, and a small mustache, was standing near the microphone. (This symbolizes seven propositions, for the modifiers are attributive in function.)

An example of a hypothetical proposition is: If it does not rain this afternoon, we shall go to the woods.

An example of a syllogism is: Eighteen is an even number because it is divisible by two. This sentence symbolizes three propositions in a syllogistic relation (to be explained in Chapter Seven):

Eighteen is a number divisible by two.

Every number divisible by two is an even number.

Therefore eighteen is an even number.

COMPOUND DECLARATIVE SENTENCE

A compound declarative sentence may symbolize two or more simple propositions or a disjunctive proposition.

An example of two or more simple propositions is: Wages are high, but so are prices.

An example of a disjunctive proposition is: Either the train is late or we have missed it.

LESS THAN A SENTENCE

Less than a sentence may sometimes symbolize a simple proposition, for example: Fire! This is equivalent to, and more idiomatic than, "Fire has broken out." To cry "Fire!" is to give an alarm that is either true or false. This proves that under such circumstances the word is understood as a proposition. "Fire!" meaning "Shoot!" is a command and does not symbolize a proposition.

A declarative sentence which is grammatically complete but which violates the rules governing common names and general descriptions or proper names and empirical descriptions (see Chapter Two, Language and its Symbols) symbolizes no proposition, for it symbolizes fewer than two logical terms.

6 RELATIONS OF SIMPLE PROPOSITIONS

From the time of Aristotle, it has been recognized that both logic and rhetoric, as arts of composition, have in common invention and disposition. Invention is the art of finding material for reasoning or discourse, and disposition is the art of properly relating or ordering the material.

In logic, disposition includes definition, division, the framing of propositions, and the relating of them. In rhetoric, disposition is the proper ordering of the parts of a composition—its introduction, body, and conclusion—according to the principles of unity, coherence, and emphasis.

Cicero simplified Aristotle's treatment of invention and distinguished sixteen logical topics, collectively exhaustive, by which any subject may be amplified through analysis: definition, division (of a whole, either logical or physical, into its parts), genus, species, adjuncts (of a subject, including all the categories of accident: quantity, quality, relation, action, passion, *when, where,* posture, and habiliment), contraries, contradictories, similarity, dissimilarity, comparison (greater, equal, less), cause, effect, antecedent, consequent, notation (the name), and conjugates (names derived from the same root, as *just, justice, justly*). A seventeenth topic, testimony, is external to the subject of inquiry and includes all recourse to authority, such as laws, contracts, witnesses, proverbs, apothegms, oaths, pledges, prophecies, revelation.

Note that the relation of subject to adjuncts is broader than that of a substance to the accidents which inhere in it because one accident, while itself inhering in a substance, may become the subject in which another accident inheres as its adjunct; for example, The man is walking slowly. Here *man* is the subject in which the adjunct *walking* inheres, while *walking* is at the same time the subject in which the adjunct *slow* inheres.

The logical topics of invention are general. The rhetorical topics are particularized by time, place, persons, and circumstances. They include such questions as what was done, who did it, when, where, how, was it possible, necessary, credible, honest, prudent, just, profitable, difficult, easy, pleasant?

THE RELATIONS OF PROPOSITIONS

The relations of propositions are four: conjunction, opposition, eduction, and the syllogism.

Conjunction

Conjunction is the mere joining of two or more propositions.

IMPLICIT OR EXPLICIT CONJUNCTION

The joining may be either explicit or implicit.

Explicit: The telephone rang and John answered it (two propositions).

Implicit: The large, sunlit lake is tranquil (three propositions).

BARE OR MATERIAL CONJUNCTION

The conjunction may be either a bare conjunction or a material conjunction. A bare conjunction violates the unity required by rhetoric for the sentence, the paragraph, and the whole composition, whereas material conjunction is the very basis of that unity. A bare conjunction joins propositions unrelated in thought. For example: The cherry trees are in bloom, and many students are enrolled in colleges and universities.

A material conjunction joins propositions that have a real or a logical relation, such as that of parts to a whole, of place, time, cause, effect, comparison, contrast, or any of the other topics mentioned above.

1   A temporal relation, expressed by *while, before, after, then*, etc.

The child slept after her mother had given her the medicine.
The visitors had left before the telegram was delivered.

2   A causal relation, expressed by *because, for, since, consequently*, etc.

She carried an umbrella because the dark clouds threatened rain.
The father died; consequently, the mother is raising the children alone.

3 An excellent example of development by effects, along with cause, is Dante's description of the gates of hell:

> Through me the way is to the city of woe;
>> Through me the way unto eternal pain;
>> Through me the way unto the lost below.
> Justice commoved my high Creator, when
>> Made me Divine Omnipotence, combined
>> With Primal Love and Wisdom Sovereign.
> Before me nothing was of any kind
>> Except eterne, and I eterne abide;
>> Leave, ye that enter in, all hope behind!
>> —*Inferno*, III, 1–9[1]

4 This paragraph from Aristotle's *Rhetoric* is an outstanding illustration of development by division. It will be used again as an example in Chapter Eight.

> Every action of every person either is or is not due to that person himself. Of those not due to himself some are due to chance, the others to necessity; of these latter, again, some are due to compulsion, the others to nature. Consequently all actions that are not due to a man himself are due either to chance or to nature or to compulsion. . . . Those things happen through compulsion which take place contrary to the desire or reason of the doer, yet through his own agency. . . . All actions that *are* due to a man himself and caused by himself are due either to habit or to rational or irrational craving. Rational craving is a craving for good, that is, a wish—nobody wishes for anything unless he thinks it is good. Irrational craving is twofold, namely, anger and appetite. Thus every action must be due to one or other of seven causes: chance, nature, compulsion, habit, reasoning, anger, or appetite.
> —Aristotle, *Rhetoric* 1.10[2]

RULES GOVERNING VALUE IN THE CONJUNCTION OF PROPOSITIONS
In Chapter Five it was stated that every proposition must be either true or false, whether it is asserted categorically as a matter of fact or modally as a necessity or a possibility. Whatever is probable must, of course, be possible. Sometimes, however, for practical purposes, it is desirable to distinguish three values: true, probable, and false. The rules of conjunction deal with these three values.

Rule 1. A conjunction of propositions is true only when every proposition conjoined is true. Conversely, if each of the propositions conjoined is true, their conjunction is true.

Rule 2. A conjunction of propositions is false if any one of the propositions conjoined is false. Conversely, if at least one proposition is false, the conjunction is false.

Rule 3. A conjunction of propositions is probable if at least one of the propositions conjoined is merely probable, and none is false. Conversely, if one proposition is probable and none is false, the conjunction is merely probable.

Applying these rules, we find that when only two propositions are conjoined, there are nine possible combinations of value; if more propositions are conjoined, the number of possible combinations of value increases accordingly.

These rules are summarized in the following table where X and Y each symbolize a proposition; 1 symbolizes truth; 0, falsity; and .n, probability.

Rule	Prop. X	Prop. Y	Props. X and Y
1	1	1	1
2	0	1	0
2	1	0	0
2	0	.n	0
2	.n	0	0
2	0	0	0
3	1	.n	.n
3	.n	1	.n
3	.n	.n	.n x .n

6-1   *Values in the Conjunction of Propositions*

Note that the final formula of Rule 3 shows a conjunction of propositions in which each proposition states a probable value. When two or more propositions are merely probable, their conjunction becomes less probable, which is indicated by the formula, .n x .n. For example, if a mutilated corpse has a triangular scar on the left shin, it may or may not be the body of a certain missing man, for a number of persons are likely to have that mark; but if it also has webbed toes and an x-shaped scar on the left shoulder from an operation, and if the missing man had these marks, it becomes less probable that the corpse is that of any person other than this missing man, for it is very improbable that these three peculiar marks should be conjoined in any other one person.

PRACTICAL APPLICATIONS OF CONJUNCTION

1 In a true-false test, the rules of conjunction must be applied. A statement is to be marked true only when every part of it is true; it is to be marked false when any part of it is false.

2 In estimating the chances of a candidate to win both nomination and election, and in estimating the probability of guilt of a person accused of a crime, one may apply the principles of the conjunction of probabilities.

3 Often one needs to distinguish clearly which part of a conjunction he accepts and which part he rejects. Many young people will agree with Perdita that true love persists through affliction.

> *Camillo*. Prosperity's the very bond of love,
> Whose fresh complexion and whose heart together
> Affliction alters.
> *Perdita*. One of those is true,
> I think affliction may subdue the cheek,
> But not take in the mind.
> —*The Winter's Tale* 4.4.573–577

When King Cymbeline declares him a banished traitor, Belarius replies:
> Indeed a banished man;
> I know not how a traitor.
> —*Cymbeline* 5.5.318–319

4 Misunderstandings may result from ignoring the rules of conjunction. In a group, someone remarks that Jane is a beautiful, brilliant, honest girl. Jane's friend says she doesn't agree. (She doesn't think Jane is brilliant.) A busybody later tells Jane that her friend said she wasn't honest.

5 In discussing politics, religion, and similar subjects with others, one should remember that the human mind is made for truth and

instinctively seeks truth; that it often embraces error along with truth because it fails to distinguish the error that is mixed with the truth; that seldom does the mind embrace what is all error and no truth; and never does it embrace error except under the misapprehension that it is truth. Consequently, in discussion it is a good idea to focus on truths held in common and to point out the errors that are mixed with the truth. A person naturally resents having his convictions attacked as all wrong; he will be much more receptive to the ideas of one who first takes account of what truth he does hold before proceeding to point out errors.

Opposition of Propositions

OPPOSITION
Propositions are in opposition when they have the same matter, that is, the same subject and the same predicate, but differ in form, that is, in quality, in quantity, or modality, or in two of these. Remember that quality refers to affirmative and negative; quantity, to total or partial; and modality, to necessary or contingent.

The four relations of opposition exist between the A E I O forms of any given proposition. These forms may be either quantitative or modal.

Quantitative Forms (Categorical)

A	All S is P.	All lions are animals.
E	No S is P.	No lions are animals.
I	Some S is P.	Some lions are animals.
O	Some S is not P.	Some lions are not animals.

Modal Forms

A	S must be P.	A lion must be an animal.
E	S cannot be P.	A lion cannot be an animal.
I	S may be P.	A lion may be an animal.
O	S may not be P.	A lion may not be an animal.

6-2   *Opposition in A E I O Forms*

THE FOUR RELATIONS OF OPPOSITION AND THE RULES GOVERNING THEM
1   The contradictories are A and O as well as E and I. Two propositions are opposed as contradictories if they differ both in quality and

in either quantity or modality. There is no middle ground between contradictory propositions (just as there is no middle ground between contradictory terms, for example, white and nonwhite). Contradictory propositions represent a clean-cut difference.

Rule 1. Of contradictory propositions, one must be true and the other must be false.

2   The contraries are A and E. Two propositions are opposed as contraries if they differ in quality and if both are either total in quantity or necessary in modality. There is a middle ground between contrary propositions (just as there is a middle ground between contrary terms, for example, white and black). Contrary propositions represent the greatest degree of difference.

Rule 2. Of contrary propositions, both cannot be true, but both may be false. Hence, if one is known to be true, the other must be false; but if one is known to be false, the value of the other is unknown.

The fallacy which most frequently occurs in opposition is the assumption that if one contrary is false the other is true (instead of unknown).

Note that the truth or falsity of a proposition involved in a formal relation is said to be unknown if its value cannot be known from the form alone but is determined by the matter, that is, if it must be learned from a knowledge of its terms.

ANALOGY: Comparison of form and matter

Standard measures may be regarded as empty forms. For example, two pints equal one quart. Four quarts equal one gallon. The truth or falsity of these statements can be known from the forms alone without a knowledge of what these measures contain.

These forms may, however, contain various kinds of matter, such as milk, water, mercury, wine, nitric acid, maple syrup. About these one may make various statements. Some examples are: A quart is healthful. A gallon is sickening. A pint is poisonous. A half-pint is not intoxicating. The truth or falsity of these statements cannot be known from the forms alone but is determined by the matter, that is, by the content of these forms. A pint of milk is not poisonous. A pint of nitric acid is poisonous.

3   The subcontraries are I and O. Two propositions are opposed as subcontraries if they differ in quality and if both are either partial in quantity or contingent in modality.

Rule 3. Of subcontrary propositions, both cannot be false, but both may be true. Hence, if one is known to be false, the other must be true; but if one is known to be true, the value of the other is unknown.

4   The subalterns are A and I as well as E and O. A proposition is subaltern to another if it has the same quality but differs from it either in being partial instead of total or in being contingent instead of necessary.

Strictly speaking, subalterns are not opposed, for they do not differ in quality. Traditionally, this relation has, however, been treated with opposition, for it is present among the A E I O forms of a given proposition.[3]

The normal relation of subject and predicate in an I proposition was stated in Chapter Five as that of partial inclusion of the subject in the predicate, and that of an O proposition as the exclusion of part of S from P. Both I and O propositions were represented by overlapping Euler's circles; I and O differ in the parts of the circles shaded, indicating the different parts of the subject being talked about.

In the opposition of propositions, however, I and O propositions are to be understood as including the following (the parts talked about are shaded):

If it is true that all S is P, it must be true that some of that S is P. All lions are animals. Some lions are animals. (Both are true.)

If it is true that no S is P, it must be true that some of that S is not P. No lions are elephants. Some lions are not elephants. (Both are true.)

Rule 4. Of subalterns, if the total (or necessary) proposition is true, the partial (or contingent) must be true; but if the former is known to be false, the value of the latter is unknown. Conversely, if the partial (or contingent) proposition is false, the total (or necessary) must be false; but if the former is known to be true, the value of the latter is unknown.

In categorical forms, the opposition of singular empirical propositions is restricted to contradiction, and this relation is achieved through a difference of quality alone, for example: Mary is tall. Mary is not tall.

A   Mary is tall.
E   Mary is not tall.

In modal forms, the opposition of singular empirical propositions includes all four relations.

A   Mary must be courteous.

E   Mary cannot be courteous.
I   Mary may be courteous.
O   Mary may not be courteous.

THE SQUARE OF OPPOSITION

The four relations of opposition are graphically represented by the square of opposition. The lines represent the four relations as numbered:

1   Contradictories: A and O; E and I.

2   Contraries: A and E.

3   Subcontraries: I and O.

4   Subalterns: A and I; E and O.

To use a familiar analogy, on this square of opposition, the lines between contradictories, AO and EI, represent the only "two-way streets"; for if A is true, O is false, and if O is false, A is true; or if A is false, O is true, and if O is true, A is false; the same holds for the relations of E and I. But all the other lines represent only "one-way streets": AE, IO, AI, EO; thus, if A is true, E is false, but if E is given false, the value of A is unknown.

When one form is given as either true or false, one can arrive at the value of the other three forms by applying only two of the rules of opposition, namely, that of contradictories and that of contraries.

Given A is true, then O is false, for of contradictories, one must be true and the other must be false (*Rule 1*); E is false, for of contraries both cannot be true (*Rule 2*); I is true, for it is the contradictory of E, which we have just shown must be false (*Rule 1*). (We can, of course, also know that I is true by applying *Rule 4*.)

Given A is false, then: O is true (*Rule 1*); E is unknown, for of contraries both may be false; I is also unknown, for it is the contrary of E, and if the truth or falsity of one were known, that of the other could be known from it. (Also according to *Rule 4*, if A is false, I is unknown; that is, it may be either true or false, depending on the terms related.)

In both the following sets of propositions, A is false; but in the one set E is false and I is true, whereas in the other set E is true and I is false. The possibility of having such contrasting results demonstrates that when A is false, the truth or falsity of E and I is determined by the matter, not by the form, for different matter involved in the same formal relation yields different results. Remember that 1 symbolizes truth and 0 symbolizes falsity.

EXAMPLES: Opposition

0	A	All roses are red.	0	A	All squares are circles.
0	E	No roses are red.	1	E	No squares are circles.
1	I	Some roses are red.	0	I	Some squares are circles.
1	O	Some roses are not red.	1	O	Some squares are not circles.

Following is a summary of all other relations involved in the square of opposition:

Given E is true, then I is false (*Rule 1*); A is false (*Rule 2*); O is true (*Rules 2, 1, and 4*).

Given E is false, then I is true (*Rule 1*); A and O are unknown (*Rules 2, 1, and 4*).

Given I is true, then E is false (*Rule 1*); A and O are unknown (*Rules 2, 1, 3, and 4*).

Given I is false, then E is true (*Rule 1*); A is false (*Rules 2 and 4*); O is true (*Rules 1 and 4*).

Given O is true, then A is false (*Rule 1*); E and I are unknown (*Rules 2, 1, 3, and 4*).

Given O is false, then A is true (*Rule 1*); E is false (*Rules 2 and 4*); I is true (*Rules 1 and 3*).

Sometimes a sentence which seems to symbolize but one proposition actually symbolizes a conjunction or two or more propositions. Such a conjunction must be resolved into its constituent simple propositions before it can be expressed in A E I O forms. A conjunction is: All the crew save one were drowned. Its simplification is: One of the crew was not drowned. The rest of the crew were drowned.

THE NATURE OF A FORMAL RELATION
Since opposition is the first formal relation we have studied, and since logic is concerned chiefly with formal relations, it will be profitable to

consider here the essential difference between a formal relation, such as opposition, and a material relation, such as conjunction.

1   Unlike a conjunction of propositions, which is either true or false or probable, a formal relation of propositions, such as opposition, is neither true nor false nor probable; it is either formally correct or formally incorrect.

2   The basic distinction between a material and a formal relation of propositions is this: The truth or falsity of a conjunction of propositions depends upon the truth or falsity of each of the propositions conjoined, and the value of each must be ascertained independently by reference to the facts; but the truth or falsity of propositions formally related is interdependent, and if the value of one proposition is known, the value of the others can be ascertained therefrom by applying the rules of the formal relation, without a knowledge of the terms related or any knowledge of the facts, that is, without any material knowledge at all. Thus the formal correctness of the opposition of the contradictory propositions A and O does not determine whether A is true or false or whether O is true or false. But it does determine that if A is true, O must be false, and that if A is false, O must be true; likewise that if O is true, A must be false, and that if O is false, A must be true.

3   A material relation holds between any propositions, regardless of their forms, whereas a formal relation holds only between propositions having certain forms.

4   A formal relation is really a relation of propositional forms, a formula. It holds regardless of what matter, what terms, are substituted for the symbols of the formula.

ANALOGY: Opposition to algebra and conjunction to arithmetic

A relation of propositional forms, such as opposition, is analogous to an algebraic formula. The relations are correct, regardless of what matter, what numbers are substituted for the symbols of the formula.

$(x + y)^2 = x^2 + 2xy + y^2$
$C = 2(\pi)R$

In contrast, a material relation of propositions, such as conjunction, is analogous to an arithmetical equation; the truth or falsity of every such equation must be checked independently with the facts and is determined altogether by the matter, not at all by a form, for such an equation is not a formula.

$3 \times 8 = 2 \times 12$
$6 \times 3 = 9 \times 2$

5 A propositional formula, such as that of opposition, eduction, or the syllogism, operates as a rule of assertion thus: If a given proposition having a certain form has a given value, then another proposition related to it by a correct formula must have the value required by the formula.

Eduction

Eduction is the formal process of making explicit all that is implicit in a given proposition. Hence it is not an advance in knowledge. In this it differs radically from deduction, of which the syllogism is the form, for through the syllogism the mind advances to new knowledge. Through eduction we turn a proposition, as it were, inside out and upside down until we have explored all its content.

In the following bit of doggerel, an anonymous parodist has expressed a very simple idea with an explicit thoroughness analogous to that of eduction.

Hiawatha's Mittens

He killed the noble Mudjokivis.
Of the skin he made him mittens,
Made them with the fur side inside,
Made them with the skin side outside.
He, to keep the warm side inside,
Put the inside skin outside;
He, to get the cold side outside,
Put the warm side fur side inside.
That's why he put the fur side inside,
Why he put the skin side outside,
Why he turned them inside outside.

Eduction is a formal process which never involves a change of value. Provided that the eductions are correctly made, if the original proposition is true, the eductions must be logically equivalent; if the original proposition is false, the eductions must be false.

Eduction employs two processes, obversion and conversion. By applying these two processes alternately, seven eductive forms (their names appear below where they are derived) may be obtained from a general or a total proposition, fewer from a partial or a contingent one.

OBVERSION

Obversion turns a proposition around by changing the quality and the predicate but not the meaning.

Rules for obverting a proposition:
1 Change the quality (determined by the copula).
2 Substitute for the predicate (P) its contradictory (P').

To avoid illicit obversion: Do not confuse a contradictory modifier of a term with the full contradictory term. Contradictory terms are always dichotomous; they divide all being, not merely a genus. For example, the contradictory of starchy food is not nonstarchy food; it is nonstarchy-food. Pencils and doorknobs and stars are nonstarchy-food; they are not nonstarchy food, for they are not food at all.[4]

Obversion of A E I O forms. Each of these can be obverted. In the following formula, P' symbolizes non-P.

S a P is obverted to S e P'.	All voters are citizens. No voters are noncitizens.
S e P is obverted to S a P'.	No Mohammedans are Christians. All Mohammedans are non-Christians.
S i P is obverted to S o P'.	Some chairs are comfortable. Some chairs are not uncomfortable.
S o P is obverted to S i P'.	Some pupils are not attentive. Some pupils are inattentive.

A principle of obversion is: If S is included in P, it is certainly excluded from non-P. Obversion is an application of the Law of Excluded Middle: Between contradictories there is no middle ground.

PRACTICAL APPLICATIONS OF OBVERSION

The rhetorical figure named litotes, used extensively in Old English literature and still used widely in modern English and in other literatures, is an application of obversion. It has an important effect on tone.

Original: I was successful in that undertaking. (S a P)
Obverse: I was not unsuccessful in that undertaking. (S e P′)

Original: She is aware of her charms. (S a P)
Obverse: She is not unaware of her charms. (S e P′)

Original: He has acted nobly in these difficult circumstances. (S a P)
Obverse: He has not acted ignobly in these difficult circumstances. (S e P′)

Original: I found his book interesting. (S a P)
Obverse: I found his book not uninteresting. (S e P′)

Adam observed, and with his eye the chase
Pursuing, not unmoved to Eve thus spake.
  —John Milton, *Paradise Lost* 11.191

One of the heavenly host, and by his gait
None of the meanest.
  —John Milton, *Paradise Lost* 11.230

Be that as may, my oracles from hence
Shall be unveiled, far as to lay them bare
May be not unbefitting thy rude sense.
  —Dante Alighieri, *Purgatorio* Canto 33

As to courage, the world knows that I don't lack it.
  —Jean-Baptiste Moliere, *The Misanthrope*

I remained upon the field wholly discomfited.
  —James Boswell, *The Life of Samuel Johnson*, L.L.D.

My death's sad tale may yet undeaf his ear.
  —*Richard II* 2.1.1

I have no hope that he's undrown'd.
  —*The Tempest* 2.1.237–238

Let me unkiss the oath 'twixt me and thee.
  —*Richard II* 5.1.74

Lest her beauty . . . unprovide my mind again.
  —*Othello* 4.1.204–206

Tremble, thou wretch, That hast within thee undivulged crimes
Unwhipped of justice.
  —*King Lear* 3.2.51–53

CONVERSION

Rules for converting a proposition:

1   Reverse the subject and predicate.

2   If it is necessary to do so in order to avoid an illicit process, change the quantity (or the modality), and thereby convert by limitation or *per accidens*.

3   Do not change the quality (determined by the copula).

To avoid an illicit process in converting: No term may be distributed in the converse that was undistributed in the proposition from which it was derived. An illicit process is an attempt to get more out of a proposition than there is in it by using in its full extension a term which in the original proposition was used in only a part of its extension. Illicit conversion is among the most prolific sources of error to which the mind of man is prone. The fallacies occasioned by it are discussed in Chapter Nine.

CONVERSION OF A E I O FORMS
Not every proposition can be converted. S a P is regularly converted by limitation (that is, by loss of total quantity or of necessary modality) to P i S in order to avoid an illicit process. An example is: All lions are animals. Some animals are lions. P a S cannot ordinarily be correctly derived from S a P, for to attempt this involves an illicit process of P.

		In this original proposition, P is undistributed (u),
d	u	for it is the predicate of an affirmative proposition.
S	a P	In this illicit converse, P is distributed (d), for it
d	u	has become the subject of a total (or a necessary)
P	a S	proposition. The line drawn from u to d indicates
		the illicit process.

S a P is correctly converted to P a S when P is known to be either the definition or the property of S, for then P is distributed through the matter, not through the form. It is the test of definition and of property that these predicates be convertible with the subject.

EXAMPLES: Correct conversions of S a P

Definition: Man is a rational animal. A rational animal is a man.
Property: Man is mirthful. A mirthful being is a man.

S e P is converted simply to P e S, for since an E proposition distributes both S and P, an illicit process cannot occur when the terms are transposed in converting the proposition. No lions are elephants. No elephants are lions.

S i P is converted simply to P i S, for since an I proposition distributes neither S nor P, an illicit process cannot occur when the terms are transposed in converting the proposition. Some roses are red. Some red things are roses.

S o P cannot be converted at all, for to convert it simply would involve an illicit process of S. In the original proposition, S is undistributed, for it is the subject of a partial (or a contingent) proposition. In an illicit converse, S is distributed, for it has become the predicate of a negative proposition. It cannot be converted by limitation (as in the case of S a P), for S o P is already partial in quantity (or contingent in modality). Since conversion never involves a change in quality, there is no possible way validly to convert O. It is a fact that often S o P remains true when converted to P o S, but the process is, nevertheless, always formally invalid.

EXAMPLES: Invalid conversion of S o P

Some roses are not red. Some red things are not roses.

Here *roses* is distributed in the converse and is undistributed in the original proposition. Therefore, the conversion involves an illicit process of S. That both these propositions are materially true is merely an accident of the matter. Their truth cannot be guaranteed through the formal process; hence the process itself is always invalid, regardless of whether the proposition derived from a true S o P is materially true or false.

In the following examples the converse proposition is both materially false and formally invalid.

Categorical: Some animals are not lions. Some lions are not animals.

Modal: An animal may not be a lion. A lion may not be an animal.

THE EDUCTIVE FORMS

Seven eductive forms can be derived from S a P and from S e P, and three from S i P and from S o P, by alternately and successively applying the two eductive processes, obversion and conversion; whenever, because of having had to convert S a P by limitation to S i P, one arrives at S o P to be converted, one can go no further but must return to the original proposition, applying to it the process alternate to that first applied. In these eductions all implications of a given proposition are made explicit. In the following table the word *contrapositive* refers to the proposition that results when the quality of a proposition is changed and the predicate is converted to its contradictory. The word *inverse* is the term for a proposition that uses the contradictory of the subject and the predicate of the original proposition.

Eductions of S a P

		Process	
Original proposition	S a P	*Process*	All voters are citizens.
Obverse	S e P'	Obversion	No voters are noncitizens.
Partial contrapositive	P' e S	Conversion	No noncitizens are voters.
Full contrapositive	P' a S'	Obversion	All noncitizens are nonvoters.
Full inverse	S' i P'	Conversion	Some nonvoters are noncitizens.
Partial inverse	S' o P	Obversion	Some nonvoters are not citizens.
Converse (of original)	P i S	Conversion	Some citizens are voters.
Obverted converse	P o S'	Obversion	Some citizens are not nonvoters.

6-3 *Eductions of S a P*

Consider carefully the exact meaning of each of the propositions above. Euler's circles may prove helpful by graphically showing the content of each of the propositions. This series may remind the reader of "Hiawatha's Mittens," but it seriously performs the function of expressing all the possible relations between citizens, voters, and the contradictory of each of these terms.

Eductions of S e P

The process of obversion is noted by an "o," and the process of conversion, by a "c."

		Process	
Original proposition	S e P	*Process*	No Mohammedans are Christians.
Obverse	S a P'	o	All Mohammedans are non-Christians.
Partial contrapositive	P' i S	c	Some non-Christians are Mohammedans.
Full contrapositive	P' o S'	o	Some non-Christians are not non-Mohammedans.
Converse (of original)	P e S	c	No Christians are Mohammedans.
Obverted converse	P a S'	o	All Christians are non-Mohammedans.
Partial inverse	S' i P	c	Some non-Mohammedans are Christian.
Full inverse	S' o P'	o	Some non-Mohammedans are not non-Christians.

6-4 *Eductions of S e P*

Eductions of S i P

Original proposition	S i P	*Process*	Some chairs are uncomfortable.
Obverse	S o P'	o	Some chairs are not uncomfortable.
Converse (of original)	P i S	c	Some comfortable things are chairs.
Obverted converse	P o S'	o	Some comfortable things are not nonchairs.

6-5   *Eductions of S i P*

Eductions of S o P

Original proposition	S o P	*Process*	Some pupils are not attentive.
Obverse	S i P'	o	Some pupils are inattentive.
Partial contrapositive	P' i S	c	Some inattentive beings are pupils.
Full contrapositive	P' o S'	o	Some inattentive beings are not nonpupils.

6-6   *Eductions of S o P*

It can only be known through the matter (for it cannot be known through the form) that P is either the definition or a property of S. When this occurs, then S a P is throughout the series correctly convertible to P a S because P and S are both in full extension and therefore distributed. In this case, the seven eductions can be derived by one continuous process of alternate conversion and obversion (it does not matter which process is applied first, and if the eduction is carried one step further, the original proposition is again obtained).

Eductions of S a P with P Fully Distributed

Original proposition	S a P	*Process*	All men are rational animals.
Converse	P a S	c	All rational animals are men.
Obverted converse	P e S'	o	No rational animals are nonmen.
Partial inverse	S' e P	c	No nonmen are rational animals.
Full inverse	S' a P'	o	All nonmen are nonrational animals.
Full contrapositive	P' a S'	c	All nonrational animals are nonmen.
Partial contrapositive	P' e S	o	No nonrational animals are men.
Obverse (of original)	S e P'	c	No men are nonrational animals.
Original	S a P	o	All men are rational animals.

6-7   *Eductions of S a P with P a Definition of S*

SUPPLEMENTARY EDUCTIONS

There are three categories of supplementary eduction: eduction by added determinants, eduction by omitted determinants, and eduction by converse relation.

1   Eduction by added determinants (attributive modifiers)

The formula is S is P; therefore Sa is Pa. The principle of the formula is: An added determinant decreases the extension of a term and increases its intension. This process of eduction is valid if the added determinant affects S and P to the same degree and in the same respect. The eduction is invalid if it does not modify them to the same degree or in the same respect.

EXAMPLES: Determinant not affecting terms to the same degree

Original: Kings are men.
Invalid: A majority of kings is a majority of men.

Original: An ant is an animal.
Invalid: A large ant is a large animal.
Valid: A small ant is a small animal.

EXAMPLES: Determinant not affecting terms in the same respect

Original: A contralto is a woman.
Invalid: A low contralto is a low woman.[5]
Valid: A blonde contralto is a blonde woman.

2   Eduction by omitted determinants

The formula is S is Pa; therefore S is P. The principle of the formula is: A subject that is included in a more determined (less extended) predicate is necessarily included in that predicate when it is less determined (more extended). This principle is especially evident when the two predicates are related to the subject as species and genus or as proximate and remote genera. Examples include: Socrates is a rational animal; therefore Socrates is an animal. A rattlesnake is a poisonous reptile; therefore a rattlesnake is a reptile.

Mere grammatical likeness (of words) must not be mistaken for true logical likeness (of terms). The following example may seem to disprove the principle stated above, but the difficulty is only verbal. Original: The pauper is a pretended prince. Invalid inference: The pauper is a prince. Only verbally do these sentences appear to exemplify the formula S is Pa; therefore S is P. *Pretended prince* does not express the logical term *prince* plus a determinant decreasing its extension; it expresses an altogether different term which is equivalent to *impostor*, a term which is incompatible with prince and excluded from it, certainly not included in it.

3   Eduction by converse relation

The formula is S r¹ P; therefore P r² S. (Here r¹ and r² symbolize copulas with correlative modifiers, not simple copulas.) The principle of the formula is: Because relative terms necessarily imply their correlatives, the subject and predicate of a proposition with a relative copula may be transposed if the relative copula is supplanted by its correlative. Action and passion as well as genus and species are correlatives. It is also correct with propositions stating quantitative relations to draw inferences by converse relation. Hence the change from the active to the passive verb form symbolizes eduction by converse relation.

EXAMPLES: Correlatives

Original: Aristotle taught (or was the teacher of) Alexander the Great.
Valid Inference: Alexander the Great was taught by (or was the pupil of) Aristotle.

Original: Mary saw the sand dunes.
Valid inference: The sand dunes were seen by Mary.

Original: Lily is a species of flower.
Valid inference: Flower is a genus of lily.

Original: A is greater than B.
Valid inference: B is less than A.

The Syllogism

This is the most important of the four relations of propositions, for it is the characteristic form of reasoning. According to the kind of propositions syllogistically related, we distinguish four types of syllogism: the simple (usually categorical) syllogism, the hypothetical syllogism, the disjunctive syllogism, the dilemma. These types of syllogism will be studied in succeeding chapters.

SUMMARY OF THE RELATIONS OF PROPOSITIONS

There are four relations: conjunction, opposition, eduction, the syllogism. Conjunction is a material relation; the others are formal relations. A formal relation is a process of either mediate or immediate inference.

1   Immediate inference involves only two propositions; it proceeds directly from one to the other without the mediating function of a third term or of a third proposition. There are three processes of immediate inference: opposition, obversion, and conversion. Eduction is a common name given to the two processes of obversion and conversion.

2   Mediate inference involves three terms in three propositions. Two terms, S and P, are related to each other by virtue of the relation of each to a third term M, which is the medium for relating them. The function of the third term, which is the middle term (M), will be fully explained in Chapter Seven.

ANALOGY: Relation of propositions

Two rods can be related to each other in length by virtue of the relation of each to a yardstick, which serves as a medium between them.

7 THE SIMPLE SYLLOGISM

Definition

The syllogism is the act of reasoning by which the mind perceives that from the relation of two propositions (called premises) having one term in common there necessarily emerges a new, third proposition (called the conclusion) in which the common term, called the middle term (M), does not appear.

EXAMPLE: The syllogism

A bat is a mammal.
No bird is a mammal.
∴ A bat is not a bird.

Since all bats are included in mammals and all mammals are excluded from birds, all bats must be excluded from birds. It is by virtue of the relation of each of the terms bat and bird to the mediating term mammal, common to both premises, that their relation to each other is understood and expressed in the conclusion as one of total exclusion from each other.

A premise is a proposition so related to another proposition by means of a common term that from their conjunction a new proposition, the conclusion, necessarily follows.

The syllogism is a formal relation of three terms in three propositions. Each term occurs twice: the middle term in each premise; each of the other terms, in one premise and in the conclusion. Every premise is a proposition, but not every proposition is a premise. A proposition becomes a premise by being joined to another proposition which has one term in common with it; the rules governing the valid conjunction of premises are stated below. The conclusion, a new truth, is implicit in the conjunction of the premises; it is not implicit in either one of them alone. Hence the syllogism results in an advance in knowledge achieved by the conjunction of the premises.

ANALOGY: A new truth through the syllogism

Every wife is a woman, but not every woman is a wife. A woman becomes a wife by being joined to a husband through a bond of mutual love. The child, a new being, owes its existence to both parents, not to one alone.

The syllogism is the very formula of reasoning.[1] It is a relation of propositional forms. The syllogism itself is neither true nor false; it is valid or invalid. In a valid syllogism the truth or falsity of its propositions is interdependent and can be ascertained from the formula. An invalid syllogism is one whose conclusion does not follow from its premises.

Matter and Form of the Syllogism

1 The matter of the syllogism consists of its three propositions relating its three terms (minor, major, middle). To analyze a syllogism, we must begin with the conclusion because the placement of terms in the conclusion determines how those terms function in the first two propositions of the syllogism. S, the minor term of a syllogism, is the subject of the conclusion. P, the major term, is the predicate of the conclusion. The conclusion is always symbolized S___P (with a, e, i, or o inserted in the space left blank).

"A bat is not a bird." Bat is the subject of the conclusion and the minor term. Bird is the predicate of the conclusion and the major term. They would be marked thus:

   S   P
A bat is not a bird.

The minor premise is one which contains the minor term S and the middle term M. M is the term present in both premises but not in the conclusion. "A bat is a mammal" is the minor premise of the sample syllogism. Bat is the minor term, and mammal is the middle term. This premise would be marked thus:

   S   M
A bat is a mammal.

The major premise is one which contains the major term P and the middle term M. "No bird is a mammal" is the major premise of the syllogism. Bird is the major term, and mammal is the middle term. This premise would be marked thus:

P   M
No bird is a mammal.

2   The form of the syllogism is the logical necessity with which the conclusion follows from the premises by virtue of their valid relation, which is achieved by a combination of figure and mood (explained below).

Dictum de Omni et Nullo: Principle of Syllogistic Reasoning

Whatever is affirmed of a logical whole must be affirmed of the parts of that whole; whatever is denied of a logical whole must be denied of the parts of that whole.

This means that if P is affirmed of M, it must be affirmed of S, which is a part of M; if P is denied of M, it must be denied of S, which is a part of M (or, less frequently, if P is affirmed of M and M is denied of S, P must be denied of S). In the example, bird, the major term, is denied of mammal, the middle term, and thus is denied of bat, which is included in mammal.

Another way of stating the relation is this: If S is included in M, and M is included in P, S must be included in P; if S is included in M, and M is excluded from P, or if S is excluded from M, and M is included in P, S must be excluded from P. These relations can be made clearer by means of Euler's circles.

Hence the function of the middle term, the logical whole, is, as it were, to draw the meaning out of the major term and transmit it to the minor. It is a mediating term which, having served in the premises as a means of comparison, is dropped from the conclusion.

Rules of the Syllogism and Formal Fallacies

The following rules govern the syllogism.

Rule 1. A syllogism must contain three and only three terms. The fallacy that results from violating this rule is four terms.

Rule 2. A syllogism must contain three and only three propositions. The fallacy that results from violating this rule is four propositions.

Rule 3. The middle term must be distributed in at least one of the premises (because it must serve as the logical whole on which the principle of syllogistic reasoning is based). The fallacy that results from violating this rule is undistributed middle term.

Rule 4. No term may be distributed in the conclusion which was undistributed in its own premise. The fallacy that results from violating this rule is illicit process of the major term or of the minor term. Note that a term that is distributed in its premise may, however, be undistributed in the conclusion, for it is not an illicit process to take out of something less than there is in it. There cannot be an illicit process of the middle term, for the two premises are independent. One premise is not derived from the other as the conclusion is derived from the two premises.

Rule 5. From two negative premises no conclusion can be drawn. One cannot infer a relation between two given terms unless at least one of them is related to a common, third term; this is the very principle on which syllogistic reasoning is based. The fallacy that results from violating this rule is two negative premises.

Rule 6. If one premise is negative, the conclusion must be negative. Conversely, in order to prove a negative conclusion, one premise must be negative. If one term is included in the middle term, and the other is excluded from it, the two terms in the conclusion must accordingly be excluded from each other. The fallacy that results from violating this rule is a negative conclusion without a negative premise.

Rule 7. From two partial or singular (or contingent) premises, no conclusion can be drawn. (This is a corollary of *Rules* 3, 5, and 6.) The fallacy that results from violating this rule is two partial (or contingent) premises.

Rule 8. If one premise is partial, the conclusion must be partial. (This is a corollary of *Rules* 3 and 4.) The fallacy that results from violating this rule is a general conclusion in a syllogism with one or more partial premises.

Rule 9. If one premise is contingent, the conclusion must be contingent. In order to prove a necessary conclusion, both premises must be necessary in modality. The fallacy that results from violating this rule is a necessary or categorical conclusion with a contingent premise.

Rule 10. If one or both premises are empirical, the conclusion must be empirical. In order to prove a general conclusion, both premises must be general propositions. The fallacy that results from violating this rule is a general conclusion with an empirical premise.

Two of the general rules of the syllogism are concerned with its matter (*1* and *2*); two with distribution, the most important consideration (*3* and *4*); two with quality (*5* and *6*); two with quantity (*7* and *8*); two with modality (*7* and *9*); one with the reference to reality, to essence, or to the individual (*10*).

Mood

The A, E, I, or O forms of its three component propositions constitute the mood of a syllogism. The mood is designated by these letters placed in a definite, conventional order. We shall adopt this order: the minor premise, the major premise, the conclusion.[2]

Because there are four propositional forms, A, E, I, and O, there are sixteen possible combinations of premises, namely: AA, AE, AI, AO; EA, EE, EI, EO; IA, IE, II, IO; OA, OE, OI, OO.

Rule 5, forbidding two negative premises, requires the elimination of four of these combinations: EE, EO, OE, and OO.

Rule 7, forbidding two partial (or contingent) premises, requires the elimination of three more (OO is eliminated under *Rule 5*, but it also would be eliminated by *Rule 7*): II, IO, and OI. We shall discover later that an eighth combination, EI, must be eliminated because, although it violates none of the general rules, it conforms to none of the special rules. (The special rules will be explained later in Chapter Seven.)

There remain eight valid combinations of premises. We can determine whether the conclusion derived from each of these combinations will be A, E, I, or O by applying *Rules* 6 and 8.

The table below lists the valid combination of premises. The "adaptation to avoid a fallacy" column anticipates the problem which arises from the placement of terms. The placement of terms is explained in the next section, Figures.

Valid Combination of Premises

Eight Standard	*Adaptation to Avoid a Fallacy*
AAA	AAI
AEE	AEO
AII	
AOO	
EAE	EAO
IAI	
IEO	
OAO	

7-1 *Valid Combination of Premises*

Figures

The figure of a syllogism is determined by the position of the middle term in the premises. Figure and mood together constitute the form of a syllogism, that is, the logical necessity by which the conclusion must follow from the premises.

There are four possible positions for the middle term, and consequently there are four figures.

Figure I	Figure II	Figure III	Figure IV
S___M	S___M	M___S	M___S
M___P	P___M	M___P	P___M
S___P	S___P	S___P	S___P

7-2 *Four Figures: Determined by Position of Middle Term*

It is of no consequence whether the major premise is placed first or second; the figure and the rules of the figure remain the same. The first figure is that in which the middle term is the predicate of the minor premise and the subject of the major; the second figure is that in which the middle term is the predicate of both premises; the third, that in which it is the subject of both; the fourth, that in which it is the subject of the minor premise and the predicate of the major. Note, however, that the diagram of Figure I and Figure IV would look different if the major premise was first and the minor premise second.

The sample syllogism is in Figure II because the middle term is the predicate of both premises.

   S   M
A bat is a mammal.

   P   M
No bird is a mammal.

   S   P
A bat is not a bird.

Testing the Validity of a Syllogism

To determine the validity of a syllogism, merely test it by the general rules, particularly those of distribution. The rules of distribution, first explained in Chapter Five, are repeated here to guide the reader since distribution is such an important component in analyzing a syllogism.

Distribution in A E I O Forms

d u
S a P   Because an A proposition is total (or necessary), it distributes its subject. Because an A proposition is affirmative, its predicate it undistributed. (All lions are animals.)

d d
S e P   Because an E proposition is total (or necessary), it distributes its subject. Because an E proposition is negative, it distributes its predicate. (No lions are horses.)

u u
S i P   Because an I proposition is partial (or contingent), it has its subject undistributed. Because an I proposition is affirmative, its predicate is undistributed. (Some lions are tame.)

u d
S o P   Because an O proposition is partial (or contingent), its subject is undistributed. Because it is negative, it distributes its predicate. (Some lions are not tame.)

7-3 *Distribution in A E I O Forms*

To analyze a syllogism, follow the procedure outlined in this section.

1 Find the conclusion, and write S over its subject, P over its predicate.

   S   P
A bird is not a bat.

2 Write S and P over the same terms where they appear in the premises.

   S
A bat is a mammal.

   P
No bird is a mammal.

3 Write M over the term which appears in both premises but not in the conclusion.

     M
A bat is a mammal.

     M
No bird is a mammal.

4   Determine the mood and the figure of the syllogism. To determine the mood, note the A E I O form of each of the premises. The combination, both the type and the order, of propositions within the syllogism constitutes its mood. Determine the figure of the syllogism. To determine the figure of the syllogism, note the position of the middle term. At the right of the formula, name the figure and mood.

A bat is a mammal.	A E E
No bird is a mammal.	Figure II
A bat is not a bird.	

5   Mark the distribution of terms in accordance with the form of each proposition (but if one proposition is a definition, either by genus and differentia or by property, write *def.* over its predicate to indicate that it is distributed through its matter). Notice (1) whether the middle term is distributed in at least one premise, (2) whether either P or S is distributed in the conclusion but undistributed in its premise. Draw a line between the undistributed and the distributed use of the same term as in the examples below, to indicate any error in distribution. Such a line is not necessary in the example since it has no error in distribution.

A bat is a mammal.	d u S a M	
No bird is a mammal	d d P e M	No error in distribution
A bat is not a bird.	d d S e P	

6   Test the formula further to see whether there are (1) two negative premises, (2) two partial (or contingent) premises, (3) four terms, (4) four propositions.

7   If no fallacy is discovered, write *Valid* at the right; if one is discovered, write *Invalid* and name the fallacy; if there are two or more fallacies, name each.

A bat is a mammal.	d u S a M	Figure II
No bird is a mammal.	d d P e M	Mood A E E

A bat is not a bird.	d d S e P	Valid

ILLUSTRATION: Testing the validity of syllogisms

S M Some salesmen are not polite.	u d S o M	Figure II
P M All true gentlemen are polite.	d u P a M	Mood O A O
S P ∴ Some salesmen are not true gentlemen.	u d S o P	Valid

S M No squares are oblongs.	d d S e M	Figure I
M P All oblongs are rectangles.	d u M a P	Mood E A E
S P ∴ No squares are rectangles.	d d S e P	Invalid: Illicit process of the major term

M S All men are capable of mirth.	d def. M a S	Figure III
M P All men are mortal.	d u M a P	Mood A A A
S P ∴ All mirthful beings are mortal.	d u S a P	Valid: Illicit process of the minor term is avoided through definition

M S Some football teams are not good losers.	u d M o S	Figure IV
P M No basketball team is a football team.	d d P e M	Mood O E O
S P ∴ Some good losers are not basketball teams.	u d S o P	Invalid: Two negative premises

Enthymeme

DEFINITION

An enthymeme is a syllogism logically abridged by the omission of one proposition, either the major premise, the minor premise, or the conclusion. It contains three terms and can be expanded into a full syllogism.

An enthymeme is to be distinguished from a syllogism logically complete but grammatically abridged. An example would be: Climbing the Alps is a fascinating but dangerous undertaking. Therefore some fascinating undertakings are dangerous.

In this logically complete syllogism, the minor premise is only grammatically abridged, and the rules of grammar suffice for the expansion which must be made before its validity can be determined. Only one expansion can or need be made, for, if the sentence is analyzed or diagrammed, it is perfectly clear that "Climbing the Alps" is the subject of the minor premise (as well as of the major) and that a "fascinating undertaking" is its predicate. The formula of the syllogism is M a P, M a S, S i P; it is in Figure III, Mood A A I, and it is valid.

In an enthymeme the omitted proposition is logically abridged because there is no rule of grammar or of logic to determine the position of its terms in the expansion which must be made before the validity of the enthymeme can be determined. An example is: An oak is a plant because it is a tree.

RULES FOR DETERMINING THE VALIDITY OF AN ENTHYMEME
Find the conclusion using the following clues: (1) *because, for,* or *since* introduces a premise (a cause, of which the conclusion is the effect) and therefore the other proposition is the conclusion; (2) *therefore, consequently,* or *accordingly* introduces the conclusion; (3) *and* or *but* connects two premises and indicates that the proposition omitted is the conclusion.

Write S above the subject of the conclusion and P above its predicate. One of these terms will appear with M in the other proposition given (if the enthymeme is of the usual type with the conclusion and one premise stated). Mark both terms in the premise given. Substitute for pronouns the nouns for which they stand. Since there is no rule of logic or of grammar to determine the position of the terms in the missing proposition, that proposition may be stated in either of two ways. Hence there are two expansions possible, in two different figures.

The principles for determining the validity of an enthymeme are: (1) If an enthymeme is valid in one expansion, it is a valid enthymeme regardless of whether it is valid in the other expansion. (2) If an enthymeme is found to be invalid in the first expansion, it is necessary to expand it in the alternate figure in order to be certain whether it is a valid enthymeme or not; but if it is found valid in the first expansion, it need not be expanded both ways.

EXAMPLES: Expanded enthymemes

An oak is a plant because it is a tree.

Expansion a

S	M		d		u			
An oak is a tree.			S	a	M		Figure 1	
M	P		d		u			
A tree is a plant.			M	a	P		Mood A A A	
S	P		d		u			
∴ An oak is a plant.			S	a	P		Valid	

Since this enthymeme thus expanded into a full syllogism is valid, it need not be expanded in the alternate figure. But if it is, it is found to be invalid in Figure II. It must be clearly understood, however, that an enthymeme is a good, sound argument if it is formally valid in *one* of its possible expansions. It cannot be pronounced an invalid argument unless it has an error in *both* expansions.

Expansion b

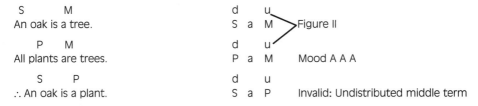

S	M		d	u			
An oak is a tree.			S	a	M	Figure II
P	M		d	u			
All plants are trees.			P	a	M	Mood A A A
S	P		d	u			
∴ An oak is a plant.			S	a	P	Invalid: Undistributed middle term

These shoes will not hurt your feet, because they are not too short. (The major premise is omitted.)

Expansion a

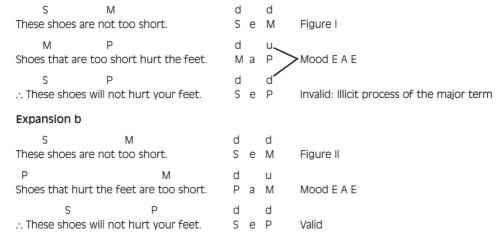

S	M		d	d		
These shoes are not too short.			S	e	M	Figure I
M	P		d	u		
Shoes that are too short hurt the feet.			M	a	P	Mood E A E
S	P		d	d		
∴ These shoes will not hurt your feet.			S	e	P	Invalid: Illicit process of the major term

Expansion b

S	M		d	d		
These shoes are not too short.			S	e	M	Figure II
P	M		d	u		
Shoes that hurt the feet are too short.			P	a	M	Mood E A E
S	P		d	d		
∴ These shoes will not hurt your feet.			S	e	P	Valid

Although expansion b is formally valid, the major premise is false. It is true that shoes that are too short hurt the feet, but it is not true that all shoes that hurt the feet are too short, for they may hurt the feet because they are too narrow, or for other reasons. An A proposition is not validly convertible to A unless it is a definition, and this A proposition is not a definition. This enthymeme is an erroneous argument because there is an error in both expansions.[3]

Blessed are the clean of heart, for they shall see God.

The conclusion is stated in an abnormal word order, with the predicate (a participle or adjective) first, for emphasis. The natural expansion is as follows:

S M	d u	
The clean of heart shall see God.	S a M	Figure I
M P	d u	
Those who shall see God are blessed.	M a P	Mood A A A
S P	d u	
∴The clean of heart are blessed.	S a P	Valid

Since this enthymeme is valid in this expansion, it is not necessary to expand it in the second figure.

That is too good to be true.

In this sentence there are three terms and two propositions. (For the sake of saving space, the terms and the distribution are not marked in some of the expansions that follow.)

That is too good.	S a M	Figure I
Whatever is too good cannot be true.	M a P	Mood A A A
∴ That cannot be true.	S a P	Valid

Although this syllogism is valid, both premises are false. Nothing can be literally and absolutely too good; if, however, too good be taken to mean very good, the minor premise can be accepted as true. But only a confirmed cynic could assert the major premise as true. Nonetheless, this enthymeme is repeated glibly by many who would deny the implicit major premise if they adverted to it explicitly.

You are a thief, and a thief ought to be behind bars.

In this enthymeme, the omitted proposition is the conclusion.

You are a thief.	S a M	Figure I
A thief ought to be behind bars.	M a P	Mood A A A
∴ You ought to be behind bars.	S a P	Valid

A reward is an incentive to effort, for people desire to win it.

This enthymeme illustrates the fact that the grammatical expression frequently obscures logical relations. Restatement is necessary to clarify them. Be particularly careful where there is a direct object. This usually requires conversion to the passive voice. By this means, the direct object can be extricated from other terms with which it is mixed and can be placed as an unconfused term on one side of the copula. Unless one can discern logical relations as they are actually expressed in daily life, the study of logic is not really practical. Seldom do people adhere to strict logical forms of expression.

A reward is something people desire to win.	S a M	Figure I
What people desire to win is an incentive to effort.	M a P	Mood A A A
∴ A reward is an incentive to effort.	S a P	Valid

A whale is not a fish, for it has not scales and gills, and it nourishes its young with milk.

This is a double enthymeme; the same conclusion is reached from two different sets of premises. Expansion:

A whale has not scales and gills.	S e M	Figure II
A fish has scales and gills.	P a M	Mood E A E
∴ A whale is not a fish.	S e P	Valid

Note that if this syllogism is constructed in Figure IV by stating the major premise M a P, an illicit process of the major term would not be present, for having both scales and gills is a property of fish; therefore both terms are distributed, the one through the form, the other through the matter.

A whale nourishes its young with milk.	S a M	Figure II
A fish does not nourish its young with milk.	P e M	Mood A E E
∴ A whale is not a fish.	S e P	Valid

The following is a quintuple enthymeme because one and the same conclusion is drawn from five different sets of premises. While the paragraph clearly illustrates this logical structure, it also illustrates the rhetorical principle of variety: in diction, in sentence structure and sentence length, in rhythm, in introducing a Biblical allusion and some emphatic repetition, in first naming together those who hold the third and fourth reasons, then giving the reasons they hold, and finally in substituting the contrary, the abstract, and the negative in stating them.

There is a chorus of voices . . . raised in favor of the doctrine . . . that everybody must be educated. The politicians tell us, "You must educate the masses because they are going to be masters." The clergy join in the cry for education, for they affirm that the people are drifting away from church and chapel into the broadest infidelity. The manufacturers and the capitalists swell the chorus lustily. They declare that ignorance makes bad workmen; that England will soon be unable to turn out cotton goods, or steam engines, cheaper than other people; and then, Ichabod! Ichabod! the glory will be departed from us. And a few voices are lifted up in favor of the doctrine that the masses should be educated because they are men and women with unlimited capabilities of being, doing, and suffering, and that it is as true now, as ever it was, that the people perish for lack of knowledge.

—Thomas H. Huxley, "A Liberal Education"[4]

Importance of the Enthymeme

The enthymeme has been given careful consideration because of its great practical importance.

In the enthymeme one proposition, most often the major premise, is merely implied, not explicit; and therefore it is more likely to be carelessly assumed as true, without examination, and thereby to become a source of error and fallacious reasoning.

The enthymeme is the form of reasoning which we constantly employ in our thinking, conversation, and writing, and that which we should notice in our reading and listening. Logic is really practical when it is thus habitually used as a tool in daily life.

The enthymeme is used extensively in exposition and in debate. Whenever the three, four, or any number of reasons for an event in history are given, they constitute a multiple enthymeme—triple, quadruple, etc. The formal brief for a debate is a series of interlinked enthymemes: each main point states a conclusion, and the subheads, introduced by *for*, are the reasons which support it. When the main points have been established and are summarized, the reasoning moves forward to the final conclusion, as in the epicheirema, discussed below.

SORITES

A sorites is a chain of enthymemes or abridged syllogisms, in which the conclusion of one syllogism becomes a premise of the next; one premise of every syllogism but the first and the conclusion of all but the last are unexpressed, that is, merely implicit.

There are two types of sorites: (1) that in which the conclusion of one syllogism becomes the major premise of the next; (2) that in which it becomes the minor premise of the next.

Although it is possible to construct valid sorites in each of the four figures and to combine syllogisms of different figures in one sorites, we shall consider only the two traditional types in Figure I, the Aristotelian sorites and the Goclenian sorites, both of formally unlimited length. They are the only forms likely to be actually used in our reasoning.

The formal unity of each of these sorites is emphasized by regarding it as a syllogism in Figure I with many middle terms.

EXAMPLE: Aristotelian sorites

Socrates is a man.	S	a	M^1
A man is an animal.	M^1	a	M^2
An animal is an organism.	M^2	a	M^3
An organism is a body.	M^3	a	M^4
A body is a substance.	M^4	a	P
∴ Socrates is a substance.	S	a	P

Note that the exponent numbering distinguishes one middle term from another. For instance M^1 is man; M^2 is animal etc.

EXAMPLE: Goclenian sorites

A body is a substance.	M^1	a	P
An organism is a body.	M^2	a	M^1
An animal is an organism.	M^3	a	M^2
A man is an animal.	M^4	a	M^3
Socrates is a man.	S	a	M^4
∴ Socrates is a substance.	S	a	P

A sorites of six propositions is expanded to one of twelve propositions (four syllogisms) by making explicit the suppressed premises and conclusions of each of the syllogisms.

ILLUSTRATION: Aristotelian sorites expanded

Socrates is a man.	S	a	M^1
Man is an animal.	M^1	a	M^2
∴ Socrates is an animal.	S	a	M^2
Socrates is an animal.	S	a	M^2
An animal is an organism.	M^2	a	M^3
∴ Socrates is an organism.	S	a	M^3
Socrates is an organism.	S	a	M^3
An organism is a body.	M^3	a	M^4
∴ Socrates is a body.	S	a	M^4
Socrates is a body.	S	a	M^4
A body is a substance.	M^4	a	P
∴ Socrates is a substance.	S	a	P

ILLUSTRATION: Goclenian sorites expanded

A body is a substance.	M^1	a	P
An organism is a body.	M^2	a	M^1
∴ An organism is a substance.	M^2	a	P
An organism is a substance.	M^2	a	P
An animal is an organism.	M^3	a	M^2
∴ An animal is a substance.	M^3	a	P
An animal is a substance.	M^3	a	P
A man is an animal.	M^4	a	M^3
∴ A man is a substance.	M^4	a	P
A man is a substance.	M^4	a	P
Socrates is a man.	S	a	M^4
∴ Socrates is a substance.	S	a	P

Aristotelian and Goclenian Sorites

In the **Aristotelian** sorites the first proposition is the minor premise of its syllogism and all the rest are major premises, except the last, which is a conclusion; and the omitted conclusion in each syllogism becomes the minor premise of the following syllogism.

Rule 1. Only one premise, the last, may be negative. (Otherwise there will be an illicit process of the major term.)

Rule 2. Only one premise, the first (the minor), may be partial, contingent, or singular. (Figure I requires that the minor premise be affirmative; it may be partial or contingent.)

In the **Goclenian** sorites the first proposition is the major premise of its syllogism and all the rest are minor premises, except the last which is a conclusion; and the omitted conclusion in each syllogism becomes the major premise of the following syllogism.

Rule 1. Only one premise, the first, may be negative. (Otherwise there will be an illicit process of the major term.)

Rule 2. Only one premise, the last (the minor), may be partial, contingent, or singular. (The other propositions are major premises and must be total or necessary in Figure I.)

The Aristotelian sorites is more important than the Goclenian, for it represents a more natural movement of the mind and is more often used.

THE EPICHEIREMA

An epicheirema, like a sorites, is an abridged polysyllogism; but unlike a sorites, it is of formally limited length, and the movement of thought is partly backward and partly forward.

Definition

An epicheirema is an abridged polysyllogism combining any figures, at least one of whose premises is an enthymeme. If both premises are enthymemes, the epicheirema is double; if only one premise is an enthymeme, the epicheirema is single.

EXAMPLE: Single epicheirema

Beefsteak (that is eaten) is not stored in the body because it is protein.
Food that is not stored in the body is not fattening.
∴ Beefsteak is not fattening.

In dealing with negatives, it is very important to remember that the negative may be placed either in the copula or in the term; but it is never permissible to place the negative in the copula in one premise and in the middle term in the other, for this would create four terms: M, M′, S, and P. To make clear that a *term* is negative, it is often necessary to insert a word after the copula. If the enthymeme which is the minor premise in this epicheirema stood alone, the implied major premise "Protein is not stored in the body" would normally be treated as an E proposition. But since the middle term in the major premise of the epicheirema is negative, it is not only permissible but necessary to treat this as an A proposition, as in the following expansion.

ILLUSTRATION: An epicheirema expanded

Beefsteak is protein.	S a M	Figure IV
Protein is food that is not stored in the body.	M a P	Mood A A A
∴ Beefsteak is food that is not stored in the body.	S a P	Valid
Beefsteak is food that is not stored in the body.	S a M	Figure IV
Food that is not stored in the body is not fattening.	M e P	Mood A E E
∴ Beefsteak is not fattening.	S e P	Valid

Note that beefsteak is not pure protein, and over fifty percent of protein is converted in the body to carbohydrates; but beefsteak is nonetheless among the least fattening of nourishing foods.[5]

EXAMPLE: A double epicheirema

These stones are not diamonds, for they do not cut glass.
The stolen gems are undoubtedly diamonds, for they were pronounced such by the world's greatest diamond experts.
∴ These stones are not stolen gems.

Expanding the two enthymemes, we have in this epicheirema three complete syllogisms (the maximum number), the conclusions of the first two furnishing the premises of the third. (To save space, the distribution of terms is not marked here.)

ILLUSTRATION: A double epicheirema expanded

These stones do not cut glass.	S e M	Figure II
Diamonds cut glass.	P a M	Mood E A E
∴ These stones are not diamonds.	S e P	Valid

The stolen gems were pronounced diamonds by the world's greatest diamond experts.	S a M	Figure I
Stones pronounced diamonds by the world's greatest diamond experts are undoubtedly diamonds.	M a P	Mood A A A
∴ The stolen gems are undoubtedly diamonds.	S a P	Valid
These stones are not diamonds.	S e M	Figure II
The stolen gems are undoubtedly diamonds.	P a M	Mood E A E
∴ These stones are not the stolen gems.	S e P	Valid

The double epicheirema is the five-part form of argument which Cicero[6] particularly admired and used in his orations. The five parts are (1) the major premise; (2) the proof of the major; (3) the minor premise; (4) the proof of the minor; (5) the conclusion. In its rhetorical dress, this form of argument was elaborately illustrated and thereby considerably amplified.

A multiple enthymeme differs from an epicheirema in having only one conclusion but stating many reasons that support it. A single epicheirema has two conclusions, and a double epicheirema has three, for the conclusions of its two enthymemes become premises which lead to a third conclusion.

From a Sorites to an Epicheirema

The transformation of a sorites into an epicheirema allows for a comparison of structure. A sorites not exceeding five propositions may be transformed into a double epicheirema.

EXAMPLE: A sorites transformed into a double epicheirema

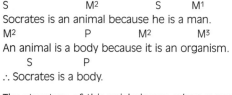

S $\quad$ M^2 $\qquad$ S $\quad$ M^1
Socrates is an animal because he is a man.
M^2 $\qquad$ P $\qquad$ M^2 $\qquad$ M^3
An animal is a body because it is an organism.
$\quad$ S $\qquad$ P
∴ Socrates is a body.

The structure of this epicheirema, when expanded, is as follows:

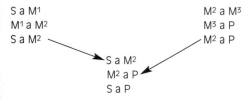

S a M^1 $\qquad\qquad\qquad$ M^2 a M^3
M^1 a M^2 $\qquad\qquad\qquad$ M^3 a P
S a M^2 $\qquad\qquad\qquad$ M^2 a P
$\qquad\qquad$ S a M^2
$\qquad\qquad$ M^2 a P
$\qquad\qquad$ S a P

The conclusion of the first syllogism becomes the minor premise of the last.

The conclusion of the second syllogism becomes the major premise of the last.

An epicheirema may likewise be transformed into a sorites.

ANALOGICAL INFERENCE OR ARGUMENT FROM EXAMPLE

This is a form of inference based on similitude. The conclusion from an analogical inference can be only probable. If it is proved to be certain, the argument ceases to be analogical.

Analogy has been used extensively throughout this book. It is common in poetry and in both literary and scientific prose. Commonly used analogies are the ship of state and the body politic.

Analogy is a mode of inference which has pointed the way to many of the discoveries of science. For example, Benjamin Franklin noted the similarity between sparks from an electrical machine and streaks of lightning and hazarded the guess, a tentative conclusion from the analogy, that lightning is electricity.

EXAMPLE: Benjamin Franklin's Analogy

Analogy	Formula
S^1 P Sparks from an electrical machine are electrical discharges,	S^1 is P, for
S^1 M for they are characterized by rapid motion and conductivity.	S^1 is M.
S^2 S^1 Lightning resembles these sparks in rapid	S^2 resembles S^1 in
M motion and conductivity.	M
S^2 P ∴ Lightning is probably an electrical discharge.	∴ S^2 is probably P.

In 1749, Franklin flew his kite and found that lightning was conductible. The lightning rod was a practical result of this experiment; it conducts the electrical discharge to the ground where it does no harm.

The worth of an analogical inference depends upon the importance of the resemblances rather than upon the number of resemblances. The validity of the argument requires that the point of resemblance M be probably a property resulting from the nature P and be not the differentia of S^1. As Aristotle has remarked, the argument from example is an inference, not from the logical whole to its parts (deduction), but from part to part when both fall under a common genus (M) but one of the two (S^1) is better known to us than the other (S^2).

MEDIATED OPPOSITION

Definition

Mediated opposition is the opposition between two propositions which together contain three terms, one term being common to both.

EXAMPLE: Mediated opposition

The witness is lying.
The witness is telling the truth.

Mediated opposition probably occurs more frequently in disputes than immediate opposition does. Immediate opposition would oppose the first proposition, in the example given above, with its contradictory: The witness is not lying.

Mediated opposition combines the rules of opposition with the rules of syllogism. Since two propositions mediately opposed have three terms, they can be formed into a syllogism, which, combined with immediate opposition, clearly expresses the relations of all the propositions involved.

Let X symbolize the minor premise, Y the major premise, and Z the conclusion of a syllogism. Let X′ symbolize the contradictory of X, and Z′, that of Z.

ILLUSTRATION: Mediated opposition

X	The witness is lying.	X′	The witness is not lying.
Y	Whoever lies does not tell the truth.		
Z	The witness is not telling the truth.	Z′	The witness is telling the truth.

Rules Determining the Validity of Mediated Opposition

1   The syllogism involved in relating the propositions mediately opposed must be formally valid.

2   The third proposition (Y), which serves to establish mediated opposition between two others, must be materially true.

The following fallacies result from the violation of these rules: illicit, illusory, or merely seeming mediated opposition.

Relations of Mediated Opposition

These relations can be understood by applying the rules of mediated opposition to the illustration above.

Provided that Y is materially true, X and Z′ are validly opposed as genuine mediated contraries, and both cannot be true. Recall that contraries are propositions which differ in quality (affirmative / negative) and are either total in quantity or necessary in modality. With contraries, both cannot be true, but both may be false.

Provided that Y is materially true, Z and X′ are validly opposed as mediated subcontraries, and both cannot be false. Recall that subcontraries are propositions which differ in quality and are either partial in quantity or contingent in modality. With subcontraries, both cannot be false, and both may be true.

Mediated opposition is frequently a source of fallacy because the disputants usually do not know the formal rules for determining its validity, nor do they consciously advert to and examine the third proposition (Y) to which each of their contentions is related and by virtue of which they are mediately opposed (just as in any enthymeme the omitted premise which is not consciously adverted to is often the source of fallacy). The terms of Y must be repugnant. Recall that "repugnant" means that the terms are incompatible. Each term symbolizes a reality that excludes the other term.

The following illustration shows how fundamental to genuine mediated opposition is the rule that Y must be materially true.

ILLUSTRATION: Y must be materially true

X   John was in New York last Monday.   X′ John was not in New York last Monday.

Y   A man who was in New York last Monday could not have been in Chicago last Monday.

Z   John was not in Chicago last Monday.   Z′ John was in Chicago last Monday.

If John were accused of a crime committed in New York last Monday, would this argument establish an alibi, provided that Z′ could be proved? We have here a valid syllogism; but in order that X and Z′ be validly opposed as mediated contraries, it is necessary also that Y be materially true. Y would have been materially true a hundred years ago but not now; hence now X and Z′ are not validly opposed as genuine mediated contraries but merely seem to be such, and both may be true.

The source of many fallacies in the daily use of mediated opposition is the false, hidden assumption that the terms not common to the propositions mediately opposed are mutually exclusive terms. For example, one person says, "Mary has a degree in law." The other replies, "That isn't true; she has a degree in philosophy." Neither disputant adverts to the full, explicit argument, which is explained in the following illustration.

ILLUSTRATION: Y must be materially true

X   Mary has a degree in law.   X′ Mary does not have a degree in law.

Y   Whoever has a degree in law cannot have a degree in philosophy.

Z   Mary does not have a degree in philosophy.   Z′ Mary has a degree in philosophy.

We see at once that although the syllogism is valid, Y is not materially true. Therefore X and Z′ may both be true, and X′ and Z may both be false. As a matter of fact, this Mary has a degree in law and also a degree in philosophy. Each disputant happened to know only about the one degree, not the other. In this, as in many arguments in daily life, there is not genuine opposition, for both disputants are right. A realization of this and a knowledge of the rules of mediated opposition would forestall much needless and futile contention. This misunderstanding applies to many arguments about the spelling or the pronunciation of words, for the dictionary shows many instances in which two or more ways are valid.

UTILITY OR WORTH OF THE SYLLOGISM

The various forms and combinations of the syllogism discussed in this chapter are useful only if the syllogism itself is a means whereby the mind advances in knowledge. John Stuart Mill and other logicians of the Empiricist School have attacked the syllogism, contending that the conclusion is contained in the major premise, and has to be known before the major premise can be stated; that it therefore begs the question in thus assuming the very proposition to be proved; and that it is therefore not an advance in knowledge.[7]

A refutation of the Empiricists' argument is that while it may be true of a syllogism whose major premise is a mere enumerative empirical proposition that the conclusion has to be known before the major premise can be stated, but it is never true of a syllogism whose major premise is a general proposition, for the truth of a general proposition is known, not from counting instances and adding them together, but from an analysis of the terms in relation to each other; its truth is not dependent on investigation of the individual facts, for it is understood in intension, not in extension. In other words, the terms are understood by their meaning rather than by their application.

EXAMPLE: Syllogism in which major premise is an enumerative empirical proposition

Every new car built for the American market has airbags.
The Smiths' new car was built for the American market.
∴ The Smiths' new car has airbags.

EXAMPLE: Syllogism with a general proposition as the major premise

A blind man cannot umpire a football game.
Tom Jones is a blind man.
∴ Tom Jones cannot umpire a football game.

The second syllogism is not begging the question, because the conclusion, that is, the proposition to be proved, is not implicit in the major premise, nor in the minor premise, but in the conjunction of the two premises.

The syllogism is an advance in knowledge because its conclusion is a truth distinct from that of each of the premises and apparent only through their conjunction.

It is a common experience that a person may have knowledge of only one of the premises, and that as soon as he discovers the second, he recognizes the truth of the conclusion which instantly emerges in a spontaneous act of syllogistic reasoning. For example, one may have known that "A bird is not a mammal." But one may not have known that "A bat is a mammal." The conclusion that "A bat is not a bird" was, then, not only a distinctly new piece of knowledge, but the contradictory of what had been believed, namely, that "A bat is a bird."

It may be further contended against Mill that even the conclusion from two empirical premises sometimes represents an advance in knowledge, arising from the conjunction of the premises. This is the very means used to create suspense and interest in many stories and parts of stories. For example, in Hawthorne's *The House of the Seven Gables*,[8] the reader knows that the Maule family has been hostile to the Pyncheon family, for Matthew Maule had cursed Colonel Pyncheon and his descendants after Colonel Pyncheon had persecuted him. The reader also knows that Holgrave is interested in Phoebe Pyncheon. But it comes as a surprise, as an advance in knowledge, to discover at the end of the story that Holgrave is a Maule. The situation may be stated thus:

> The Maules have no love for the Pyncheons.
> Holgrave is a Maule.
> ∴ Holgrave will not love a Pyncheon.

Since, however, living human beings, although rational, are not ruled altogether by cold logic, especially that of a dead ancestor's curse, but by emotion and independent judgment as well, the lovers disregard the major premise and end the family feud.

Another example is in Dickens' *A Tale of Two Cities*.[9] Dr. Manette knows that Charles Darnay, a young man whom he likes and admires, wishes to marry Lucie Manette, his daughter. He also knows that the St. Evremonde family has grievously injured him. But when he learns Charles Darnay's true family name, these separate, previously known propositions suddenly conjoin in the following disturbing sorites made up of two syllogisms:

> My daughter loves Charles Darnay.
> Charles Darnay is a St. Evremonde.

The St. Evremondes have grievously injured me.
∴ My daughter loves one of a family which has grievously injured me.

Dr. Manette finally consents to let Charles Darnay become his son-in-law, but so great is the emotional shock of the new knowledge arising from the conjunction of the premises that Dr. Manette temporarily loses the use of his reason.

Examples could be multiplied indefinitely both from literature and from life—cases of mistaken identity, of proving an alibi in court, and the like.

THE SYLLOGISM AS A FORMULA OR RULE OF INFERENCE

A valid syllogism, like every other relation of propositional forms, is a formula or rule of inference requiring that a given assertion must be made if certain other assertions are made. Provided that the syllogism is valid, it operates as a rule of inference in the following manner:

Rule 1. If both premises are true, the conclusion must be true.

Rule 2. If the conclusion is false, at least one of the premises must be false. The premises together constitute a conjunction of propositions. Hence when one is false, the conjunction is false.

Rule 3. If one or both of the premises are false, the value of the conclusion is unknown.

EXAMPLES: Syllogisms with false premises

	1		2
0	All squares are circles.	0	All squares are circles.
1	No circle is a triangle.	1	No circle is a rectangle.
1	No square is a triangle.	0	No square is a rectangle.

Since in both these examples, one of the premises is false, and since in the one the conclusion is true whereas in the other the conclusion is false, it is evident that if the premises are false, the value of the conclusion is unknown through the form although it may be learned from the matter.

Rule 4. If the conclusion is true, the value of the premises is unknown.

Rule 5. If one or both of the premises are probable, the conclusion can be only probable; it cannot be categorically true or false.

Rule 6. If the conclusion is probable, the value of the premises is unknown; for in the first example illustrating *Rule 3* the conclusion is true and one of the premises is false, whereas in every sound syllogism the conclusion is true and the premises are true. Hence when the conclusion is true the value of the premises cannot be known through the form but must be learned from the matter.

These first two rules are the most important. Rules 3 to 6 are implied in Rules 1 and 2.

SPECIAL RULES OF THE FOUR FIGURES OF THE SYLLOGISM

As has been stated earlier in this chapter, a knowledge of the general rules of the syllogism, particularly those of distribution, suffices to determine the validity of any syllogism.

It is, however, a good logical exercise to apply the general rules to each figure abstractly in order to determine the special rules for each. It is easiest to understand the rules for Figure II, and we shall therefore begin with that.

Special Rules of Figure II

S___M	Since the middle term, which must be distributed
P___M	at least once, is predicate in both premises, and
S___P	since only a negative proposition formally distributes its predicate, the first rule is apparent at once:

Rule 1. One premise must be negative in order to distribute M (in accordance with general *Rule 3*).

A second special rule follows from this. Since the conclusion will be negative (*Rule 6*), the major term P will be distributed there and must accordingly be distributed also in its own premise (*Rule 4*); but there it stands as subject, and since only a total or a necessary proposition distributes its subject, the second special rule is:

Rule 2. The major premise must be total or necessary in order to avoid an illicit process of the major term.

Applying these special rules to the nine combinations of premises permitted by the general rules one finds that the valid moods in Figure II, with minor premise first, are AEE, EAE, IEO, OAO.

Special Rules of Figure I

S____M	In considering the position of the terms, we do not
M____P	see at once, as we did in Figure II, what special rule is
S____P	necessary, because the reasoning is indirect, by disproof
	of the contradictory of the special rule.

Rule 1. The minor premise must be affirmative.

The necessity of this rule becomes clear only in considering what would follow if the minor premise were negative: the conclusion would then be negative (*Rule 6*), and consequently the major term P would be distributed there and would have to be distributed in its own premise (*Rule 4*), where it occupies the position of predicate; the major premise would then have to be negative, since only a negative proposition distributes the predicate. But we have assumed that the minor is negative, and from two negative premises no conclusion can be drawn. Therefore, in order to avoid, on the one hand, an illicit process of the major term or, on the other hand, the formal fallacy of two negative premises, it is obvious that the minor premise must be affirmative. The second special rule follows from this:

Rule 2. The major premise must be total or necessary in order to avoid an undistributed middle term.

Since in Figure I the minor premise must be affirmative, the middle term M, as its predicate, cannot be distributed there by the form (although, if it is a definition, it will be distributed by the matter); in this figure, therefore, M can be distributed formally (*Rule 3*) only as subject of the major premise, which, consequently, must be total or necessary because only those distribute the subject.

Applying these special rules, we find that the valid moods of this figure are AAA, AEE, IAI, IEO.

Special Rules of Figure III

M____S	Since in this figure, as in Figure I, the major term is
M____P	predicate in the major premise, the same special rule
S____P	follows, for the same reasons, which need not be re-
	peated here.

Rule 1. The minor premise must be affirmative.

Rule 2. This follows from the first rule. Since the minor premise must be affirmative, the minor term S, its predicate, is formally undistributed there and must likewise be undistributed in the conclusion (*Rule 4*), where it stands as subject. But only partial or contingent propositions have the subject undistributed; therefore the conclusion must be partial or contingent.

Applying these special rules, one finds that the valid moods of Figure III are AAI, AII, IAI, AEO, AOO, IEO.

Special Rules of Figure IV

Although Aristotle knew Figure IV, both he and logicians of the Renaissance discussed only the first three figures. Figure IV has, however, been treated in logic for a long time. It is not a very satisfying figure, and it is unstable in the sense that its rules are a series of ifs, two of which (without the *if*) have been discussed in relation to other figures.

M_____S
P_____M
S_____P

Rule 1. If the major premise is affirmative, the minor must be total or necessary.

If the major premise is affirmative, the middle term M, its predicate, is formally undistributed in the major premise and must be distributed in the minor (*Rule 3*); but there it occupies the position of subject, and since only a total proposition distributes the subject, the minor premise must be total or necessary.

Rule 2. If the minor is affirmative, the conclusion must be partial or contingent. See *Rule 2* of Figure III.

Rule 3. If the conclusion is negative, the major premise must be total or necessary. See *Rule 2* of Figure II.

Applying these special rules, we find that the valid moods of Figure IV are AAI, EAE, AII, AEO, IEO.

COMPARISON OF THE FOUR FIGURES OF THE SYLLOGISM

Figure I is called the perfect figure because it alone can yield a total or a necessary general affirmative proposition as conclusion. Such conclusions are the goal of science, of philosophy, and of all general knowledge, for negative and partial or contingent propositions usually express limitations of knowledge rather than the perfection of knowledge. The perfect mood of the perfect figure is therefore Mood AAA in Figure I.

Figure I is also called the perfect figure because in it alone is the middle term really in the natural, middle position; in it alone is the natural synthesis of the terms given in the premises themselves. It represents the spontaneous, natural movement of thought in the process of reasoning. In Figure I the *dictum*, the fundamental principle of syllogistic reasoning, has immediate and obvious application, for as the major term is affirmed (or denied) of the middle term, the logical whole, so is it affirmed (or denied) of the minor term, the logical part.

Note that in this book the minor premise has regularly been placed first because (1) it is thereby more clearly evident that the middle term is in the middle (S____M, M____P, therefore S____P); (2) it corresponds more closely to our experience, for we usually become interested first in a particular object, then place it mentally in a class, perhaps after careful examination (This is a toadstool, not a mushroom), join to it what we know of that class (Toadstools are poisonous), and draw a conclusion therefrom (This is poisonous, and I must not eat it)—the second conclusion making this, by the implied premise (Whatever is poisonous I must not eat) two syllogisms; (3) this is the natural movement of thought, as is evident from the fact that we find the Aristotelian sorites, which places the minor premise first, much more comfortable than the Goclenian sorites, which places the major premise first. It is, of course, true that certain arguments seem more satisfactory with the major premise first, others with the minor premise first. So far as validity or formal correctness goes, it makes no difference which is placed first.

Figure II, except when one premise is a definition, can yield only negative conclusions. It is therefore particularly adapted to disproof.

Figure III is the weakest figure because, except when one premise is a definition, it can yield only a conclusion that is partial or singular or contingent. It is adapted to proving exceptions.

Figure IV, whose premises are the converse of Figure I, is so unnatural in the movement of its thought that it gives the mind the least satisfaction and the least sense of conviction, whereas the first figure gives the mind the most in both of these respects.

REDUCTION OF SYLLOGISMS

This is an ingenious exercise of little practical importance. Reduction is the process by which a syllogism in one of the imperfect figures (II, III, or IV) is expressed as a syllogism of the first figure, which is called the perfect figure.

The purpose of reduction is to demonstrate the validity of an imperfect figure as a formal process of reasoning by showing that an argument carried on according to the rules of an imperfect figure is valid in the perfect figure.

The assumptions of reduction are two: that the premises of the imperfect figure are true as given and that the first or perfect figure is formally valid.

The mnemonic lines that follow are a clever medieval device enumerating the nineteen[10] valid moods of the four figures and indicating the methods for reducing the moods of the imperfect figures to the corresponding moods of the perfect figure.

> Barbara, Celarent, Darii, Ferio, *que prioris*,
> Cesare, Camestres, Festino, Baroco, *secundae*.
> *Tertia* Darapti, Disamis, Datisi, Felapton
> Bocardo, Ferison *habet*, *Quarta insuper addit*
> Bramantip, Camenes, Dimaris, Fesapo, Fresison.[11]

The key to the mnemonic lines is that the vowels indicate the mood in this traditional order: major premise, minor premise, conclusion. B, C, D, F signify to what corresponding mood of the first figure the moods of the other figures are to be reduced; s (*simpliciter*) signifies that the proposition indicated by the preceding vowel is to be converted simply; p (*per accidens*) signifies that the proposition indicated by the preceding vowel must be converted by limitation (A to I and in one case, I to A, namely, Bramantip to Barbara); m (*muta*) signifies that the premises are to be transposed; c (*per contradictorian propositionem*) signifies that the reduction is to be indirect, by disproving a contradictory conclusion in a syllogism of the first figure; r, b, l, n, t, d have no significance.

ILLUSTRATION: Reduction (Camestres to Celarent): (a to b)

Camestres decoded means:

a All circles are curvilinear.   P a M   m—Transpose the premises.

   No square is curvilinear.   S e M   s—Convert simply.

   ∴No square is a circle.   S e P   s—Convert simply.

b No curvilinear figure is a square.   M e P

   All circles are curvilinear.   S a M

   ∴ No circle is a square.   S e P

ILLUSTRATION: Reduction (Bocardo to Barbara): (a to b)

Bocardo decoded means: c—Show that the conclusion of a corresponding syllogism in Figure I contradicts a premise given as true in Figure III. The method is: From Barbara, using as premises the A of Bocardo and the contradictory of its conclusion draw the conclusion implicit in these premises.

a Some lions are not tame.   M o P

   All lions are animals.   M a S

   ∴ Some animals are not tame.   S o P

b All animals are tame.   M a P

   All lions are animals   S a M

   ∴ All lions are tame   S a P

This conclusion in Barbara, since it is the contradictory of the O premise of Bocardo, which was given as true, must be false. But Barbara is accepted as a valid process of reasoning. The error therefore must be in the matter, since it is not in the form; for if the conclusion of a valid syllogism is false, at least one of the premises must be false. But the minor premise of Barbara, borrowed from Bocardo, is given as true; therefore the major premise of Barbara must be false. Since this major premise is the contradictory of the conclusion of Bocardo, that conclusion must be true.

Thomas Fuller (1608–61) in "The General Artist"[12] notes the many uses of logic:

> Logic is the armory of reason, furnished with all offensive and defensive weapons. There are syllogisms, long swords; enthymemes, short daggers; dilemmas, two-edged swords that cut on both sides; sorites,

chain-shot. And for the defensive, distinctions, which are shields; re-
tortions, which are targets with a pike in the midst of them, both to defend and oppose.

EXERCISES

Examine the following arguments. Expand those that are abridged.
Concerning each determine (1) the type, (2) figure, (3) mood, (4) validity, (5) the fallacy, if any.

Coral is used in jewelry. Coral is an animal skeleton. Therefore some animal skeletons are used in jewelry.

All humans are intelligent. All humans are finite. Therefore all intelligent
beings are finite.

Rita is an aunt because she has a niece.

Neither an elm nor an oak is an evergreen. Therefore an oak is not an elm.

A horse is a mammal. A mammal is a vertebrate. A vertebrate is an animal.
An animal has sense knowledge. Therefore a horse has sense knowledge.

He has had a liberal education, for he is, as completely as a man can be,
in harmony with Nature.
—T. H. Huxley, "A Liberal Education"

Eggs darken silver, for they contain sulphur. Eggs darken these spoons.
Therefore some silver is in these spoons.

Some politicians are grafters. All grafters are dishonest. All dishonest people are a social menace. People who are a social menace should be punished by law. Therefore some politicians should be punished by law.

This chemical substance must be a base, for it turns red litmus paper blue
and phenolphthalein red.

The present is the only thing of which a man can be deprived, for that is
the only thing which he has, and a man cannot lose a thing that he has not.
—Marcus Aurelius, *Meditations*

I thrice presented him a kingly crown,
Which he did thrice refuse.
Was this ambition?
—*Julius Caesar* 3.2.96–97

A balloon filled with helium will rise, for it is lighter than air. This balloon does not rise. Therefore this balloon is not filled with helium.

Since cultivation of mind is surely worth seeking for its own sake . . . there is a knowledge which is desirable, though nothing come of it.
—John Henry Newman, *The Idea of a University Defined*

Light rays are energy rays, for they produce an image of an obstructing body on a photographic film. Rays emitted from uranium resemble light rays in producing an image of an obstructing body on a photographic film. Therefore rays emitted from uranium are probably energy rays.
—Henri Becquerel

Olivia. Y'are servant to the Count Orsino, youth.
Cesario. And he is yours, and his must needs be yours.
Your servant's servant is your servant, madam.
—*Twelfth Night* 3.1.100–102

The specific purpose for which a college exists is the development of the intellectual virtues. The development of the intellectual virtues demands intellectual honesty. Whatever demands intellectual honesty is incompatible with cheating. Therefore the specific purpose for which a college exists is incompatible with cheating.

Flavius. Have you forgot me, sir?
Timon. Why dost thou ask that? I have forgot all men.
Then, if thou grant'st th'art a man, I have forgot thee.
—*Timon of Athens* 4.3.473–5

A lie is intrinsically evil, for it is the perversion of a natural faculty. Whatever is intrinsically evil can never be justified, for it cannot become good through any extrinsic circumstance whatsoever. Therefore a lie can never be justified.

That we cannot bear. Better to die, for death is gentler far than tyranny.
—Aeschylus, *Agamemnon*

Death certainly, and life, honor and dishonor, pain and pleasure, all these things equally happen to good men and bad, being things which make us neither better nor worse. Therefore they are neither good nor evil.
—Marcus Aurelius, *Meditations*

Each man holds that to be the highest good which he prefers before all others. The highest good is defined as happiness. Therefore each man esteems that estate happy which he prefers before all others.

—Boethius, *Consolation of Philosophy*

Seriousness is gravity. Gravity is a law of nature. Therefore seriousness is a law of nature.

"C-e-l-t is pronounced *kelt*." "That isn't true; it is pronounced *selt*."

Happiness is a virtuous activity of the soul. Therefore neither a brute animal nor a very young child is truly happy.

—Aristotle, *Ethics*

Loving in truth, and fain in verse my love to show.
That she, dear she, might take some pleasure of my pain,
Pleasure might cause her read, reading might make her know,
Knowledge might pity win, and pity grace obtain.

—Philip Sidney, "Sonnet I"

Macbeth [speaking of Duncan] He's here in double trust:
First as I am his kinsman and his subject.
Strong both against the deed; then as his host
Who should against his murderer shut the door,
Not bear the knife myself.

—*Macbeth* 1.7.12–16

Paris has no sound courage. Therefore I deem that he will gather bitter fruit.

—Homer, *Iliad*

8 RELATIONS OF HYPOTHETICAL AND DISJUNCTIVE PROPOSITIONS

HYPOTHETICAL PROPOSITIONS

A hypothetical proposition is one that asserts the dependence of one proposition on another. An example is: If a man drinks poison, he will die. It is usually an *if* proposition; *unless* meaning *if not*, *provided that*, and sometimes *when* may also express this relation. The proposition which depends on the other is called the consequent; the proposition on which it depends is called the antecedent. The dependence itself is the nexus, which is the connection, the link between the propositions.

The hypothetical proposition expresses a relation of propositions, whereas the simple proposition expresses a relation of terms. The hypothetical proposition expresses a conditional relation of dependence, and hence of limitation, whereas the simple categorical proposition expresses without limitation a relation between a subject and a predicate.

Because a hypothetical proposition expresses a dependence primarily in the logical order, the antecedent is more correctly called the reason, rather than the cause, of the consequent. A reason is the relation in the logical order, whereas a cause is, strictly speaking, a relation in the metaphysical order. Thus, the existence of the world is a reason for believing in the existence of God, but it is not a cause of His existence; on the contrary, it is an effect of His existence.

Types of Hypothetical Propositions

There are two types of hypothetical propositions: the type having three terms and the type having four terms.

1   In the type having three terms, one term being common to both antecedent and consequent, the formula is If S is M, it is P. If you study, you will learn.

2   In the type having four terms, no term being common to both antecedent and consequent, the formula is If B is C, D is E. If he comes, I will go.

Reduction of Hypothetical Propositions

The hypothetical proposition can be reduced to a categorical proposition and vice versa, but usually this involves a change of import or a distortion of meaning. Distortion occurs especially in reducing the second type. Were there no difference whatever except in form, there would be no real justification for regarding the categorical and the hypothetical propositions as logically distinct types instead of verbally distinct. The genuine hypothetical is one in which the dependence between antecedent and consequent cannot be adequately expressed in categorical form or in which such dependence persists even in the categorical form.

Formula for Reduction of Hypothetical Propositions

1. The first type: If S is M, it is P becomes SM is P.

2. The second type: If B is C, D is E becomes BC is DE.

8-1   *Reduction of Hypothetical Propositions*

EXAMPLES: Reduction of hypothetical propositions

Hypothetical propositions

1. If a man drinks poison, he will die.

2. If a man is virtuous, he will be rewarded.

3. If she attended the freshman class meeting last week, she is an American citizen.

4. If you do not return the book to the library on time, you will be fined.

5. If a child goes wrong, the mother will grieve.

Categorical propositions

1. Whoever drinks poison will die.

2. A virtuous man will be rewarded.

3. All who attended the freshman class meeting last week are American citizens.

4. Your failure to return the book to the library on time is the cause of your being fined.

5. A child's going wrong is a cause of the mother's grieving.

It will be noted that all these examples, except the last, represent the first type: SM is P. The first two suffer little distortion; the last two suffer much, and in them especially the dependence between antecedent and consequent persists and is felt even in the categorical form, for causality is the relation expressed in both forms.

Just as clearly, the categorical nature of the third persists and is felt when it is expressed in hypothetical form because its antecedent is not the reason of the consequent, nor does the one depend on the other. This is an empirical proposition, to which the categorical form is natural.

The compound nature of all these propositions (especially categorical example 2, "A virtuous man will be rewarded.") becomes obvious if we recall that grammatical modification is implicit logical predication; therefore, each of these examples is a conjunction of propositions, not one simple proposition. It is not bare conjunction, however, but one expressing a relation of dependence. Therefore, although the hypothetical proposition is compound and can be reduced to its component simple propositions or to one simple proposition with compound terms, it represents a species of judgment, a particular kind of relationship between propositions and not merely between terms, and so it merits treatment as a distinct logical form.

Special Characteristics of Hypothetical Propositions

TRUTH OR FALSITY
The hypothetical proposition does not assert either one of its component simple propositions as true or false; it asserts only that one depends on the other, that there is a nexus between them. Hence a hypothetical proposition is true when the nexus holds in the real order and false when it does not.

EXAMPLES: Hypothetical propositions and dependence on truth of nexus

If a man drinks poison, he will die. (True)

If a man drinks water, he will die. (False)

QUALITY
The hypothetical proposition is always affirmative in the sense that it always affirms the nexus, that is, the connection of its component simple

propositions; these, however, taken separately, may be both affirmative, or both negative, or one may be affirmative and the other negative.

EXAMPLES: Hypothetical propositions always affirmative

If you stop eating, you will die.

If you do not eat, you will die.

If you do not eat, you will not live.

If you stop eating, you will not live.

The proposition which denies a hypothetical proposition denies the nexus, yet such a proposition is not really a hypothetical proposition, for it does not assert the dependence of one proposition on another but denies such dependence.

EXAMPLE: Hypothetical proposition and its contradictory

If a man drinks water, he will die.

If a man drinks water, he will not die.

Taken in relation to the first proposition, which is false, the second, its denial (contradictory), is true; but, taken by itself, the second proposition is not true, for by drinking water a man cannot keep from dying. Nevertheless, in relation to a given proposition, such denials provide the change of quality needful to the opposition and eduction of hypothetical propositions.

DISJUNCTIVE PROPOSITIONS

A disjunctive proposition is one which asserts that of two or more suppositions, one is true. It is an *either . . . or* proposition.

Types of Disjunctive Propositions

There are three types represented by the following formulas. The first is the most important type.

1   S is P or Q or R.

A triangle is either equilateral or isosceles or scalene.

A rectangle is either a square or an oblong.

This type of disjunctive proposition is usually a summary of the results of a logical division of a genus into its constituent species and conforms to the same rules; for the alternatives are (1) collectively exhaustive, (2) mutually exclusive, (3) species resulting from division according to a single basis.

    2   S or T or U is P.

Either John or Helen or Henry will win the scholarship.

    3   B is C or D is E.

Either the man committed suicide or someone murdered him.

Either the captain failed to give the order or the soldier failed to obey it.

Reduction of Disjunctive Propositions

A disjunctive proposition having only two alternatives can be expressed in a hypothetical proposition which denies one alternative and affirms the other.

If this man did not commit suicide, someone murdered him.

If a rectangle is a square, it is not an oblong. (If S is M, it is not P.)

The reduction may be carried further by reducing the hypothetical proposition to a simple proposition (SM___P).

EXAMPLES: Reducing converted disjunctive to a simple proposition

A rectangle that is a square is not an oblong. (SMeP)

A nonsquare rectangle is an oblong. (SM'aP)

If the disjunctive proposition has more than two alternatives, it may, it is true, be expressed in a hypothetical proposition, but in that case the consequent will be disjunctive. For example: If a triangle is not equilateral, it is either isosceles or scalene.

Special Characteristics of Disjunctive Propositions

TRUTH OR FALSITY

A disjunctive proposition is strictly true if it enumerates all the possibilities, that is, if the alternatives are mutually exclusive and collectively exhaustive. Otherwise, strictly speaking, it is false.

The strict purpose, then, of the disjunctive proposition of every type is so to limit the choice of alternatives that if one is true, any other must be false.[1] Only under this condition does it serve as a true instrument of reasoning toward truth. It is this limitation of choice that makes the disjunctive proposition distinct from the hypothetical and the categorical. It is itself a conjunction of simple propositions joined by *or*, but it is not a bare conjunction, for the series of alternatives is fixed; to add to or subtract from the alternatives would falsify the series.

In ordinary discourse the disjunctive proposition is often used loosely without the strict disjunctive purpose, yet this purpose is often present in the context even when it is absent from the proposition itself. An example is: The package is in either the living room or the dining room.

This proposition does not seem to exhaust the possibilities, but it does so implicitly if the context in the mind of the speaker is this: Since I had the package when I entered the house, and now, having left the house, I do not have it, and since I was in only the two rooms mentioned, the package must be in either the one room or the other.

To deny a disjunctive proposition, one may either:

1. Deny the possibilities as well as the choice.
   Original: A student is either a laborer or a gentleman.
   Denial: A student is neither.

2. Deny that the alternatives are mutually exclusive.
   Denial: A student is both a laborer and a gentleman.

3. Deny that the alternatives are collectively exhaustive.
   Denial: A student is *not* either a laborer or a gentleman.

The last is the most effective method of denying this example, for a student may be a woman; the original proposition is false, however, on all three counts.

QUALITY

The disjunctive proposition is always affirmative, in the sense that it affirms a series of possibilities. The proposition which denies a disjunctive proposition is not really a disjunctive proposition, as may be seen in the first and third examples above, for it does not assert that of two or more suppositions one is true; rather it is the negation of such an assertion. In relation to a given disjunctive proposition, however, such denials provide the change of quality needful to the opposition and eduction of the disjunctive proposition.

The hypothetical and the disjunctive proposition are effective in drama or story. Shakespeare often used the hypothetical proposition to state an important problem.

ILLUSTRATION: Shakespeare's use of the hypothetical proposition

Hamlet [of Claudius]. If his occulted guilt
Do not itself unkennel in one speech,
It is a damned ghost that we have seen.
  —*Hamlet* 3.2.80–82

Carlisle [of Bolingbroke]. And if you crown him, let me prophesy,
The blood of English shall manure the ground
And future ages groan for this foul act.
  —*Richard II* 4.1.136–138

Ford. If I suspect without cause . . . let me be your jest.
  —*The Merry Wives of Windsor* 3.3.149–151

The disjunctive proposition is particularly fitted to express choices upon which character or action depends.

ILLUSTRATION: Disjunctive propositions, significant in creating either action or character

Antony. These strong Egyptians fetters I must break
Or lose myself in dotage.
                    —*Antony and Cleopatra* 1.2.116–17

Prince Hal. The land is burning; Percy stands on high;
And either we or they must lower lie.
                    —*1 Henry IV* 3.3.203–4

Bastard. Straight let us seek, or straight we shall be sought.
The Dauphin rages at our very heels.
                    —*King John* 5.7.79–80

The following paragraph illustrates the use of continued disjunction or subdivision in closely knit reasoning. The final sentence gathers together the parts disclosed by division.

ILLUSTRATION: Continued disjunction

Every action of every person either is or is not due to that person himself. Of those not due to himself some are due to chance, the others to necessity; of these latter, again, some are due to compulsion, the others to nature. Consequently all actions that are not due to a man himself are due either to chance or to nature or to compulsion. . . . Those things happen through compulsion which take place contrary to the desire or reason of the doer, yet through his own agency. . . . All actions that are due to a man himself and caused by himself are due either to habit or to rational or irrational craving. Rational craving is a craving for good, that is, a wish—nobody wishes for anything unless he thinks it is good. Irrational craving is twofold, namely, anger and appetite. Thus every action must be due to one or other of seven causes: chance, nature, compulsion, habit, reasoning, anger, or appetite.
                    —Aristotle, Rhetoric 1,10[2]

RELATIONS OF HYPOTHETICAL AND DISJUNCTIVE PROPOSITIONS

Hypothetical and disjunctive propositions have all the relations that simple propositions have, and the rules governing these relations are practically the same.

One who understands the grammatical structure of the simple sentence has only to apply the same principles to the more complicated but not altogether new patterns of the compound-complex sentence.

Conjunction

Although hypothetical and disjunctive propositions are themselves relations of simple propositions, they are capable of being conjoined. The conjunction may be a bare conjunction or a material conjunction.

Opposition

OF HYPOTHETICAL PROPOSITIONS

Although, as has been said, every hypothetical proposition, taken by itself, is, strictly speaking, affirmative, by varying the consequent, one can construct A E I O forms of hypotheticals which, in relation to each other, differ in quality and in either quantity or modality. The square of opposition of hypotheticals may be construed of either quantitative or of modal A E I O forms.

EXAMPLES: Hypothetical propositions in A E I O forms

Quantitative Forms

A   If an animal is striped, it is always a zebra.
E   If an animal is striped, it is never a zebra.
I   If an animal is striped, it is sometimes a zebra.
O   If an animal is striped, it is sometimes not a zebra.

Modal Forms

A   If a man's heart stops beating, he will necessarily die.
E   If a man's heart stops beating, he will necessarily not die.
I   If a man's heart stops beating, he may die.
O   If a man's heart stops beating, he may not die.

The modal forms are better suited to hypothetical propositions. The quantitative forms in the example above do not convey the relations as well as the modal forms would.

OF DISJUNCTIVE PROPOSITIONS

The opposition of disjunctive propositions also can be expressed in either quantitative or modal forms.

EXAMPLES: Disjunctive propositions in A E I O forms

Quantitative Forms

A   Every number is either odd or even.
E   No number is either odd or even.
I   Some numbers are either odd or even.
O   Some numbers are not either odd or even.

Modal Forms

A   A triangle must be either equilateral or isosceles or scalene.
E   A triangle cannot be either equilateral or isosceles or scalene.
I   A triangle may be either equilateral or isosceles or scalene.
O   A triangle may not be either equilateral or isosceles or scalene.

Eduction

OF HYPOTHETICAL PROPOSITIONS

All seven forms may be derived.

EXAMPLE: Eduction of hypothetical proposition

Original: If a tree is a pine, it is necessarily an evergreen.

Obverse: If a tree is a pine, it is necessarily not a nonevergreen.

Partial contrapositive: If a tree is a nonevergreen, it is necessarily not a pine.

Full contrapositive: If a tree is a nonevergreen, it is necessarily a nonpine.

Full inverse: If a tree is a nonpine, it may be a nonevergreen.

Partial inverse: If a tree is a nonpine, it may not be an evergreen.

Converse: If a tree is an evergreen, it may be a pine.

Obverted converse: If a tree is an evergreen, it may not be a nonpine.

Note that *sine qua non* hypothetical proposition is one whose antecedent is that without which the consequent will not follow. *Sine qua non* means that the item so labeled is essential. The sense of the Latin phrase is that without this element, the subject under discussion cannot be what it is. Its antecedent is the only reason of its consequent; and its consequent cannot follow from any other antecedent. Therefore a *sine qua non* hypothetical proposition, like a definition, is convertible simply. An example is: If a substance turns blue litmus paper red, it is an acid. If a substance is an acid, it turns blue litmus paper red.[3] The seven eductions of a *sine qua non* hypothetical proposition can, therefore, like those of a definition, be derived in one continuous process of alternate obversion and conversion, and the eighth operation returns the original.

The ignorant assumption that a hypothetical proposition is convertible when it is not is illustrated by an incident narrated by Saint Thomas More:

ILLUSTRATION: Erroneous conversion of a hypothetical proposition

Witness: This doctor said to me that if Hunne had not sued the premunire he should never have been accused of heresy.

Doctor: I said indeed, that if Hunne had not been accused of heresy he would never have sued the premunire.

Witness: Lo, my lords, I am glad you find me a true man.

Lord: I have espied, good man, so the words be all one, it makes no matter to you which way they stand; but all is one to you, a horse mill and a mill horse, drink ere you go, and go ere you drink.

Witness: Nay, my lords, I will not drink.

And therewith he went his way, leaving some of the lords laughing to see that as contrary as their two tales were, yet when he heard them both again, he took them both for one because the words were one.

—*The Confutation of Tyndale's Answers*[4]

OF DISJUNCTIVE PROPOSITIONS

A strict disjunctive proposition which expresses the results of a logical division is, like a *sine qua non* hypothetical proposition and a definition, convertible simply. Therefore its seven eductions can be derived in one continuous process of alternate obversion and conversion and the eighth operation returns the original.

EXAMPLE: Eduction of disjunctive proposition

Original:	A material substance must be either a gas, a liquid, or a solid.
Converse:	A substance that is either a gas, a liquid, or a solid must be a material substance.

Obverted converse:	A substance that is either a gas, a liquid, or a solid cannot be a nonmaterial substance.
Partial inverse:	A nonmaterial substance cannot be either a gas, a liquid, or a solid.
Full inverse:	A nonmaterial substance must be neither a gas, a liquid, nor a solid.
Full contrapositive:	A substance that is neither a gas, a liquid, nor a solid must be a nonmaterial substance.
Partial contrapositive:	A substance that is neither a gas, a liquid, nor a solid cannot be a material substance.
Obverse:	A material substance cannot be neither a gas, a liquid, nor a solid.
Original:	A material substance must be either a gas, a liquid, or a solid.

Syllogism

THE HYPOTHETICAL SYLLOGISM

There are two types of hypothetical syllogism: the pure hypothetical syllogism and the mixed hypothetical syllogism.

The Pure Hypothetical

All three of the following propositions are hypothetical.

EXAMPLES: Pure hypothetical syllogism

If goods become scarce, prices will advance (other things being equal).

If prices advance, our savings cannot buy as much as at present.

If goods become scarce, our savings cannot buy as much as at present.

The Mixed Hypothetical

The mixed hypothetical syllogism is extensively used. The major premise is a hypothetical proposition, and the minor premise is a simple proposition.

Rules for the Mixed Hypothetical Syllogism

The minor premise must either

1   posit the antecedent or
2   sublate the consequent of the major premise.[5]

Fallacies:

1   to sublate the antecedent;
2   to posit the consequent.

8-2   *Rules for the Mixed Hypothetical Syllogism*

To posit the antecedent is to restate it as a fact, retaining the same quality: if it is negative in the major premise, it should be negative in the minor; if it is affirmative in the major, it should be affirmative in the minor.

To sublate the consequent is to restate as a fact its contradictory. This requires a change of quality: if it is affirmative in the major premise, it should be negative in the minor; if it is negative in the major, it should be affirmative in the minor.

Note that the rule has reference only to what the minor premise does to the major. Whenever the minor premise posits the antecedent, the conclusion posits the consequent. And whenever the minor premise sublates the consequent, the conclusion sublates the antecedent. This is correct and does not conflict with the rule.

There are two moods of the mixed hypothetical syllogism: the constructive, which posits, and the destructive, which sublates. Only two forms are valid.

The valid constructive mood posits the antecedent.

EXAMPLE: Positing the antecedent

If a man is not honest, he is not a fit public officer.
This man is not honest.
∴ This man is not a fit public officer.

The valid destructive mood sublates the consequent.

EXAMPLE: Sublating the consequent

If all students were equally competent, each would acquire the same amount of knowledge from a given course.
But each does not acquire the same amount of knowledge from a given course.
∴ All students are not equally competent.

Note that when the consequent is sublated, the conclusion should be the contradictory, not the contrary, of the antecedent. Contradictory and contrary terms are explained in Chapter Four. There is no middle ground between contradictory terms; they divide everything into one sphere or another (tree or nontree). Contrary terms can have a middle ground. They express degrees of difference; for example, good and evil are contrary terms. Most people or behaviors are not either good or evil but shadings of both.

Equivalent Fallacies of Mixed Hypothetical and Simple Syllogisms
1   The fallacy of sublating the antecedent in a mixed hypothetical syllogism is equivalent to the fallacy of an illicit process of the major term in a simple syllogism.

EXAMPLE: Sublating the antecedent

If a man drinks poison, he will die.   **Fallacy**: Sublating the antecedent
This man has not drunk poison.
∴ He will not die.

Equivalent simple syllogism:

Whoever drinks poison will die.   M a P   **Fallacy**: Illicit process of the major term
This man has not drunk poison.   S e M
∴ He will not die.   S e P

2   The fallacy of positing the consequent in a mixed hypothetical syllogism is equivalent to the fallacy of an undistributed middle term in a simple syllogism.

EXAMPLE: Positing the consequent

If a man drinks poison, he will die.   **Fallacy**: Positing the consequent
This man died.
∴ He must have drunk poison.

Equivalent simple syllogism:

Whoever drinks poison will die.   P a M   **Fallacy**: Undistributed middle term
This man died.   S a M
∴ He must have drunk poison.   S a P

Note that if the hypothetical proposition is a *sine qua non*, no fallacy can result in a mixed hypothetical syllogism for in that circumstance the minor premise may posit or sublate either the antecedent or the consequent. Similarly, if one of the premises of a simple syllogism is a definition, neither an illicit process nor an undistributed middle will occur, even if the special rules of the figures are disregarded.

Formal Basis for the Rules Governing the Syllogism as a Formula of Inference

By applying the rule of the mixed hypothetical syllogism, we can show formally the ground for the rules governing the syllogism as a formula of inference. We may state each of the rules in a formally correct mixed hypothetical syllogism, thus:

1 If the premises of a valid syllogism are true, the conclusion must be true.
    In this valid syllogism the premises are true.
    ∴ The conclusion is true.

This mixed hypothetical syllogism is correct, for the minor premise posits the antecedent. It would be incorrect to sublate the antecedent. Therefore, if the premises are not true, the value of the conclusion is formally unknown.

2 If the premises of a valid syllogism are true, the conclusion must be true.
    The conclusion of this syllogism is not true.
    ∴ The premises are not true.

This mixed hypothetical syllogism is valid, for the minor premise sublates the consequent. It would be incorrect to posit the consequent. Therefore, if the conclusion is true, the value of the premises is formally unknown.

The point may be demonstrated further by constructing two more correct mixed hypothetical syllogisms, the minor premise of the one positing the antecedent, that of the other sublating the consequent of the following major premise, which states the second important rule: If the conclusion of a correct syllogism is false, at least one of the premises must be false. In the same way one could prove the rules of opposition which work in only one direction; for example: If A is true, E is false.

THE DISJUNCTIVE SYLLOGISM

This is a syllogism in which the major premise is a disjunctive proposition and the minor premise is a simple categorical proposition positing or sublating one of the alternatives.

Moods of the Disjunctive Syllogism

There are two moods of the disjunctive syllogism: *ponendo tollens* and *tollendo ponens*.[6]

1 *Ponendo tollens*, in which the minor premise posits one alternative, and the conclusion sublates the other.

EXAMPLE: *Ponendo tollens* **disjunctive syllogism**

S is either P or Q.	This woman's long-unheard-from husband is either living or dead. (Stated before making investigation.)
S is P.	He is living. (Stated after long investigation.)
∴ S is not Q.	He is not dead.

---

2 *Tollendo ponens*, in which the minor premise sublates one alternative, and the conclusion posits the other.

EXAMPLE: *Tollendo ponens* **disjunctive syllogism**

S is either P or Q.	The soul is either spiritual or material.
S is not Q.	The soul is not material.
∴ S is P.	The soul is spiritual.

Note that this mood is valid only when the disjunctive proposition is of the strict type, its alternatives being collectively exhaustive and mutually exclusive.

Fallacies of the Disjunctive Syllogism

There is only one purely formal fallacy, which will seldom occur. It is present when both the minor premise and the conclusion both posit and sublate each alternative.

EXAMPLE: Fallacy of disjunctive syllogism

John is either a rabbit or not a rabbit.	(Only two alternatives.)
John is not a rabbit.	(You say, removing one alternative.)
∴ John is a rabbit.	(The only alternative left.)

This appears at first sight to exemplify the second formula above. But notice that the minor premise sublates the first alternative and posits the second and does both these things simultaneously. The conclusion simultaneously posits the first alternative and sublates the second.

The root of the error lies in the ambiguity of *not* in the major premise; as worded, it may be understood with *is* or with *rabbit,* either with the copula or with the term. The ambiguity can be removed by a clearer statement in which the negative is clearly attached to *rabbit* and the alternatives are dichotomous.

EXAMPLE: Syllogism with ambiguity resolved

John is either a rabbit or a nonrabbit.
John is not a rabbit.
∴ John is a nonrabbit.

ANALOGY: Billiards and the disjunctive syllogism

In billiards or in croquet, it is permissible to move two balls with one stroke. But to move both alternatives by one statement is not permissible in the disjunctive syllogism. Each stroke, each proposition, must affect only one alternative at one time.

The material fallacy of imperfect disjunction, which also has a formal aspect, occurs when the alternatives are either not mutually exclusive or not collectively exhaustive.

EXAMPLE: Alternatives not collectively exhaustive

Roses are either red or white.
The roses he sent are not red.
∴ The roses he sent are white.

THE DILEMMA

The dilemma is a syllogism which has for its minor premise a disjunctive proposition, for its major premise a compound hypothetical proposition, and for its conclusion either a simple or a disjunctive proposition.

The dilemma, correctly constructed, is a valid and useful form of reasoning, as all but the first of the four following examples and also some of the examples in the exercises at the end of this chapter illustrate. In actual use, a part of the argument is usually only implicit.

If the disjunctive offers three alternatives, the argument is more correctly called a trilemma; if many, a polylemma.

The dilemma is constructive if the minor premise posits the two antecedents of the major and destructive if it sublates the two consequents.

The dilemma has four moods: simple constructive, complex constructive, simple destructive, and complex destructive.

EXAMPLES: Four moods of the dilemma

Simple constructive

The accused lives either frugally or lavishly.
If he lives frugally, his savings must have made him wealthy; if he lives lavishly, his expenditures prove him to be wealthy.
∴ The accused is wealthy.

Empson, a tax-gatherer of Henry VII of England, used this argument to prove that everyone whom he haled[7] into court could and should pay higher taxes to the king.[8]

Complex constructive

Either the Christians have committed crimes or they have not.
If they have, your refusal to permit a public inquiry is irrational; if they have not, your punishing them is unjust.
∴ You are either irrational or unjust.

Tertullian, the Christian apologist, used this argument in an appeal to the Roman Emperor Marcus Aurelius, who was regarded as both a philosopher and an upright man, to stop the persecution of the Christians.

Simple destructive

If a student has earned graduation with the honor *summa cum laude*, he must have shown both talent and diligence.
But (his grades indicate that) either this student has not shown talent or he has not shown diligence.
∴ This student has not earned graduation with the honor *summa cum laude*.

In the simple destructive dilemma, the two consequents of the major premise are conjoined by *both* and *and* instead of being disjoined by *either* and *or*. They are therefore not alternatives; if they were, to sublate one or the other of them in the minor premise would not necessarily involve sublating the antecedent in the conclusion, as is required in a destructive dilemma.

Complex destructive

If this man had been properly instructed, he would know that he is acting wrongly; and if he were conscientious, he would care.

But either he does not know that he is acting wrongly or he apparently does not care.
∴ Either he has not been properly instructed or he is not conscientious.

THE TRILEMMA

The trilemma, which is a dilemma in which the disjunctive proposition offers three alternatives, follows the rules for the dilemma.

EXAMPLE: Trilemma

The priest can avoid capture only by flight, by combat, or by suicide.
If there is no exit but the one we guard, he cannot escape by flight; if he has no weapons, he cannot combat our armed forces; if he values his eternal salvation, he will not commit suicide.
∴ He cannot avoid capture.

Note that such an argument might have been used by priest hunters in sixteenth-century England.

FALLACIES OF THE DILEMMA

There are three fallacies of the dilemma: (1) false major premise; (2) imperfect disjunction in the minor premise; (3) the dilemmatic fallacy, occasioned by a shifting point of view.

There are three methods of attack in exposing these three sources of error.

1 *Taking the dilemma by the horns:* This method of attack is used when the major premise is false, that is, when the nexus affirmed between antecedent and consequent in the major premise does not hold in fact.

EXAMPLE: Taking the dilemma by the horns

If this man were intelligent, he would see the worthlessness of his arguments; if he were honest, he would admit that he is wrong.
But either he does not see the worthlessness of his arguments or, seeing it, he will not admit that he is wrong.
∴ Either he is not intelligent or he is not honest.

In attacking the dilemma, the controversialist would deny the nexus of the first part of the major premise by asserting that he is intelligent and thereby recognizes his arguments not as invalid but as valid.

---

2 *Escaping between the horns:* This method of attack is used when the minor premise presents an imperfect disjunction in that the alternatives stated are not collectively exhaustive. The discovery of an unmentioned alternative offers an escape from the conclusion, between the horns.

EXAMPLE: Escaping between the horns

If I tell my friend that her new dress is unbecoming, she will be hurt; if I tell her that it is becoming, I shall tell a lie.
But I must either tell her that it is becoming or that it is unbecoming.
∴ I must either hurt my friend or tell a lie.

Here escape between the horns, the alternatives presented in the minor premise, is easy. I can refrain from making any comment on the dress; or, better, I can remark on some point that I can really commend, such as the color, the material, etc., avoiding any statement that will be either untruthful or offensive.

3 *Rebutting the dilemma:* This method of attack is used when both the dilemma open to rebuttal and the rebutting dilemma contain the dilemmatic fallacy, which is both a formal and a material fallacy; sometimes a condition has two consequents, and each dilemma states only one (half-truth, optimistic or pessimistic), as in the Empson example above; sometimes each adopts a shifting point of view, as in the Protagoras example below.

The method of rebuttal is to accept the alternatives presented by the minor premise of the original dilemma but to transpose the consequents of the major premise and change them to their contraries. Hence a conclusion exactly opposite to the conclusion of the original dilemma is derived.

Formal rebuttal is a rhetorical device, a mere manipulation of the material in order to show up the weakness of an opponent's position. The very fact that a rebuttal to a given dilemma can be constructed shows that the dilemmatic fallacy of a shifting point of view is present in both dilemmas and that neither one is valid.

A famous ancient example is the argument between Protagoras and Euathlus, his law pupil. According to the contract between them, Euathlus was to pay half his tuition fee when he completed his studies and the other half when he had won his first case in court. Seeing that his pupil deliberately delayed beginning the practice of law, Protagoras sued him for the balance of the fee. Euathlus had to plead his own case.

ILLUSTRATION: Rebutting the dilemma

Protagoras' argument

If Euathlus loses this case, he must pay me by the judgment of the court; if he wins it, he must pay me in accordance with the terms of the contract.
But he must either win or lose it.
∴ He must pay me in any case.

Euathlus' rebuttal

If I win the case, I need not pay, by the judgment of the court; if I lose it, I need not pay, by the terms of the contract.
But I must either win it or lose it.
∴ I need not pay in any case.

A dilemma is open to rebuttal only when there is room for a real shift in the point of view, not merely a shift in the position of the terms. For example, a child might be faced with the following dilemma.

ILLUSTRATION: Dilemma not open to rebuttal

I must take either castor oil or bitter cascara.
If I take castor oil, I shall suffer an ugly taste; and if I take bitter cascara, I shall suffer an ugly taste.
∴ I shall suffer an ugly taste in either case.

This dilemma is not open to rebuttal. There is no room for a real shift from pessimism to optimism.

The following is not a rebuttal but only a meaningless shifting of the terms.

ILLUSTRATION: False rebuttal

If I take the bitter cascara, I shall escape the ugly taste of castor oil; and if I take the castor oil, I shall escape the ugly taste of bitter cascara.
But I must take either bitter cascara or castor oil.
∴ I shall escape an ugly taste in either case.

If this dilemma really constituted a rebuttal to the first one, any dilemma could be rebutted. But such is not the case. Even though a dilemma open to rebuttal and its rebuttal are both fallacious, neither of them is so patently empty an argument as this second dilemma about the medicine.

State the type and mood of each of the following arguments, expand any that are abridged, and determine the validity of each; if invalid, name the fallacy. Consider also whether the propositions are true. Re-state the mixed hypothetical syllogisms in their equivalent simple forms. Where imperfect disjunction is seen, *state* the missing alternative. Some of these exercises, because they are concrete, may be understood differently by different persons.

The patient will either die or get well. The patient did not die. Therefore he will get well.

The wind is blowing from either the west or the south. It is not blowing from the south. Therefore it is blowing from the west.

Being told that a certain person maintained that there is no distinction between virtue and vice, Samuel Johnson replied: If the fellow does not think as he speaks, he is lying; and I cannot see what honor he can propose to himself from having the character of a liar. But if he does really think that there is no distinction between virtue and vice, why, sir, when he leaves our houses let us count our spoons.
     —James Boswell, *The Life of Samuel Johnson L.L.D.*

Agamemnon . . . Iphigenia, my virgin daughter,
I to Diana, goddess of this land
Must sacrifice. This victim given, the winds
Shall swell our sails, and Troy beneath our arms
Be humbled in the dust; but if denied
These things are not to be.
     —Euripides, *Iphigenia at Aulis*

The prisoner is either guilty or not guilty. He is guilty (jury's verdict). Therefore he is not guilty.

An Athenian mother sought to dissuade her son from entering politics by means of the following argument: If you act justly, your fellow politicians will hate you; and if you act unjustly, the gods will hate you. But you must act either justly or unjustly. Therefore you will be hated in either case.

Henry V. If we are marked to die, we are enough
To do our country loss; and if to live,
The fewer men, the greater share of honor.
God's will! I pray thee wish not one man more.
                                        —*Henry* V 4.3.20–23

Three men had five hats, three white and two black. In a dark room each put on one of the hats and stepped into a lighted room, A first, B next, C last. C, who could see A's and B's hats, said, "I do not know what color my hat is." B, who could see A's hat and who had heard C speak, said, "I do not know what color my hat is." A, who merely heard C and B speak, said, "I do know what color my hat is." What color is A's hat? Express syllogistically the reasoning by which he knew.

You are given twelve balls that look exactly alike, but one is either lighter or heavier than the others. In three weighings with balance scales that show only comparative weight, find the odd ball. Express syllogistically the reasoning involved in satisfying all the possibilities.

Either the understanding of ourselves is a constant and lively and ever-renewed obligation of reasonable men or it is not. If it is our obligation, the humanist is something far different from a transmitter of the past, and the subject of his studies is something far subtler and more profound than societies; it is nothing less than a human being.
                        —G. K. Chalmers, *Poetry and General Education*

9   FALLACIES

The proper attitude in argument is expressed by Socrates:

> What sort of man am I? I am one of those who would be glad to be re-
> futed when saying a thing that is untrue, glad also to refute another if he
> said something inexact, not less glad to be refuted than to do it, since I
> deem it the greater blessing, in proportion as it is a greater good, to be re-
> leased from that which is the greatest evil than to release another from it.
> —Plato, *Gorgias*[1]

In so far as an argument is fallacious, it is not logical. But as logic is concerned with truth, it is incidentally concerned with the negation of
truth, namely errors—falsity and fallacies.

A fallacy is a violation of logical principle disguised under an appearance of validity; it is an error in process. Falsity is an error in fact.
Fallacy arises from an erroneous relation of propositions; falsity, from
an erroneous relation of terms. A premise may be false; reasoning may
be fallacious.

To discover a fallacy is to discover the reason why the mind was de-
ceived into regarding error as truth. To classify fallacies is to attempt to
find common ground for such deception. But a given argument may be
fallacious for more reasons than one, and hence it may exemplify more
than one fallacy. Consequently, a classification of fallacies is neither exhaustive nor mutually exclusive.

A fallacy is either formal or material or both simultaneously.

Formal fallacies arise from the violation of rules governing the formal relations of propositions and have been treated where these formal relations have been treated. The fallacies of opposition are
violations of the rules of opposition; the commonest one is to assume
of contraries that when one is false the other is true instead of unknown. The fallacies of eduction are two: illicit obversion and illicit
conversion. The fallacies of the syllogistic relation are: undistributed
middle term; illicit process of the major term or of the minor term;

four terms; four propositions; two negative premises; two partial premises; merely seeming mediated opposition; sublating the antecedent or positing the consequent in the minor premise of a mixed hypothetical syllogism; simultaneously positing and sublating both alternatives of a disjunction; imperfect disjunction; the dilemmatic fallacy.

Material fallacies have their root in the matter—in the terms, in the ideas, and in the symbols by which the ideas are communicated. They vitiate an argument that may be formally correct.

Aristotle grouped them in two classes: six fallacies *in dictione*, occasioned by a hidden assumption not conveyed in the language, and seven fallacies *extra dictionem*, characterized by a hidden false assumption not warranted by the language in which the ideas are expressed.

Fallacies were devices used in oral controversy in Athens by the Sophists, who sought not truth but victory over their opponents by these merely apparent refutations. These fallacies continue to be used, however, to deceive others and sometimes even to deceive the one using them.

FALLACIES *IN DICTIONE*

Fallacies *in dictione* arise from ambiguity of language, whether of words or of construction. They have their root in the grammar (the language) that seeks to symbolize the logic (the thought), and they may all be regarded as special instances of the fallacy of four terms. This fallacy is simultaneously a formal and a material fallacy because it both violates a rule of the form and lies in the matter. Six types of fallacies *in dictione* may be distinguished: equivocation, amphiboly, composition, division, accent, and verbal form.

Equivocation

Equivocation is a fallacy occasioned by the ambiguity of a word which symbolizes two or more different terms.

EXAMPLE: Equivocation

Feathers are light.
Light is the opposite of darkness.
∴ Feathers are the opposite of darkness.

Light in the minor premise means "not heavy"; in the major premise it means "not dark."

Amphiboly

Amphiboly is a fallacy produced by ambiguity of syntax or grammatical structure, such as a misplaced or a dangling modifier, ambiguous reference of pronouns, or ambiguity of word order. Such ambiguity is especially likely to occur in an uninflected language like English. It is always an error in grammar, but, strictly speaking, it occasions the fallacy of four terms in logic only when the ambiguous sentence becomes a premise in a syllogism.

EXAMPLES: Amphiboly

The duke yet lives that Henry shall depose.
                    —*2 Henry VI* 1.4.30

Translated into an inflected language, like Latin, this passage would lose its ambiguity. The argument would become syllogistic if the duke should interpret it by adding the minor premise, "I am this duke," and conclude, "Therefore I shall depose Henry." Or, if he should give the alternate meaning to the major premise and conclude, "Therefore Henry shall depose me."

He told his brother that he had won the prize. (Who won it?)

Feed a cold and starve a fever.

Here *feed* is subjunctive. The sentence is a warning; it means: If you feed a cold, you will have a fever to starve. As commonly interpreted, however, *feed* is taken to be imperative, and a meaning just the opposite of the one intended is derived.[2]

Clown. I was a gentleman born before my father, for the king's son took me by the hand and called me brother; and then the two kings called my father brother.

                    —*The Winter's Tale* 5.2.139–143

The clown has been using the words *gentleman born* to mean "born a gentleman." Literally, the clown is using the word *gentleman* to refer to the social status of the gentleman class, but the reference to his father leaves open the possibility that *gentleman* is a synonym for man, thus creating a paradox. This quote illustrates both amphiboly and equivocation.

Composition

The fallacy of composition occurs when the properties of the parts are illicitly predicated of the whole.

Sodium and chlorine are toxic elements.
Toxic elements are harmful.
∴ Sodium chloride is harmful.

Here are present simultaneously four fallacies, one material and three formal:

1 Composition. Sodium and chlorine are referred to as discrete entities in the premises and as combined in the conclusion.

2 The formal fallacy of four terms, for composition is a fallacy *in dictione*.

3 The formal fallacy of four propositions, for the major premise is a conjunction of two propositions: Sodium is a toxic element. Chlorine is a toxic element.

4 The formal fallacy of an illicit process of the major term.

Division

Division, just the reverse of composition, occurs when the properties of the whole are illicitly predicated of the parts.

EXAMPLE: Division

Nine and seven is sixteen.
Sixteen is an even number.
∴ Nine and seven are even numbers.

In addition to the material fallacy of division, there are present here also the formal fallacies of four terms and four propositions.

It is this fallacy of division that produces such erroneous conclusions as: A single straw broke the camel's back. A single justice of the Supreme Court determined the constitutionality of a law in a five-to-four decision.

Accent

The accent fallacy occurs when a meaning different from that intended is conveyed through a special emphasis on certain letters, syllables, words, or ideas. Emphasis of words can be produced orally by stress or indicated in written language by italics or another visible device. Such misleading emphasis may occur in syllables of the same word or in different words of the same sentence.

EXAMPLES: Accent

A master said to his servant: "Go heat this capon's leg," who immediately did eat it. Then his master, being angry, said, "I bade you heat it, with an *h*." "No, sir," said the servant, "I did heat it with bread."

This misunderstanding of a word, peculiar to a certain class of Englishmen, is given as an example of this fallacy by Thomas Blunderville in *The Art of Logic* (1599).

The servants incensed the king.

Here the alternative pronunciations, in'-censed and in-censed', convey strongly contrasted meanings and imply different conclusions if a premise is added.

He is my friend.

Here not only does the meaning change as the emphasis is made to fall successively on each of the words, but an ironical emphasis will convey a meaning which actually contradicts the statement spoken in an ordinary manner.

Note that this form of the fallacy of accent must not be confused with amphiboly. In this sentence there is no doubt about syntax, whereas there always is in amphiboly.

Quotations taken out of context are sometimes gross examples of the fallacy of accent. For example, the Bible says: There is no God. No one can be trusted.

It is a fact that these propositions are in the Bible, but in their context the meaning is altogether different: "The fool hath said in his heart: There is no God" (Ps. 4:1–2). "I said in my excess: No one can be trusted" (Ps.116:11).

To introduce italics into quoted material without stating that one has done so may be an instance of the fallacy of accent. Headlines, arrangement of copy, and the use of different-sized fonts to misrepresent are also examples of the fallacy of accent.

In extended discourse, by overemphasizing certain aspects of a subject and either slighting or completely neglecting other related aspects, one may, without actual misstatement, convey a very false idea of the subject in its entirety. This is called special pleading or propaganda and is a very frequent source of misrepresentation.

EXAMPLE: Special pleading or propaganda

Propaganda is the coloring of the news through overemphasis of some facts and underemphasis or omission of others, for instance at the time of a political campaign.

In a certain history textbook, after eulogizing the achievements of Roger Bacon, the author remarked that Bacon had been left to die in poverty. He created a very false impression by ignoring the fact that in becoming a Franciscan friar, Roger Bacon freely chose both to live and to die in poverty.

Verbal Form

Verbal form is a fallacy that results from erroneously supposing that similarity in the form of language signifies a corresponding similarity in meaning.

This fallacy occurs, for instance, when the identity of the prefix or suffix of words leads one to conclude erroneously that they are therefore analogous in meaning. For instance, *inspiration* and *inexplicable* are both negative terms, and if *in* means "not" in the one, it must mean "not" in the other.

EXAMPLES: Verbal form

The words *flammable* and *inflammable* both mean "easily ignited," and yet the suffix *in* with *flammable* misleads people into thinking that *inflammable* means *nonflammable* because frequently *in* means "not."

John Stuart Mill commits this fallacy when he argues:

The only proof capable of being given that an object is visible is that people actually see it. . . . The only proof that a sound is audible is that people hear it. . . . In like manner, the sole evidence it is possible to give that anything is desirable is that people do actually desire it.

Since the whole force of the argument lies in the assumption of a strict analogy between *visible*, *audible*, and *desirable*, the argument fails when it is understood that, according to the dictionary, *visible* and *audible* mean "capable of being seen" or "heard," or "actually seen" or "heard," whereas *desirable* means "worthy of desire" or "that which ought to be desired."

A fallacy in verbal form may also arise from the similarity of phrases, particularly verb phrases.

EXAMPLE: Fallacy in verb phrase

He who sleeps least is most sleepy.
He who is most sleepy sleeps most.
∴ He who sleeps least sleeps most.

Here the verb phrases *sleeps least* and *sleeps most* appear to be contraries; but if the tenses are more carefully discriminated, we have the following valid syllogism (true of normal, healthy persons):

He who has slept least is most sleepy.
He who is most sleepy will sleep most.
∴ He who has slept least will sleep most.

A fallacy in verbal form also includes an illicit transition from one category in the ten categories of being to another, as in the following, from substance to relation.

EXAMPLE: Fallacy in verbal form

A boy who has six marbles and loses one no longer has what he once had.
He who no longer has the six marbles he once had has not necessarily lost six marbles.
∴ He who no longer has what he once had has not necessarily lost it.

Objects collectively considered are related as members of a given group. If one is lost all that remain have lost the relation, a member of six, even though as independent substances, they have not been lost.

FALLACIES *EXTRA DICTIONEM*

Common to the seven fallacies *extra dictionem* is a hidden false assumption not warranted by the language in which the ideas are expressed. The fallacies *extra dictionem* are fallacy of accident, confusion of absolute and qualified statements, fallacy of consequent, arguing beside the point, false cause, begging the question, and complex question.

Fallacy of Accident

This fallacy arises from the false assumption that whatever is predicable of a subject (usually the middle term) is predicable of its accident (the minor term), and in the same sense; or that whatever is predicable of a term understood in one aspect (for example, specifically or concretely) is predicable of the same term understood in another aspect (for example, generically or abstractly) or vice versa.

Every predicate, except one in a definition or an identical proposition, is accidental to its subject in the sense that it is by accident that the given subject and the predicate are related in the given proposition. A lion is an animal. A square is an equilateral. It is an accident that an animal should be a lion rather than a mouse or a horse or that an equilateral figure should be a square rather than a triangle or an octagon. This situation exists whenever the extension of a predicate affirmed is greater than the extension of the subject, in other words, when the proposition is convertible only *per accidens*, that is, by limitation, hence the name.

Any one of the three terms of a syllogism may be the source of the fallacy of accident, but most often it is the middle term.

EXAMPLE: Fallacy of accident

To communicate knowledge is commendable.
To gossip is to communicate knowledge.
∴ To gossip is commendable.

Here knowledge is understood in the generic sense in the major premise and in a specific and even trivial sense hardly worthy of the general name in the minor premise. Therefore, while it is commendable to communicate knowledge understood in its essential, abstract, and general meaning, it is not commendable to communicate trivial or even mischievous information.

Aristotle remarks that the fallacy of accident results when we fail to distinguish the sameness and otherness of terms, or when we substitute an accident for an essential attribute.

According to Renaissance logicians, the fallacy of accident occurs when anything belonging to the substance of something is attributed also to some accident of that substance. Thomas Wilson[3] gives the following examples and explanations.

EXAMPLES: Attributing qualities of the substance to the accidents

Fish is not the same that flesh is.
Flesh is food.
∴ Fish is not food.

In the first proposition one understands the substance of flesh, and in the second proposition the speaker means the accident that is in both flesh and fish. Therefore, the argument is not lawful because the speaker referred both the substance and the accident to one and the same subject.

This man is a witty fellow.
This man is lame.
∴ This man has a lame wit.

This is evidently false because the accidents of the body are referred to the substance of the mind.

Aristotle gives an example similar to Wilson's second.

This dog is a father.
This dog is yours.
∴ This dog is your father.

The fallacy of accident may seem much like that of equivocation; but whereas the fallacy of equivocation involves a shifting of terms, the fallacy of accident involves a shifting of usage of the same term. To shift from one first imposition to another first imposition on the same word is to shift from one term to another, and this is the fallacy of equivocation. But to shift from a generic to a specific usage of the same term or from first imposition of a term to second or zero imposition, or from first to second intention is a shift in usage, and this is the fallacy of accident.

EXAMPLE: Word in two impositions

Feathers are light.
Light[4] is an adjective.
∴ Feathers are adjectives.

Here we have the fallacy of accident because the same term is understood as an adjective and as a noun. *Light* has the same meaning, although not the same usage, in both propositions. It is only *light* in the first proposition that is an adjective.

Every term can be used in either of the two intentions, and every word can be used in each of the three impositions. The intentions and impositions are reviewed in the box below.

Intention and Imposition

Second intention: logic

Second imposition: grammar

First imposition and first intention: reference to reality

Zero imposition: phonetics and spelling

9-1   *Possible Intentions and Impositions of a Word*

EXAMPLE: Accident and equivocation

Feathers are light.
Light is a noun.
∴ Feathers are nouns.

Here we have simultaneously two fallacies, accident and equivocation, for in the major premise, *light* is classified grammatically as "the opposite of darkness"; this is not the same term symbolized by *light*, meaning "not heavy" in the minor premise.

Every term can be used in either of the two intentions, and every word can be used in each of the three impositions. Particularly enlightening species of the fallacy of accident are those that involve a shift from one plane or plateau of discourse to another by a change of intention or of imposition. The ordinary plane of discourse is that of first imposition and first intention. There are three others: that of second intention, of second imposition, and of zero imposition. A valid argument can be maintained if each term is used consistently in any one of these planes of discourse, but if the same term is shifted from one plane to another, the argument is invalid.

SHIFT OF IMPOSITION

The shift of imposition fallacy involves the false assumption that what is true of a word understood in one imposition is true of the same word understood in other impositions. Consider the following syllogism: A banana is yellow. *Yellow* is an adjective. Therefore, *banana* is an adjective. Here *yellow* is understood in first imposition in the minor premise and in second imposition in the major.

The parts of speech and other grammatical concepts are terms of second imposition in the sense that when used as predicates, that is, as modes of conceiving their subjects, they cause their subjects to be understood in second imposition, that is, as grammatical entities. But the terms of grammar may themselves be understood in all of the impositions, as the following examples illustrate.

Fallacious syllogisms occur when the part of speech itself is shifted from one imposition to another in the premises.

EXAMPLES: Grammar terms used in two impositions

Carry is a verb.
Verb is a noun.
∴ *Carry* is a noun.

Verb shifts from first to second imposition in the premises.

Hippopotamus is a noun.
Noun is a monosyllable.
∴ *Hippopotamus* is a monosyllable.

Noun shifts from first to zero imposition in the premises.

Valid syllogisms occur when the term of grammar is understood in first, zero, or second imposition throughout, and the argument is not erroneously shifted from one plane of discourse to another.

EXAMPLES: Valid syllogisms with terms in second and zero imposition

Sing is a verb.
A verb has tense.
∴ *Sing* has tense.

Here *verb* is understood in the first imposition in both premises, and *sing* is understood in second imposition in the minor premise and in the conclusion.

Adjective is often mispronounced.
A word often mispronounced is often misspelled.
∴ *Adjective* is often misspelled.

Here *adjective* is understood in zero imposition both in the minor premise and in the conclusion.

The terms of phonetics and of spelling, or orthography, are terms of zero imposition in the sense that when used as predicates, that is, as modes of conceiving their subjects, they cause their subjects to be understood in zero imposition, that is, as mere sounds or notations. But that the terms of phonetics and of orthography may themselves be understood in all of the impositions is illustrated by the following examples.

EXAMPLES: Terms of phonetics and orthography used in all impositions

The following is a fallacious syllogism in which the terms of phonetics or orthography are themselves shifted in imposition in the premises.

Cat is a notation.
Notation has three syllables.
∴ *Cat* has three syllables.

Here *notation* is understood in first imposition in the minor premise and in zero imposition in the major.

The following are valid syllogisms in which the term of phonetics or orthography is understood in first or in second imposition throughout and in which, consequently, the argument is not shifted from one plane of discourse to another.

Indivisibility is a polysyllable.
A polysyllable may be divided between lines.
∴ *Indivisibility* may be divided between lines.

Invisibility is a notation.
A notation is visible.
∴ *Invisibility* is visible.

In these syllogisms, *polysyllable* and *notation* are understood in first imposition in both premises; *indivisibility* and *invisibility* are understood in zero imposition in the minor premise and in the conclusion.

Notation is a noun.
A noun may be the object of a preposition.
∴ *Notation* may be object of a preposition.

Here *notation* is understood in second imposition in both the minor premise and in the conclusion.

SHIFT OF INTENTION
Shift of intention involves the false assumption that what is true of a term understood in first intention is true of the same term understood in second intention, and vice versa.

EXAMPLES: Shift of intention

A lion is an animal.
Animal is a genus.
∴ A lion is a genus.

A square is equilateral.
Equilateral is a differentia.
∴ A square is a differentia.

In these syllogisms, *animal* and *equilateral* are understood in first intention in the minor premise and in second intention in the major.

The predicables are terms of second intention in the sense that when used as predicates, that is, as modes of conceiving their subjects, they cause their subjects to be understood in second intention, that is, as concepts, as mental entities. The predicables themselves may be understood in both the intentions.

In these fallacious syllogisms the predicable itself is shifted from first to second intention in the premises.

EXAMPLES: Shift of intention

Animal is a genus.
Genus is a predicable.
∴ Animal is a predicable.

Mirthful is a property.
Property is a predicable.
∴ Mirthful is a predicable.

In these syllogisms, *genus* and *property* are understood in first intention in the minor premise and in second intention in the major.

In valid syllogisms the predicable is understood in the same intention in both premises, and the argument is not shifted from one plane of discourse to another.

EXAMPLES: Valid syllogisms with terms in second intention

Animal is a genus.
A genus is divisible into species.
∴ Animal is divisible into species.

Mirthful is a property.
A property is a term convertible with its subject.
∴ Mirthful is a term convertible with its subject.

In these syllogisms, *genus* and *property* are understood in first intention (that is, predicatively) in both premises; *animal* and *mirthful* are understood in second intention (that is, reflexively) in both the minor premise and in the conclusion.

SHIFT OF IMPOSITION AND INTENTION

An argument may shift in both imposition and intention. This is best illustrated by a sorites: Man is rational. Rational is a differentia. Differentia is a polysyllable. Polysyllable is a noun. Therefore *man* is a noun.

Here the conclusion is true, and every premise, considered separately, is true; but each of the implicit conclusions is false, and the reasoning is utterly fallacious, for the argument shifts through four planes of discourse.[5]

Confusion of Absolute and Qualified Statement or *secundum quid*

This fallacy arises from the assumption that a proposition true in certain respects or with certain qualifications is true absolutely or true without those qualifications. The term *secundum quid* means "following this." In other words, what is true in one case is assumed to be true in another.

This fallacy, which is commonly used to deceive, can also cause self-deception. It results from the seeming smallness of the difference involved in the qualification. As a tool of deception it consists (1) in getting assent to a qualified statement and proceeding as if the statement had been conceded absolutely, or (2) vice versa, or (3) in proceeding from a statement qualified one way as though the same statement had been qualified another way.

The qualified statement may be true of a particular thing or person, or with respect to a particular place, time, manner, relation (as of part to whole), comparison, etc. What is true in one respect may not be true in another respect.

EXAMPLES: Confusion of absolute and qualified statement

God says: "Thou shalt not kill." Therefore killing animals for meat is wicked.

To suffer death unjustly is preferable to suffering death justly. Therefore what takes place unjustly is preferable to what takes place justly.

Whoso drinketh well sleepeth well; whoso sleepeth well sinneth not; whoso sinneth not shall be blessed. Therefore, whoso drinketh well shall be blessed.

—Thomas Blunderville, *The Art of Logic* (1599)

The second proposition is true with respect to the time while a man sleeps; he may sin when he is awake.

Pandarus. [Helen] praised [Troilus'] complexion above Paris'.
Cressida. Why, Paris hath color enough.
Pandarus. So he has.
Cressida. Then Troilus should have too much. If she praised him above, his complexion is higher than his. He having color enough, and the other higher, is too flaming a praise for good complexion. I had as lief Helen's golden tongue had commended Troilus for a copper nose.

—*Troilus and Cressida* 1.2.99–106

Cressida makes *above*, which was qualified with respect to beauty of color, qualify with respect to intensity of color.

Fallacy of Consequent

This fallacy arises from the false assumption that an A proposition is convertible simply, when it is not. The material fallacy of consequent is present whenever one of the following formal fallacies is present: an illicit process of the major or the minor term, an undistributed middle term, sublating the antecedent, positing the consequent. As we have noted, when a premise is an A proposition that is a definition, its predicate is distributed through the matter, and therefore a fallacy of nondistribution is avoided; likewise, when a premise is a *sine qua non* hypothetical proposition, no fallacy can result. Since, however, a premise is seldom a definition or a *sine qua non* hypothetical proposition, the material fallacy of consequent is one of the most frequent causes of error in reasoning. It is most likely to occur in an enthymeme in which the major premise is only implicit.

Since we can reduce a hypothetical proposition to a simple categorical proposition, we can apply to a simple proposition the terminology of the hypothetical and call the subject of a simple proposition the antecedent and its predicate the consequent. Therefore, in both the simple and the mixed hypothetical syllogism, we distinguish two types of the material fallacy of consequent, both resulting from the nonconvertibility of a premise: one falsely assumes that because a consequent follows upon its antecedent, the antecedent must likewise follow upon its consequent (positing the consequent); the other falsely assumes that from the contrary of the antecedent the contrary of the consequent must follow (sublating the antecedent).

ILLUSTRATIONS: Fallacy of consequent

A man is an animal.   **Fallacy**: Undistributed middle term
Bucephalus is an animal.
∴ Bucephalus is a man.

A man is an animal.   **Fallacy**: Illicit process of the major term
Bucephalus is not a man.
∴ Bucephalus is not an animal.

If it rains, the ground is wet.   **Fallacy**: Positing the consequent
The ground is wet.
∴ It rained.

If it rains, the ground is wet.   **Fallacy**: Sublating the antecedent
It did not rain.
∴ The ground is not wet.

In argument, the fallacy of consequent leads a disputant to think he has refuted his opponent when he has shown the unsoundness of the reasons advanced in favor of the point urged. This amounts to the fallacy of sublating the antecedent, for, as we noted, although the conclusion does follow from true premises, one cannot disprove a conclusion by showing that its premises are false; it may be supported by other, true premises.[6] Nor does a disputant necessarily gain assent to his premises by getting his opponent to concede the truth of his conclusion, for to suppose that the truth of the premises follows from the truth of the conclusion is the fallacy of positing the consequent in the minor premise.

Arguing Beside the Point or Ignoring the Issue or *ignoratio elenchi*

This fallacy arises from falsely assuming that the point at issue has been disproved when one merely resembling it has been disproved; the point really at issue is consequently ignored.

Ignoratio elenchi means ignorance of the nature of refutation. To refute an opponent, one must prove the contradictory of his statement; and this is done only when the same predicate—not merely the name but the reality—is denied of the same subject in the same respect, relation, manner, and time in which it was asserted. To establish some other conclusion is to dodge the issue and to argue beside the point.[7]

One might think he has refuted the proposition: "The President of the United States governs the whole country" when, by citing the results of an election, he has established the proposition: The President of the United States was not elected by the majority of Americans. He has not, however, denied the same predicate as was affirmed in the proposition he attempted to refute. Authority to govern comes from the vote of the electoral college, not a majority vote in the election.

One also ignores the issue and argues beside the point, when accused of dishonesty, one replies that many others are doing the same thing, falsely assuming that when the number of dishonest people is very large, ipso facto, each ceases to be dishonest.

An argument that deals with the point at issue is *argumentum ad rem* (literally an "argument to the thing"). Arguments that evade the issue are given special names to signify on which irrelevant grounds they are based: *argumentum ad hominem, argumentum ad populum, argumentum ad misericordiam, argumentum ad baculum, argumentum ad ignorantiam*, and *argumentum ad verecundiam*.

ARGUMENTUM AD HOMINEM

The *argumentum ad hominem* (literally, an "argument to the man") fallacy confuses the point at issue with the people concerned. Attacks on the character and conduct of people and personal abuse or praise are substituted for reasoning on the point at issue.[8] *Argumentum ad hominem* seeks to persuade by unsound *ethos*. In rhetoric ethos means establishing the speaker or writer as one worthy of making an argument.

To argue that, because a certain lawyer has defrauded his relatives by getting a larger share of the inheritance than was really intended by the testator, that lawyer's arguments alleging that a certain bank official is an embezzler are worthless.

It is, however, legitimate to argue that, because a witness is known to have lied in court, his present testimony ought not to be readily accepted.

ARGUMENTUM AD POPULUM

The *argumentum ad populum* fallacy arises from substituting an appeal to the passions and prejudices of the people for logical reasoning on the point at issue, for example, the appeal to race hatred by persecutors of the Jews.

ARGUMENTUM AD MISERICORDIAM

The *argumentum ad misericordiam* (literally, an "argument to pity") fallacy replaces reason with a plea for sympathy. It is used by many criminal lawyers to divert the jurors' minds from the real question—guilty or not guilty—by moving them to pity and to a favorable verdict because the defendant is, for instance, a beautiful woman or a single parent. A scofflaw might argue that he should not receive a parking ticket because he was donating blood while the car was parked illegally. A classic example of *argumentum ad misericordiam* is that the defendant who murdered his mother and father should receive sympathy because he is an orphan.

ARGUMENTUM AD BACULUM

Argumentum ad baculum is the appeal to the "big stick." The issue is ignored in an attempt to inspire fear of the consequences of adopting a proposed opinion or program, or of allowing a movement branded as dangerous to gain strength. The threat of social ostracism or loss of a position might be used to deter a person from exposing fraud in the work place. A bully might persuade by threatening violence.

ARGUMENTUM AD IGNORANTIAM

Argumentum ad ignorantiam is the use of an argument that sounds convincing to others because they are ignorant of the weakness of the argument and of the facts that stand against it.[9]

A theory, such as evolution, is declared worthless because it has not been proved.

No one has ever proved that aliens exist; therefore aliens do not exist.

No one has ever proved that aliens do not exist; therefore aliens exist.

Argumentum ad populum, ad misericordiam, ad baculum and *ad ignorantiam* also demonstrate an unsound use of *pathos*. *Pathos* is a term used in rhetoric to mean that a speaker or a writer tries to establish empathy with the audience. *Pathos* is fully explained in Chapter Eleven.

ARGUMENTUM AD VERECUNDIAM

Argumentum ad verecundiam is an appeal to the prestige or respect in which a proponent of an argument is held as a guarantee of the truth of the argument. This is unwarranted when reasoning about an issue is required and only the authority of its upholders or opponents is given consideration. It is perfectly legitimate to supplement reasoning with authority (*argumentum ad auctoritatem*), but it is fallacious to substitute authority for reasoning in matters capable of being understood by reason. This fallacy is particularly pernicious when the authority cited is not an authority on the matter under discussion. For example, celebrity endorsement of consumer products or political causes constitutes *argumentum ad verecundiam*.

False Cause

The fallacy of false cause is present also when something accidental to a thing is held to determine its nature, character, or value, for that which is not a cause is then held to be a cause.

EXAMPLE: False cause

Football games are evil because some people gamble away too much money on the results.

A thing is not evil merely because some people abuse it. In such instances, the cause of the evil is not in the thing itself, but in those who make it an occasion for gratifying their own evil propensities.

Note that *Post hoc ergo propter hoc* is an inductive fallacy that is sometimes loosely identified with the deductive fallacy of false cause.

False cause makes a false assumption about a reason, which is a cause of knowing; *post hoc ergo propter hoc* makes a false assumption about a cause of being. The inductive fallacy *post hoc ergo propter hoc* results from the false assumption that whatever happens before a given event is the cause of that event. The error is increased by imperfect observation; often events that occur without the alleged antecedent cause pass unnoticed. A black cat crosses a person's path. The next day the stock market falls in value. The person concludes that the black cat caused the bad luck but has failed to notice how often a black cat has crossed his path and no bad luck has followed. But even if bad luck always followed, the black cat would not therefore be a cause of the misfortune, for it could not be.

Begging the Question

Begging the question is the fallacy of assuming in the premises the very proposition to be proved, namely, the conclusion—or a proposition wide enough to include the one to be proved. The conclusion assumed in the premises is usually hidden under synonyms, so that the identities of the propositions are less obvious.

EXAMPLES: Begging the question

The tautological (repetition of the same sense in different words) argument:

William Shakespeare is famous because his plays are known all over the world.

The shuttle argument:

"That boy is insane." "Why do you think so?" "Because he murdered his mother." "Why did he murder her?" "Because he is insane."

It may be a fact that the boy is insane and that may be the reason why he murdered his mother, but to reason without begging the question, other evidence of his insanity must be offered.

Arguing in a circle:

This differs from the shuttle argument only by the addition of one or more propositions, which causes the argument to go around in a circle instead of merely shuttling back and forth: "This movie is the best of the decade." "How can you prove that?" "The *New York Times* says so." "So what if the *New York Times* says so?" "The *New York Times* is the most respected paper in the entertainment industry." "How do you know that?" "Because they always pick the best movies of the decade."

Question-begging epithet:

The question-begging epithet is probably the most common instance of this fallacy. It is a phrase or a single word that assumes the point to be proved. Calling a tax bill "welfare for the rich" or labeling a proposal favorable to "Big Government" or "Big Business" are examples of the question-begging epithet.

Complex Question

The complex question fallacy is somewhat similar to that of begging the question. Begging the question assumes in the premises the proposition to be proved, and the complex question assumes in the question a part of what belongs wholly to the answer.

The fallacy of complex question occurs when, in answer to a compound question, one demands a simple answer, whereas the correct answer would divide the question and answer it part by part. Cross-examiners often employ this device to trap a witness into contradicting himself, thereby weakening the value of his testimony in favor of the opposite side. Examples of this fallacy include: Why did you steal my watch? When did you stop flirting? Where did you hide the body of the woman you murdered? How much time have you wasted studying impractical subjects like philosophy and music?

EXERCISES

Analyze the following arguments, expanding, if necessary, those that are abridged. Name the type. If the argument is fallacious, it is necessary to explain clearly wherein the fallacy lies and to name it. If there are two or more fallacies present, name each one.

The heart is an organ. An organ is a musical instrument. Therefore the heart is a musical instrument.

Speaking of the silent is impossible. John is silent. Therefore speaking of John is impossible.

Desdemona. Do you know, sirrah, where Lieutenant Cassio lies?
Clown. I dare not say he lies anywhere.
Desdemona. Why, man?
Clown. He's a soldier; and for one to say a soldier lies is stabbing.
—*Othello* 3.4.1–6

Cesario. Save thee, friend, and thy music! Dost thou live by the tabor?
Feste. No, sir, I live by the church.
Cesario. Art thou a churchman?
Feste. No such matter, sir. I do live by the church; for I do live at my house, and my house doth stand by the church.
—*Twelfth Night* 3.1.1–7

The moving train stopped. The train that stopped is standing still. Therefore the moving train is standing still.

Louise is not what Mary is. Louise is a woman. Therefore Mary is not a woman.

A mouse is small. Small is an accident. Therefore a mouse is an accident.

If the number is not even, it is odd. It is even. Therefore it is not odd.

The receiver of stolen goods should be punished. You have received stolen goods and should therefore be punished.

Not to be abed after midnight is to be up betimes; . . . To be up after midnight, and to go to bed then, is early; so that to go to bed after midnight is to go to bed betimes.

—*Twelfth Night* 2.3.1–9

To increase production in a state, men of different natures should perform different work. Now there is an opposition in nature between bald men and hairy men. Therefore if bald men are cobblers, hairy men should not be cobblers.

—Plato, *The Republic*

All the angles of a triangle are equal to two right angles; the angle x is an angle of this triangle; therefore it is equal to two right angles.

Acquiring property is good. This thief is acquiring property. Therefore this thief is doing good.

Democracy has failed in the United States because there are corrupt cities and states.

If a human being remains under water thirty minutes, he will die. This diver remained under water thirty minutes. Therefore he will die.

Cake is sweet. Sweet is an adjective. Therefore cake is an adjective.

Detective stories are excellent literature because they are preferred by learned professors of mathematics.

These strikers are lazy, for they are determined not to work.

This woman cannot be a criminal, for she has never been in prison.

The sun must move around the earth, for the Bible says that at Josue's prayer the sun stood still.

We charge King Charles II with having broken his coronation oath and we are told he kept his marriage vow.

—Thomas Babbington Macaulay, *History of England*

Prohibition did not succeed because it did not have the support of public opinion, and the people did not support it because it was a failure.

Man is an animal. Animal is a genus. A genus is divisible into species. Therefore man is divisible into species.

I do not wish to have a doctor, for I notice that all who died in this town this winter had a doctor.

When did you decide to stop posing?

Nellie is a good seamstress. Therefore she is a good woman.

The obstacle is a rock. Rock is a verb. Therefore the obstacle is a verb.

To increase wages is to raise prices. To raise prices is to increase the cost of living. To increase the cost of living is to decrease real income. Therefore to increase wages is to decrease real income.

This statue is a work of art. This statue is mine. Therefore it is my work of art.

She who swears that she will break her oath, and then breaks it, is a keeper of her oath.

No reason can be given why the general happiness is desirable except that each person, so far as he believes it to be attainable, desires his own happiness. This being a fact, we have not only all the proof that the case admits of, but all which it is possible to require, that happiness is a good, that each person's happiness is a good to that person, and the general happiness, therefore, a good to the aggregate of all persons.
—John Stuart Mill, *Utilitarianism*

Plato in his *Phaedo* proves the immortality of the soul from its simplicity. In the *Republic* he proves the soul's simplicity from its immortality.

10 A BRIEF SUMMARY OF INDUCTION

Logic is the normative science which directs the operations of the intellect so as to attain truth. Just as metaphysics, or ontology, deals with *all things as they are* in their most abstract, their most general, and, therefore, their one common aspect—being—so logic deals with *all that is thought* in its most general aspect—truth.

The requirements of truth are:

1 What is thought must represent what is. (This is the norm of conception and of induction.)

2 Thoughts must be consistent among themselves. (This is the norm of deduction.)

The first requirement is concerned with the material of reasoning; the second, with the reasoning itself. Both are necessary.

Deductive or formal logic is the only logic in the sense that it alone discovers the rules by which we think and reason correctly. But the material of thinking, the terms and propositions, must come ultimately from our experience by means of conception and induction. These processes therefore are preliminary to reasoning.

ANALOGY: Connection between deduction and induction

Raw cotton is necessary to the manufacture of muslin, organdy, and lace. But it is the machines that produce the difference between these kinds of cotton goods. It is with the machine and its operation that manufacturing is specifically concerned. The production and acquisition of raw material are not, strictly speaking, problems of manufacturing; they are preliminary, and prerequisite, to it.

ACQUISITION OF KNOWLEDGE

Knowledge—that is, whatever information the mind possesses—is derived from either the operation of one's own powers or from faith.

Human Powers

One acquires knowledge through one's own powers. The sense powers acquire an immediate perception of external objects, and the intellectual powers act on data provided by the senses.

SENSE POWERS

The sense powers comprise the external senses—sight, hearing, touch, taste, smell—as well as the internal senses. The internal senses include the imagination, which produces and retains phantasms; memory, which recalls and recognizes them as previously experienced; the common or central sense, which discriminates, coordinates, and synthesizes the sensations; and instinct, by which a sentient being estimates an object as conducive or not conducive to its physical well being.

The senses can operate intuitively or indirectly. Intuitive refers to the direct or immediate perception of the proper sensibles—color, sound, etc. Indirect refers to the indirect perception of the common sensibles, which may be perceived by more than one sense. For example, motion, rest, figure, and size may be perceived through both sight and touch; number, distance, direction, duration, and rhythm, through sight, touch, and hearing.

Note that the constructive or fictive imagination can operate by combining phantasms, for example: mermaid, satyr, centaur, griffin.

INTELLECTUAL POWERS

Intellectual powers comprise the intellect, which seeks truth; the rational memory; and the will, which seeks good. The intellect can operate intuitively (abstraction: conception, induction).

EXAMPLES: Intellectual intuition

Metaphysical: Every effect must have an adequate cause.

Logical: Contradictory propositions cannot both be true.

Mathematical: Things equal to the same thing are equal to each other.

Moral: Good ought to be done and evil avoided.

Psychological: My consciousness testifies that my will is free.

The intellect can also act inferentially, which includes both immediate and mediate or syllogistic inference.

Faith

Faith includes all that one knows from the testimony of another. This other may be human—parents, teachers, companions, books, magazines, newspapers, radio, etc.—or divine—God communicating a revelation directly or by miracles authenticating the message of His agent (angel, prophet, apostle, etc.).

The topics of invention (see Chapter Six) draw material for reasoning either from the exercise of one's own powers (the first sixteen topics) or from faith (the testimony of others).

Psychology, the philosophy of mind,[1] explains the process by which concepts and judgments are obtained from the real world. Induction, like conception, is abstractive, intuitive; but whereas conception is the abstraction of the essence, and its product is a concept expressed in a term, induction is the drawing forth and perception of a relation, and its product is a judgment expressed in a proposition. Neither process is one of merely counting or adding instances; neither is a generalization from particulars, or an inference of any sort; both are intuitions of truth drawn from reality.

The basis of conception and of intuitive induction is the same: only individuals exist, but they exist as we see them in nature, according to type. The essence is that which makes an individual a member of his species, or type; consequently, the concept, which is the intellectual apprehension of the essence present in the individual, is equally applicable to every member of the species. Similarly, a necessary general proposition which expresses the intellectual apprehension of a fundamental relation, such as cause and effect, present in the individual as a member of his species must be present in every other member of the same species.

INDUCTION: A FORM OF INTUITION

Induction is not a form of inference; it is a form of intuition. Every general proposition serving as a premise in a syllogistic inference is either the conclusion of a syllogism or of a series of syllogisms made up solely of general propositions or an induction or intuition drawn from nature. For there is no correct formula of inference[2] by which a general proposition can be derived as a conclusion from empirical premises, which alone express our knowledge of particular facts. (*Rule 10* of the general rules of the syllogism states: "If one or both premises are empirical, the conclusion must be empirical.")

Therefore, every general proposition is derived either directly or ultimately from induction.[3] Induction is a mental act but not an inference. It is preliminary and prerequisite to inference; it is an intuition of truth, either general or empirical.

Types of Induction

There are three distinct kinds of induction, none of which is inferential.

ENUMERATIVE INDUCTION

Enumerative induction[4] is the assertion of a numerically definite plural empirical proposition as a result of observing facts and counting instances, for example: fifty-three people were killed in automobile accidents in that city last year. This is the least important kind of induction, hardly worthy to be called such. Its chief value lies in contributing ascertained facts to be used in deduction or in other kinds of induction.

A statistical deduction is a conclusion in a syllogism whose minor premise is an enumerative induction and whose major premise is a statistical or mathematical law, usually expressed in a formula. The conclusion is the statement of a numerically definite probability. For example, an insurance company bases its rates on the scientifically calculated probable number of deaths in a particular group—designated by age, occupation, locality—in a year. Vital statistics provide the minor premise for this statistical deduction, and a mathematical formula for the calculation of probability is the major. The conclusion is a statement of numerically definite probability, sufficiently accurate to be the basis of a sound business enterprise.

INTUITIVE INDUCTION

Intuitive induction is the psychological act of asserting a self-evident proposition as true. This is by far the most important kind.

If the self-evident proposition is empirical, it is a datum of sense-knowledge and is relative to the sentient individual making the intuitive induction. An example is: The grass is green. A blind person could not make this induction.

If the self-evident proposition is general, it is a principle of intellectual knowledge and is relative to human reason and to the knowledge of the terms possessed by the individual making the intuitive induction. For example: The whole is greater than any of its parts.

DIALECTICAL OR PROBLEMATIC INDUCTION

Dialectical or problematic induction is the psychological act of asserting a proposition, whether general or empirical, as a possibility, without any calculation of its probability. It is an intuition of the compatibility of the terms.

EXAMPLES: Dialectical induction

A regular polygon may have a million sides.

This child may become the President of the United States.

Nature and Purpose of Induction

Induction is the legitimate derivation of general propositions from individual instances. What is invariably observed in them must be essential to their nature. Induction is a method for the discovery of truth, not a process of proof or reasoning about truth.

The physical order is, however, too complex to permit the mental act of intuitive induction without much preliminary work. Scientific methodology, the methods of science, are concerned with this preliminary work. They are systematic procedures for the investigation of natural phenomena. Their aim is to separate what is essential or typical from what is accidental or fortuitous and to present to the mind precise, relevant, simple data. The mind then abstracts the inductive judgment by an intuitive act as simple and spontaneous as that by which it abstracts the concept directly from sense data.

Scientific methodology is not a mental act at all but a safeguard to precision in the investigation of nature. It is preliminary to induction from complex phenomena, just as induction itself is preliminary to deduction. Induction and deduction are distinct, but in practice they go hand in hand.

Each of the special sciences aims to abstract from the complex natural phenomenon laws governing that aspect of nature with which it is concerned. For example, mathematics is concerned only with quantity; physics, with motion; anatomy, with the structure of living organisms; economics, with human activities in making a living.

ANALOGY: Special sciences

Petroleum is a complex natural substance from which are abstracted by fractional distillation diverse substances. Among them are gasoline, benzine, naptha, kerosene, vaseline, paraffin, artificial asphalt, and mothballs. The distinctive characteristic of each of these products is due to (1) the abstraction of part from the whole (compare the special sciences, each of which deals only with a selected phase of nature) by means of fractional distillation (compare induction) and in some instances by means of (2) a process of manufacture (compare deduction) which transforms the natural product by means of machinery (compare the mind). Thus the final products owe their being to nature's gifts modified by human ingenuity.

The aim of every science is the knowledge of facts through their causes. This is true of both deductive and inductive sciences. In deduction we know the fact, the conclusion, through its causes, the premises. In induction we apprehend the cause common to a number of observed facts; that cause is a principle, a middle term, by which their relation can be understood.

We shall consider first the nature of causality, then the uniformity of causation, and lastly the ways in which the scientific method aids in discovering causes.

Causality

Since induction is concerned mainly with the investigation of causes, it is important to understand the distinction between a cause, a condition, and a special type of condition called a determining agent, as well as the four metaphysical causes.

CAUSE

A cause is that which has a positive influence in making a thing be what it is. To the sum of its causes, it owes every one of its characteristics. A cause is not a mere antecedent in a time sequence. For instance, day and night follow each other, but they do not cause each other. The assumption that the antecedent in a time sequence is a cause is the inductive fallacy *post hoc ergo propter hoc,* which is explained in Chapter Nine.

CONDITION

A condition is that which in any way enables a cause to act in producing the effect, but to which the effect owes none of its characteristics. For instance, light is a condition requisite to the carving of a statue; food, to the health and competence of the sculptor; scaffolding, to the decoration of the ceiling of a church.

DETERMINING AGENT

The determining agent is a condition which sets in motion the causative factors. It differs from other conditions in being the origin or occasion of the effect. Examples include the mosquito which transmits the yellow fever germ and the flea which transmits the bubonic plague.

Science often seeks the determining agent rather than one of the four metaphysical causes.[5]

FOUR METAPHYSICAL CAUSES

The metaphysical causes, according to Aristotle, explain every material effect. They are the efficient, the final, the material, and the formal cause. The efficient cause and the final cause are extrinsic to the effect, the causes of a thing becoming what it is. The following explanation of the four metaphysical causes uses the example of a statue.

1   The *efficient cause* is the agent and the instruments, for example: the sculptor, and the hammer and chisel.

2   The *final cause* is the end or purpose that moved the agent, for example: desire to honor a national hero, the particular design the artist conceived, love of art, fame, money, etc. The final cause is first in intention, last in execution.

3   The *material cause* is that out of which it is made, for example: marble, bronze, wood.

4   The *formal cause* is the kind of thing into which it is made, for example: Lincoln, Napoleon, Bucephalus, Joan of Arc.

The material cause and the formal cause are intrinsic to the effect, the causes of a thing being what it is. To know an object through its formal cause is to know its essence. Thus the formal cause of man is his soul animating his body, his rational animality. The material cause is that particular matter which constitutes his physical being; it continually varies through metabolism but is supported and unified by the formal cause, the soul in the body. Thus, despite metabolism, the man remains the same man throughout his life, through the persistence of the formal cause.

Uniformity of Causation

Uniformity of causation is a postulate of all natural sciences, a physically, not a metaphysically, necessary assumption of the scientist who studies the material universe. It is not capable of proof but only of illustration. The postulate may be stated thus: The same natural cause, under similar conditions, produces the same effect.

This generalization needs to be limited in two important ways. It is not applicable to a being with free will in those activities subject to control by free will. Thus a human being is free to lift the right arm or not to lift it, to choose to think upon one subject rather than upon another. But a person has no such free control over the circulation of the blood, digestion, falling from a height when support is removed, etc. Also, the uniformity of causation requires the normal concurrence of the First Cause. Thus miracles represent a deviation from the uniformity of nature, attributable to the free will of the First Cause.

Note that the postulate of the uniformity of causation should not be confused with the philosophical principle of causality, namely: Whatever comes into being must have an adequate cause. The latter is a philosophical axiom, knowable by intuitive induction. Philosophical axioms are metaphysically necessary truths. The postulates of science are not and, accordingly, have not so high a degree of certainty.

Scientific Induction

Scientific induction as a method of discovering truth embraces five steps: observation, analogy, hypothesis, analysis and sifting of data, and verification of the hypothesis.

OBSERVATION

Observation involves asking questions of nature in order to get facts, the data of induction. Because of the complexity of nature, observation must be selective, analytic. Care should be taken to obtain facts free from inference. Ordinary observation is supplemented by (1) scientific instruments, for example: the telescope, microscope, microphone, camera, barometer, thermometer, delicate balances and (2) statistics, or enumeration, for example: a statistical study of the recurrence of depressions, of the causes of death, of the number of marriages and divorces, of the diffusion of hereditary traits among offspring.

Simple observation, aided by the use of scientific instruments and of statistics, is almost the only means available to such natural sciences as systematic zoology and astronomy and to some of the social sciences.

Experiment is observation under conditions subject to control. Its advantage lies in the opportunity it offers to simplify, to analyze, to repeat at will, to ask questions of nature, one at a time, by varying conditions one at a time. A science which can employ experiment advances much more rapidly than one which cannot. The rapid progress of physics, chemistry, bacteriology, and nutrition is due in large measure to experiment.

ANALOGY

Analogy or likeness observed in different classes of phenomena suggests to the alert scientific mind the probability of a causal relation. Analogy is a fertile source of hypotheses. The periodic table of the chemical elements had its inception in analogy; and it presents analogies which have occasioned other scientific discoveries.

HYPOTHESIS

Hypothesis is a scientific guess at general laws to explain phenomena which appear to be causally related. Hypotheses guide observation and experiment. Subsequent investigation either verifies or disproves them.

ANALYSIS AND SIFTING OF DATA (SCIENTIFIC METHODOLOGY)

Roger Bacon (1214?–1294) stressed the importance of experimental science and its place in Christian studies. Francis Bacon (1561–1626) developed a theory of induction. John Stuart Mill (1806–1873) formulated five canons or general methods of science and popularized them.

The Method of Agreement

If two or more instances of the phenomenon under investigation have only one circumstance in common, the circumstance in which alone all the instances agree is the cause or the effect of the given phenomenon.

Note that in Mill's formulas the capital letters stand for antecedents, the small letters for consequents. Each group stands for an instance. The formula is ABC—abc; ADE—ade. Hence A is causally related to a.

EXAMPLE: Method of agreement

William Stanley Jevons describes how the cause of the iridescence of mother-of-pearl was discovered:

A person might suppose that the peculiar colours of mother-of-pearl were due to the chemical qualities of the substance. Much trouble might have been spent in following out that notion by comparing the chemical qualities of various iridescent substances. But Sir David Brewster accidentally took an impression from a piece of mother-of-pearl in a cement of resin and beeswax, and finding the colours repeated upon the surface of the wax, he proceeded to take other impressions in balsam, fusible metal, lead, gum arabic, isinglass, etc., and always found the iridescent colours the same. He thus proved that the chemical nature of the substance is a matter of indifference, and that the form of the surface is the real condition of such colours.[6]

The Method of Difference

If an instance in which the phenomenon under investigation occurs and an instance in which it does not occur have every circumstance in common save one, that one occurring only in the former, the circumstance in which alone the two instances differ is the effect or the cause or an indispensable part of the cause of the phenomenon. The formula is ABC—abc; BC—bc. Hence A is causally related to a.

EXAMPLES: Method of difference

Sore eyes and retarded growth are observed in rats with no vitamin A in their diet.

A bell struck in a vacuum makes no sound; if air is admitted, it does; hence the vibration of air is seen to be causally related to the production of sound.

The Joint Method of Agreement and Difference

If two or more instances in which the phenomenon occurs have only one circumstance in common, while two or more instances in which it does not occur have nothing in common except the absence of that circumstance, the circumstance in which alone the two sets of instances differ is the effect or the cause or an indispensable part of the cause of the phenomenon. The formula is ABC—abc, ADE—ade, BDM—bdm, CEO—ceo. Hence A is causally related to a.

EXAMPLES: Method of agreement and difference

The use of diphtheria antitoxin to create immunity from diphtheria

The presence of the hydrogen ion in all acids

The Method of Residues

Subduct from any phenomenon such part as is known by previous inductions to be the effect of certain antecedents, and the residue of the phenomenon is the effect of the remaining antecedent. The formula is

ABC—abc. But it is known that A causes a, and B causes b; then C must cause c.

The exact determination of the weight of a pint of milk in a quart bottle requires that the weight of the bottle and of a pint of air be subtracted from the whole

Discovery of argon in the air

Discovery of the planet Neptune

The Method of Concomitant Variations

Whatever phenomenon varies in any manner whenever another phenomenon varies in some particular manner is either a cause or an effect of that phenomenon or is connected with it through some fact of causation. The formula is $A^1BC—a^1bc$, $A^2BC—a^2bc$, $A^3BC—a^3bc$. Hence A is causally related to a.

Effect of changes of temperature on a column of mercury—hence the thermometer

Tides and the moon

Law of supply and demand, affecting price

VERIFICATION OF THE HYPOTHESIS

Francis Bacon not only anticipated the substance of Mill's canons but also indicated the succeeding steps in the discovery of scientific law. The form of which he speaks is the formal cause of the effect in question.

> Every form which is present when the property in question is absent, or absent when the latter is present, or which does not increase or decrease concomitantly with the latter, is to be rejected as not being the form causally connected with the latter. . . . Where you cannot (as in mathematics) see that a proposition must be universally true, but have to rely for the proof of it on the facts of your experience, there is no other way of establishing it than by showing that facts disprove its rivals.

Hence the steps in verification: In the same way that in forming a concept, abstraction withdraws the attention of the intellect from what is not essential so that it may intuit what is essential, so elimination withdraws its attention from what is not causally related so that it may intuit what is causally related.

Elimination

Elimination is accomplished by means of deductive reasoning from a disjunctive proposition. The minor premises of the eliminative syllogisms are empirical propositions stating the result of observation of the facts under investigation. The major premises are the canons of the general scientific methods.

The cause of X is either A or B or C or D.

1 But A is present when X is absent.
The cause of X cannot be present when X is absent.
Therefore A is not the cause of X.

2 B is absent when X is present.
The cause of X cannot be absent when X is present.
Therefore B is not the cause of X.

3 C does not vary concomitantly with X.
The cause of X does vary concomitantly with X.
Therefore C is not the cause of X.

The cause of X is neither A nor B nor C. Therefore, the cause of X is probably D.

Note that the alternatives of the disjunctive syllogism should not be a mere enumerative catalogue of possibilities. The alternatives should be selected by scientific insight into the probable antecedents, not by a random gathering of irrelevant facts.[7] Note also that mere elimination provides no certitude.[8] The conclusion of the disjunctive syllogism merely represents the degree of simplification that scientific method can achieve. After the rival alternatives have been disproved, the data, the facts of nature, thus divested of some of their complexity, stand naked, as it were, before the mind's eye.

Intuitive Induction

If the mind sees positive reasons for asserting that the cause of X is D, there is certitude. If not, the analysis of the data was probably incomplete, and the alternatives were not exhaustive; an unknown antecedent, not listed, may be the cause of X.

Application and Demonstration by Deduction

The certitude resulting from the intuitive induction of a general law must be demonstrated by syllogistic inference using either a regressive or demonstrative syllogism.

A **regressive syllogism** is the link between induction and deduction. It is a theoretical verification of the hypothesis by deduction. Seeking the cause of natural phenomena, a law that governs them, is seeking a middle term, which is the formal cause of the relation of the terms in the conclusion of a syllogism. In contrast to the definite process by which the premises lead to the conclusion, seeking the middle term is an indefinite, inverse process, for S and P may be related by many M's. The conclusion may be supported by many reasons.

ANALOGY: Seeking the middle term

In mathematics, we proceed definitely from multiplier and multiplicand to the product, but the inverse process is indefinite as is shown in the following example.

Given: 6 × 6. What is the product? Definite answer: 36.

Given: 36. What are the factors? 3 × 12; 4 × 9; −2 × −18; −3 × −12; −4 × −9.

Induction is a similar indefinite, inverse process until it is verified by deduction and application.

In our observation of nature, we intuit the empirical proposition S is P. But S is P because it is M. The whole problem of the discovery of laws of nature is the problem of discovering M. The effect P proves the presence of the cause M. Here M must not be only the antecedent of P but the only antecedent, a property or a definition. Hence M is P must be convertible simply to P is M. In other words, science seeks the verification of a hypothesis which can be expressed in a hypothetical proposition that is reciprocal: If S is M, it is P; and if S is P, it is M. When this reciprocal relationship is found, it may be stated in a regressive syllogism in the first figure: S is P. P is M. Therefore S is M. The theoretical verification of the hypothesis, stated fully, then is: If S is M, it is P. But S is M. Therefore S is P.

A **demonstrative syllogism** is a practical verification of the hypothesis by deduction.

As a final step in its verification, the hypothesis must be applied over and over again to the facts of nature and thereby have its truth demonstrated. The hypothesis becomes the major premise in a syllogism whose minor premise is an empirical proposition derived by intuition from the observation of nature. The conclusion which follows from a correct syllogistic formula employing these premises is, then, an empirical proposition which is an inference from the hypothesis being tested. If this process is repeated again and again, with different, typical, and widely selected data as the minor premises of the testing syllogisms, and if, in every case, the empirical conclusion inferred conforms to the observed facts of nature, then the hypothesis is verified, and it is demonstrated to be a law of nature. Herein, then, by combining deduction with induction, one verifies before the tribunal of human reason the general law with which induction furnished us.

Deduction leads to consistency in the conceptual order, and induction leads to the assurance that this conceptual order truly represents the real order.

PHILOSOPHY IN THE FIELD OF KNOWLEDGE

What is the place of philosophy in the field of knowledge? Our rationality urges us to analyze, relate, organize, synthesize, and so to simplify our knowledge. Philosophy represents the greatest unity and simplicity to which unaided human reason can attain.

Progress Toward Unity

4 Experience (fact: for example, A stone falls. A chair falls.)

3 Science (law: for example, the law of gravity)

2 Philosophy (principles: for example, Every effect must have an adequate cause.)

1 Beatific vision (Unity of Perfect Truth; the all in the One. Theology and faith prepare us for the beatific vision after death.)

10-1   *Synthesis of Knowledge*

These four steps in the synthesis of knowledge are the special provinces of history, science, philosophy, and theology. History's primary function is to chronicle the facts of experience. Science's primary function is to organize facts under their proximate causes or laws. Philosophy's primary function is to discover ultimate causes. It accepts the findings of the special sciences as its data and treats of the ultimate principles and characteristics which constitute the order of the universe as a whole.

Speculative philosophy is concerned with knowledge of the real order for the sake of knowledge. According to the three classes of objects to be understood, the mind employs three kinds of abstraction and distinguishes three great fields of knowledge: (1) Physics in the wide sense, meaning all the special sciences that deal with the material world; they abstract from individual conditions and are concerned with general laws and the universal type; (2) Mathematics abstracts for consideration only quantity; (3) Metaphysics abstracts only being as being.

Practical or normative philosophy regulates actions according to some standard. Logic deals with thought; it directs the intellect to truth. Ethics deals with action; it directs the will to good. Aesthetics deals with expression; it directs the intellect, the senses, and the emotions to beauty and its contemplation.

Abstraction is the basis of science and of philosophy. Each special science adopts as its sphere of investigation one general characteristic and ignores all others. It is only by this means that human beings can make progress in knowledge. A complex being, for example, a man or a woman, is made the object of distinct special sciences such as biology, psychology, anthropology, ethics, economics, politics, each of which studies only a chosen aspect. Even chemistry, physics, mathematics contribute to our knowledge of humankind. No one science gives us the whole truth. All together give us one truth, a composite picture, limited, of course, by the inadequacies of the human mind.

It is very important to realize the selectivity of the special sciences — to understand that each represents but one aspect of reality. To know one aspect as a part of a greater complex whole is to know a part of the truth. But to think that one such aspect is the whole is to distort truth into gross error. This is the danger of specialization. Philosophy, which harmonizes the findings of the special sciences, comes closest to giving us the whole truth, insofar as we can know it by reason alone.

Theology's primary function is to supplement human knowledge with knowledge which unaided human reason cannot attain. This is Revelation, which comprises both speculative and practical knowledge, chiefly of God, who is the First Cause of all that science and philosophy study, and the Last End of man, who studies them.

DEFENSE OF PERENNIAL PHILOSOPHY

The logic of perennial philosophy presented in this book is scorned in many colleges and universities today as outmoded, inadequate, and unfit for a scientific age. Logical positivism admits as knowable only sense experience of matter and the relations of coexistence and succession in natural phenomena; it denies spirit, intellect, and the capacity to know essence.[9] Modern semantics regards as arbitrary and shifting not only words but ideas; it denies that words are signs of ideas that truly represent things. The new symbolic or mathematical logic,[10] which aims to free logic from the restrictions of words and things, becomes a mere manipulation of symbols capable of being tested for their internal consistency but having no correspondence to ideas or things (and therefore no stability or truth).

Perennial philosophy holds that symbols such as those of the syllogism, opposition, obversion, conversion represent a higher degree of abstraction and more clear relationships than words do, and therefore a more advanced knowledge; they are sound precisely because they represent words that do correspond to the ideas and things. These symbols point the way to a more complete symbolic logic which preserves the basic truths of perennial philosophy, in particular its healthy respect for intellectual knowledge derived from sense knowledge by abstraction.

11 COMPOSITION AND READING

The art of rhetoric originated in Sicily, when a democracy was established in Syracuse in 466 B.C., and Corax and his pupil Tisias assisted
those who had been dispossessed of property to convince the judges that
they had a just claim to its restoration. Corax put together some theoretical precepts based principally on the topic of general probability,
called *eikos* (see Aristotle, *Rhetoric*, 2.24.9), and Tisias developed it further, as Plato shows in *Phaedrus*. Gorgias, the Sicilian, came to Athens
in 427 B.C., introduced the art of rhetoric into many parts of Greece,
and had many disciples, among whom the most admirable and famous
was Isocrates, the orator and teacher. Gorgias, Protagoras, Prodicus, and
Hippias emphasized the graces of style, figures of speech, distinction of
synonyms, correctness and elegance in the choice of words, and rules
of rhythm. Gorgias aimed to teach how to convince, independent of
any knowledge of the subject. He admittedly taught persuasion, not
virtue. Plato and Aristotle condemned the sophists: Gorgias, Protagoras,
and others for their superficiality and disregard of truth in teaching how
to make the worse appear the better cause.

Aristotle himself constructed a well-balanced system of the arts of
discovering and communicating truth, and his treatises on these subjects profoundly influenced his own and succeeding ages. He system-
atized rhetoric and made it an instrument of truth. He explicitly
claimed to be the founder of the art of logic. His *Poetics* is the beginning of real literary criticism.

Logic and rhetoric are concerned with the discovery and communication of truth directly from the mind of the author to the mind of the
listener or reader. Poetic is a very different mode of communication, an
indirect one that imitates life in characters and situations; readers or listeners share imaginatively the characters' experiences as if they were
their own; yet poetic rises out of knowledge as well as feeling, and logic
and rhetoric are employed in the communication of the whole, which
goes beyond them. Poetic is argument through vivid representation.

Logic

Aristotle divided logic, according to its subject matter, into scientific demonstration, dialectic, and sophistic, treated in the works named below.

1 *Posterior Analytics.* Scientific demonstration has as its subject matter premises that are true, essential, and certain. In this field there are not two sides to a question but only one. The reasoning is merely expository, as in geometry, moving step by step to the conclusive demonstration of what was to be proved. *Prior Analytics* treats certainty through form. The work is concerned with inference, and it presents the syllogism.

2 *Topics.* Dialectic has as its subject matter opinion, not certain knowledge; therefore, the premises are merely probable.

In this field there are two sides to a question, and there is reasonable support for opposing views, both only probable, neither certain, although each person engaging in the discussion may be personally, even ardently, convinced of the truth of his views. Yet he cannot justly regard them as having the quality of geometric proof because each must recognize that the matter under discussion is not intrinsically clear and that his opponent's view is not so manifestly false as the proposition that two and two makes five. The argument is conducted in a spirit of inquiry and love of truth. If, in the course of the discussion, one disputant sees that the opponent's view is true and that which he has advanced is false, he may be justly said to have won the argument because he has gained truth, which, he now sees, his opponent had at the start. Plato's *Dialogues* are the perfect examples of dialectic.

3 *Sophistical Refutations* (treatise on material fallacies). Sophistic has as its subject matter premises that seem to be generally accepted and appropriate but which really are not appropriate. In this field, usually that of opinion, the sophist seeks not truth but only an appearance of truth, achieved by the use of fallacious arguments designed to put down the opponent in contentious dispute. Anyone who wins by such methods has not won truth. On the contrary, he has made error appear to have triumphed over truth, and nobody has won truth by means of the argument. It is a sad commentary that many people today attach to the word argument only the sophists' conception, entertain the sophistic notion of "winning" an argument, and ignore the fine and constructive pursuit of, or understanding of, truth to be gained by the only

forms of argument worthy of the name, namely scientific demonstration and dialectic.

Rhetoric

Rhetoric, according to Aristotle, is the counterpart of dialectic, and the rhetorical enthymeme is the counterpart of the dialectical syllogism. Both these arts, rhetoric and dialectic, deal with opinion, with probability, not certainty, and therefore these two arts, and they alone, are capable of generating arguments on two or more sides of a question. Dialectic deals with philosophical and general questions, proceeds by question and answer, employs technical language, and is addressed to philosophers. Rhetoric deals with particular questions, such as political action, proceeds by uninterrupted discourse, usually employs nontechnical language, and is addressed to a popular audience.

Rhetoric is defined by Aristotle as the art of finding in any given subject matter the available means of persuasion. The modes of persuasion are three, and since, as Aristotle remarks, one must know not only what to say but how to say it effectively in words and in a well disposed order, his basic treatment may be outlined as follows.

Persuasion is achieved by means of logos, pathos, and ethos. Logos requires one to convince the minds of the listeners or readers by proving the truth of what one is saying. Pathos requires one to put the listeners or readers into a frame of mind favorable to one's purpose, principally by working on the emotions. Ethos requires one to inspire in the audience, by courtesy and other qualities, confidence in one's character, competence, good sense, good moral character, and good will.

Style is characterized by good diction, good grammatical structure, pleasing rhythm, clear and appropriate language, effective metaphor, etc.

Arrangement is the order of parts: introduction, statement and proof, conclusion.

The five traditional components of rhetoric were invention (finding arguments for persuasion), arrangement of the parts of a composition, style, memory of a speech, and the proper use of voice and gesture in delivering it.

Poetic

Poetic, as Aristotle understands it, is imitation, an imitation of life, in which the author does not speak to the reader directly but only through his characters. The author lets them speak and act, and the readers or listeners identify imaginatively with the characters. The use of verse is not essential.

Because poetic communication is mediate, through the interposition of the characters and the situation in the story, it is more subject to misinterpretation than direct or expository communication. If, for example, one does not recognize irony, burlesque, or satire, one will understand just the opposite of what is intended by the author. It is necessary to learn how to interpret poetic communication. Often it is the easiest, most natural, and most effective means of communication, as in the parable of the prodigal son (Luke 15:11–32); but sometimes it is difficult to understand, as in the parable of the unjust steward (Luke 16:1–8).

In the *Poetics*, Aristotle discusses tragic drama and the epic, both plotted narrative. He distinguishes six formative elements or qualitative parts of drama: (1) plot, (2) characters, (3) the thought of the characters, (4) diction or style, (5) music, (6) spectacle (production in the theatre, scene, costumes).

The specific function of tragedy is to produce in the audience a purification of the emotions through pity and fear, evoked principally by the tragic suffering of the hero. To produce this effect, the tragic hero must be a man, not perfect, but on the whole good, for whom one feels liking and sympathy, whose misfortune is brought upon him not by vice or depravity but by an error of judgment or a flaw in his character.

It will be noticed that character (ethos), thought (logos), arousal of the emotions (pathos), and style (through grammar) are basic in both rhetoric and poetic.

Poetic is the imitation of an action by which agents to whom we ascribe moral qualities achieve happiness or misery. Their thought and character are shown as causes of their actions which result in success or in failure. Moreover, at any time, anywhere, a person of this kind will probably, or even necessarily, say or do this, under circumstances like this. Yet the character in the drama, even while typical of many others, is realized in this story vividly and imaginatively as an individual one has known, whose joys and sorrows one has shared. Therefore, poetic stands in a unique position between history and philosophy. It is more philosophic and of greater import than history because it is universal, not singular, and represents what might be, not merely what has been. By it one gathers the meaning of an insight as an artist perceived it. It is more moving than philosophy because the universal is realized intensely in the individual portrayed, and the appeal is to the whole person: to the imagination, the feelings, and the intellect, not to the intellect alone.

THE SHORT STORY

Poetic, as Aristotle conceived it, is plotted narrative dramatically imitating action in human life, whether in epic or drama. Consequently, poetic is realized also in the novel and the short story.

Because the short story is the shortest form of plotted narrative, this discussion focuses on the short story, although the principles are applicable to the novel, the drama, and the epic as well.

The Plot

The plot, not the characters, is the first and the essential element in poetic. The characters reveal themselves in the action.

A plot is a combination of incidents so closely connected by cause and effect that not one of them may be transposed or withdrawn without disjoining and dislocating the whole. This causal connection constitutes unity of action, the one unity essential to every poetic work.

A plot, says Aristotle, must have a beginning, a middle, and an end. The beginning is not necessarily that which is after, or caused by, something else, but is that which causes what follows it; the middle is that which is caused by what precedes it and is the cause of what follows it; the end is that which is caused by what precedes it but does not cause something to follow after it. In other words, a plot has a rising and a falling action in a sequence of cause and effect.

The topics of cause and effect[1] are the tools for analyzing poetic, just as division is the tool for analyzing rhetorical in the sense of expository or direct communication of ideas.

The plot is the story. Every plot is a narration of events, but not every narration of events is a plot. A plot is a narration of selected events causally connected, rising out of a conflict and the resulting obstacles to be overcome, all of which creates suspense which is not satisfied until the end. Thus plotted narrative has logical and artistic unity which unplotted narrative lacks. In unplotted narrative the end is simply a cessation of the story, which otherwise could be continued indefinitely beyond that point; in plotted narrative there is actual dissatisfaction unless the end is known, and there is a sense of finality when it is known—no desire to have the story go on and on.

The plot of a short story involves a single situation: one central character is facing a problem, and the plot is its solution. The problem or conflict is the driving desire or purpose of the main character, who, encountering obstacles, either overcomes them (happy ending) or is overcome by them (tragic ending); both are solutions.

Therefore, the simplest analysis of any plotted narrative is in terms of character, problem, and solution. This analysis may be made of the main plot and of subplots, if there are any, as there are in some dramas and novels.

PARTS OF THE ACTION

The parts of the action are (1) the situation or exposition; (2) the complication or rising action; (3) the resolution or falling action. The basic analysis of plotted narrative discovers the beginning of the action, the turning point (the logical climax), and the denouement or final outcome (the emotional climax).

ANALYSIS OF ACTION

In Shakespeare's *Hamlet*, the action begins when the ghost tells Hamlet that he is Hamlet's father, murdered by the king, and asks Hamlet to avenge this wrong. The turning point occurs when Hamlet, thinking it is the king whose reactions to the play within the play have revealed his guilt, kills Polonius instead. The denouement is the scene in which Hamlet kills the king with the poisoned weapon which the king had prepared for him, and from which he, too, dies.

These three points in the action, it will be noticed, are what Aristotle called the beginning, the middle, and the end of a plot.

The parts of a plot may be diagrammed thus, with the three important points of the action marked a, b, c.

PROBLEMS OF ACTION

Plausibility is absolutely essential to a story. It is the achievement of illusion and inward consistency. No matter how imaginative or even fantastic a story may be, it must create illusion; it must seem real. A writer may secure plausibility by the following means.

1   Natural, adequate motivation

2   Skillful, adequate forecast, which includes motives and details of setting, appearance, incident, etc.—all the elements that make later events plausible

3   Vivid, concrete, realistic detail

4   Effective creation of setting

5   Tone

The beginning of the story can occur at any point of the action. A writer must decide where to begin the story—at the beginning, the middle, or near the end of the series of events that constitute the story. It is often better to plunge *in medias res* (literally, "into the midst of things"), into the midst of the events, as Homer does in the *Iliad* and the *Odyssey*, and to tell what happened earlier (retrospective action) at points where the incidents will have greatest significance. For example, in the *Odyssey* the story of Odysseus' pursuit of the boar which tore his leg is told in Book XIX, when the scar causes his old nurse to recognize him, although the incident occurred earlier perhaps than any other related in the story.

Retrospective action may be introduced by letters, by dialogue, by reminiscent reverie. In *A Tale of Two Cities*, the letter which Dr. Manette wrote during his imprisonment in the Bastille, before the story opened, is introduced with intense dramatic effect at Charles Darnay's second French trial near the end of the novel. The conversation between Sidney Carton and the Sheep of the Prisons (Solomon Press) near the end of the novel clarifies the facts about the mysterious funeral of Roger Cly and Jerry Cruncher's muddy boots (bits of forecast) introduced near the beginning.

Retrospective action is very important in building a story; it is a means to secure artistic unity, dramatic effect, compactness. Prospective action is that which moves forward chronologically: the order of narration corresponds to the order of events. Retrospective action is that which moves backward chronologically: the order of narration differs from the order of the events narrated. The action is retrospective whenever an incident which occurred before another is told after it. This device is also called a flashback. A story *cannot* begin with retrospective action, although it may begin with reminiscence; these two are not identical.

Dramatic and nondramatic scenes constitute the narrative. Dramatic scenes create an experience for the reader to share imaginatively, through dialogue, reverie, detail of action, and vivid picturing details. A scene is obligatory if psychological necessity requires a dramatic presentation to satisfy the reader's interest and to make the story or the character convincing and plausible. Dialogue should forward plot, reveal character, and be natural. Dialogue cannot be created by merely putting words into quotation marks and adding *he said, she said*, etc. It must have the quality of speech and must fit the character and situation. Nondramatic narration merely gives the reader information through the author's explanation and summary of events. In most good stories there is little of this.

Angle of narration includes point of view, focus, the use of frames, and the degree of dramatization.

1 *Point of View.* A story is usually told in third- or first-person point of view. In first-person point of view, the narrator may be the main character or a less important character. In third-person point of view, the story may use omniscient narration and present the thoughts of many or all of the characters, or it may use limited omniscient narration and only present the thoughts of one character. Second-person point of view uses a narrator who speaks directly to the reader. It is rare.

2 *Focus.* From whose perspective is the story to be told? Whose story is it to be? Sometimes the choice of an unusual angle of narration gives a fresh and interesting turn to an otherwise ordinary story, for example, a family tragedy from the plumber's point of view or a fight between lovers from a cabdriver's point of view, in either first or third person. An interesting effect is sometimes produced, usually in a work longer than a short story, by telling the same story or part of a story more than once, each time from the point of view of a different character, for example: Robert Browning's *The Ring and the Book* and William Faulkner's *The Sound and the Fury.*

3 *Frame.* A story can be told within a larger story, for example: Dostoyevski's "The Thief" and Kipling's "The Man Who Would Be King."

4 *Degree of Dramatization.* A story can be objective and present only the speech and action of its characters or subjective and present the thoughts of one or more characters, for example: Shirley Jackson's

"The Lottery" (objective) and Isaac Bashevis Singer's "Gimpel the Fool" (subjective).

Forecast or foreshadowing hints about later developments in the action but does not reveal; it affects suspense and plausibility.

Suspense is curiosity or pleasurable anxiety created by interest in the story. Motivation of characters and action, forecast, and the structure of the story add to suspense. Suspense is not surprise.

Transition refers to the links between the segments of the action.

Technique of presentation includes the many devices a writer uses to tell a story. The writer enables the characters to act out the story. Sometimes a story is told through letters, diary, dream. Writers use dialogue, reverie, images, explanation, and summary. Usually many of these techniques are employed; explanation should be used sparingly.

The Structure of a Story

The structure of a story may be presented as follows. The theme is the underlying idea of the story and can be expressed in general terms in one sentence. Asterisks indicate dramatic scenes.

"The Piece Of String"

by Guy de Maupassant

Character: Maitre Hauchecorne

Problem: To clear himself of suspicion of theft.

Solution: He does not succeed in clearing himself but dies, vainly protesting his innocence.

Theme: Appearances can be deceptive.

Beginning of the action: Hauchecorne picked up a piece of string, and an enemy saw him.

Turning point: Accused by his enemy of picking up a wallet that had been lost, he told the truth, but his story was not believed even after the lost wallet was found and returned; it was thought that an accomplice had returned it. (He was freed from the legal charge but not from the suspicion of his fellow townsmen.)

Denouement: Worn out by vain efforts to make himself believed, he wasted away and died, still not believed.

Retrospective Action

2. He and Malandain had once had a quarrel and had borne each other malice ever since.

6. Malandain had brought the charge against him.

Prospective Action

1. Seeing on the ground a piece of string, Maitre Hauchecorne picked it up. He noticed that Maitre Malandain was watching him.

*3. While Hauchecorne was at Jourdain's inn, the town crier announced that Maitre Houlbreque had lost a pocketbook containing 500 francs and business papers.

*4. The corporal of gendarmes came to the inn and called for Hauchecorne, who went with him.

*5. Brought before the mayor, Hauchecorne was accused of stealing the pocketbook.

*7. Hauchecorne denied the charge and asserted he had merely picked up a piece of string, which he drew from his pocket.

8. No one believed him.

9. Searched at his own request, Hauchecorne was dismissed with a warning.

10. Hauchecorne told the story of the string to all he met. No one believed him. They laughed.

11. Hauchecorne went home

to his own village and made the rounds telling his story, which no one believed. He brooded over it all night.
12. Next day, a farm hand returned the missing pocketbook.

13. He had found it and, being unable to read, had taken it to his master.

*14. Hauchecorne repeated to everyone he met the story of the string, triumphantly adding as proof of his innocence the fact that the purse had been returned.
*15. He realized that people thought his accomplice had brought it back. The crowd jeered at him.
16. Struck to the heart by the injustice of the suspicion, Hauchecorne continued to tell his tale, adding proofs, but the more artful his arguments the less he was believed.
17. Jokers would lead him on to tell the story.
18. Exhausting himself in useless efforts to vindicate himself, he wasted away, his mind grew weak, and he died, vainly protesting his innocence.

Characters

A character is an imagined figure who takes a role in a story. Characters can be round, which means they are multidimensional, or flat, which means they can be distinguished by one outstanding trait. A flat character may be a stock character that is a recognizable stereotype.

The wicked stepmother, the sad clown, the handsome and shallow playboy are all stock characters.

Characters can be considered according to the degree to which they are developed in a story. Some characters are not well developed; they are needed only to fulfill a function in the plot, for example: Orestes in *Iphigenia at Aulis*, Iris and Chryseis in the *Iliad*, the minor wooers in the *Odyssey*. Some characters are recognizable types, for example: Euryclea, the faithful servant in the *Odyssey*; Uriah Heep, the scheming sycophant in *David Copperfield*; Jane Bennet, the ingenue in *Pride and Prejudice*. Other characters are fully developed and individualized, even if they evolve from types: for example, Shylock in *The Merchant of Venice*, Elizabeth Bennet in *Pride and Prejudice*, Hamlet.

Motivation refers to the reason the characters act as they do—hence the basic link between characters and plot. Adequate motivation is the principal means to create plausibility and suspense.

Character can be revealed either directly or indirectly. In direct characterization, the author or an observer in the story describes the character. In indirect characterization, the character is revealed by what he or she thinks, says, or does. The author presents details and creates an experience for the reader who imaginatively meets the character. A detail suggests much more than it actually states, for from it the reader spontaneously builds up a vivid image of the whole. The use of detail is the principal means to make the reader see everything with the vividness of an eyewitness, to make the story tell itself without the intrusion of the author, to make it a poetic communication that creates illusion.

Thought

The thought and moral qualities of the characters, says Aristotle, are the natural causes of the action or plot. Thought and action reveal character. Thought expressed in language is that part of poetic which is common to both logic and rhetoric, for the characters employ these arts to prove or disprove, to arouse emotion, or to maximize and minimize events and issues.

GENERAL STATEMENTS

Particularly important thoughts are the general statements or sententious utterances (general propositions, apothegms, proverbs) which express a universal view or judgment or philosophy of life. *Hamlet* owes much of its philosophical quality to the large number of such utterances in it.

. . . to the noble mind
Rich gifts wax poor when givers prove unkind.
　　　　　—*Hamlet* 3.1.99–100

. . . the good, when praised,
Feel something of disgust, if to excess
Commended.
　　　　　—Euripides, *Iphigenia at Aulis*

Even his character grew firmer, like that of a man who has made up his mind and set himself a goal.
　　　　　—Nikolai Gogol, "The Cloak"

Could we know all the vicissitudes of our fortunes, life would be too full of hope and fear, exultation or disappointment, to afford us a single hour of true serenity.
　　　　　—Nathaniel Hawthorne, "David Swan"

THEME

Theme is the underlying thought of the whole story and can be stated in one sentence. It is usually a conviction about life, which might have been the subject of an essay or a sermon but which has been expressed instead in a poetic communication: a story, drama, or novel.

A man should not be allowed to perish altogether.
　　　　　—Dostoyevski, "The Thief"

Sacrifice for the public good exalts the sorrow it entails.
　　　　　—Euripides, *Iphigenia at Aulis*

Self-knowledge is the first step to maturity.
　　　　　—Jane Austen, *Pride and Prejudice*

DICTION OR STYLE

Aristotle uses the term diction to mean communication by means of language. Modern literary criticism uses the term diction in a narrower sense to mean the words which the author uses and considers diction one element of style. Style refers to how the writer manages the elements of the story. In a broad sense, it includes every choice the writer makes, but since most of those choices are discussed under other headings, usually the focus is on the following elements of style: tone, diction, and syntax.

Tone is the author's attitude toward the subject of his literary work and the various devices by which he or she creates that attitude. Tone may be serious, earnest, realistic, romantic, flippant, cynical, satiric, etc.

Diction is the language a writer uses. Diction may be pedantic or colloquial, abstract or concrete, unadorned or poetic. Most stories use a range of diction, and these purposeful choices help to communicate character, action, and tone.

Syntax is sentence structure. Both the length and construction of sentences are components of syntax. Grammatically, sentences can be simple, compound, complex, or compound-complex. Sentence fragments, elements punctuated as sentences that are not grammatically sentences, can also be found in stories. Rhetorical elements of sentence structure, such as the use of parallel structure or periodic sentences, are part of syntax.

COSTUME AND SCENERY

Of the two remaining elements of drama discussed by Aristotle, music is not essential today, as the songs of the chorus were in Greek drama; music is dominant, however, in opera. Spectacle is essential to the production of drama; it includes costumes and scenery.

In written narrative details of setting play a strong role. Setting includes the time and the place of the story. All details of time and place fall under this general heading, so the author's description of nature, the furniture in a room, the temperature, etc. are elements of setting. Setting may create atmosphere; Poe, for instance, uses setting to add to the terror of a story.

Regional writers set stories in one geographic area. William Faulkner's Yoknapatawpha County is a fictional name for a part of Mississippi; Thomas Hardy recreates parts of Dorset, England, in his novels although he calls Dorset by its Anglo-Saxon name, Wessex, and he fictionalizes place names in the region. Local color is an aspect of regional writing that involves faithful representation of an area's locale, dress, customs, and speech. Bret Harte and Mark Twain use local color in their stories.

Most stories show that setting has a strong impact on character development and action. Naturalism, however, emphasizes the importance of setting even more because in a naturalistic story the environment directly affects character and plot. Most often, the protagonist is shown as a victim of his or her environment. The French novelist, Emile Zola, is considered the founder of naturalism. American writers Stephen Crane, Upton Sinclair, and Theodore Dreiser used elements of naturalism.

The Work as a Whole

The distinctive value of the world's great stories is that they lead the reader to share imaginatively the rich and varied experience of individual characters confronted with problems and conditions of life common to people in all ages. They present potentialities and norms of living made significant by the best writers. They may show men and women suffering as a result of their own desire to have an excess of what is good for them or of what is not good, even sinful. They show how false conceptions of happiness lead to misery. A story that portrays evil is morally sound if it shows evil as evil yet does not portray the evil so as to make it a source of temptation to a normal reader.[2] Good stories appeal to the human in us. We may love, detest, admire, pity, scorn, or ridicule.

The reader should ask: What vision of life, what insight, is gained from this story? What problems has the author stated and solved? What has been left unsolved? Does the story present the problem of conflicting duties, the claims of public good against those of private good, human rights against property rights, adjustment to environment, clashes of culture, etc.? Has the story brought to life fictional or historical personages worth knowing? Are they individualized? alive? Are they normal and fine people or are they perverted? Are they heightened above life to an ideal conception? Are their actions and dialogue appropriate? Who are the most interesting people? Why? Of which people and incidents in the story does the author seem to approve? to disapprove? What seems to be the philosophy of life? What is the dominant idea, the single impression, left by the story? Does it present other times, other places, other civilizations and cultures? Is the style distinguished? What are the literary relationships and influences that affect the story? What was the author trying to do in this work? Did she or he succeed in doing it? Was it worth doing?

Dostoyevski's "The Thief," for example, answers the question "Who is my neighbor?" Am I my brother's keeper? Yes. Is it right to let a man perish altogether? No, not even if he seems worthless, an incorrigible drunkard, lazy, ungrateful, a thief, a liar. Not even if I am poor and have very little to share with anyone, and he has no particular claim on me such as kinship or friendship. He is a human being, and I must not let him perish. That claim is sufficient. This story gives a vision of life. It asserts on the lowest level, in universal terms, the inescapable kinship of all human beings and the duty of brotherly love.

FIGURATIVE LANGUAGE

According to the ancient conception, expressed by Cicero and Quintilian,[3] figurative language includes any deviation, either in thought or expression, from the ordinary and simple modes of speaking. This would include the language of ordinary people moved by excitement to adopt short cuts and turns of expression which give their speech liveliness and vividness not ordinarily found in it.

Cicero and Quintilian distinguished about ninety figures of speech, and Renaissance rhetoricians about two hundred in all, which were divided into tropes and schemes. Schemes were fashionings of language or thought deviating from the ordinary, which were divided into grammatical and rhetorical schemes. Grammatical schemes included devices which today are treated as means to improve style through grammar: variety of structure, parallel and antithetical structure, balance, rhythm, emphasis, elliptical structure, and the use of one part of speech for another, for example, nouns used as verbs. Rhetorical schemes of repetition were frequently used to emphasize parallel structure, balance, and rhythm. They included repetition of letters in alliteration and repetition of words. Rhetorical schemes of thought corresponded to the threefold means of persuasion: logos, pathos, and ethos. One hundred and twenty-two of the two hundred figures corresponded to the topics of logic and the forms of reasoning. We have already seen that litotes is the rhetorical counterpart of logical obversion.[4] Other rhetorical schemes correspond to the enthymeme,[5] the disjunctive and hypothetical syllogisms,[6] and the dilemma.[7]

The modern concept of figures of speech is almost limited to those which ancient and Renaissance rhetoricians called tropes. A trope is the turning of a word from its ordinary and proper meaning to another not proper meaning, in order to increase its force and vividness. It is an imaginative, in contrast to a matter-of-fact, use of words. For example, "The knife is rusty" is a matter-of-fact use of *rusty*. "Their minds are rusty" is a figurative use of *rusty*, turning it to a meaning not proper to it, but nonetheless forceful.

The value of tropes lies in their power to convey ideas vividly in a condensed and picturesque style. They are means to achieve a clear, forceful, lively style. The most important trope is the metaphor.

Renaissance rhetoricians distinguished from four to ten tropes; Quintilian, fourteen. We shall distinguish eight tropes (simile, metaphor, onomatopoeia, personification, antonomasia, metonymy, synecdoche, and irony) and shall notice from which topic of invention each is derived.[8]

Tropes Based on Similarity

Simile, metaphor, onomatopoeia, personification, and antonomasia are tropes based on a similarity between the elements which are compared.

SIMILE

A simile expresses through the words, *like, as*, or *resembles* an imaginative comparison between objects of different classes. A simile is not, strictly speaking, a trope, since the similarity is expressed and no word is turned to a meaning not proper to it. Its resemblance to metaphor is so basic, however, that this technical distinction will be ignored here.

EXAMPLES: Simile

My fate cries out,
And makes each petty artery in this body
As hardy as the Nemean lion's nerve.
                    —*Hamlet* 1.4.82–84

Oh, my love is like a red, red rose
That's newly sprung in June:
My love is like the melody
That's sweetly played in tune.
  —Robert Burns, "My love is like a red, red rose"

Now, therefore, while the youthful hue
Sits on thy skin like morning dew
And while thy willing soul transpires
At every pore with instant fires,
Now let us sport us while we may,
And now, like amorous birds of prey,
Rather at once our time devour
Than languish in his slow-chapped power.
—Andrew Marvell, "To His Coy Mistress"

METAPHOR

A metaphor boldly states, without using a word of comparison, the identification of similar objects of different classes.

EXAMPLES: Metaphor

The Lord is my shepherd:
there is nothing I lack.
In green pastures, you let me graze;
to safe water you lead me;
you restore my strength.
　　　　　　—Psalms 23:1–5

It sifts from leaden sieves
It powders all the road
It fills with alabaster wool
The wrinkles of the road
—Emily Dickinson, "It sifts from leaden sieves"

. . . my way of life
Is fallen into the sere, the yellow leaf.
　　　　　　—*Macbeth* 5.3.22–23

ONOMATOPOEIA

Onomatopoeia is the use of words or rhythms whose sound imitates the sense.

EXAMPLES: Onomatopoeia

The moan of doves in immemorial elms
And murmuring of innumerable bees.
　　　　—Alfred Lord Tennyson, "The Princess"

But when loud surges lash the sounding shore,
The hoarse, rough verse should like the torrent roar;
When Ajax strives some rock's vast weight to throw
The line too labors, and the words move slow.
　　　　—Alexander Pope, "An Essay on Criticism"

Men of every station—Pooh-Bah,
Nabob, bozo, roff, and hobo—
Cry in unison, "Indubi-
Tably, there is simply nobo-

Dy, who oompahs on the tubo,
Solo, quite like Roger Bubo!"
　　　　—John Updike, "Recital"

PERSONIFICATION

Personification is the attribution of life, sensation, and human qualities to objects of a lower order or to abstract ideas. Personification is based on the relation of subject and adjuncts. An adjunct is an accident or a quality that inheres in a subject.

I would hate that death bandaged my eyes, and forebore,
And bade me creep past.
— Robert Browning, "Prospice"

Life's but a walking shadow, a poor player
That struts and frets his hour upon the stage
And then is heard no more.
— *Macbeth* 5.5.24–26

Season of mists and mellow fruitfulness!
Close bosom-friend of the maturing sun;
Conspiring with him how to load and bless
With fruit the vines that round the thatch-eaves run.
— John Keats, "To Autumn"

ANTONOMASIA

Antonomasia is of two kinds: (1) a proper name is substituted for a quality associated with it and is used much like a common name; (2) a phrase descriptive of attributes is substituted for a proper name. Like personification, it is based on the relation of subject and adjuncts.

He was an Einstein in problem solving.

Wall Street tumbled today after fourth quarter earnings were announced.

In the *Odyssey*, epithets[9] such as "gray-eyed goddess" and "daughter of Zeus" frequently substitute for Athena's name.

The White House issued a statement.

Trope Based on Subject and Adjunct and Cause and Effect: Metonymy

Metonymy is a trope based on subject and adjunct and also on cause and effect. Metonymy substitutes subject for adjunct, adjunct for subject, cause for effect, or effect for cause, including each of the four causes: efficient, final, material, and formal.[10]

EXAMPLES: Metonymy

. . . to have thy prison days prolonged through middle age down to decrepitude and silver hairs, without hope of relief or respite.

—Charles Lamb "The Superannuated Man"

. . . malt does more than Milton can
To justify God's ways to man.
   —A. E. Housman, "Terence, this is stupid stuff"

The days are evil.
      —Eph. 5:16

Calais was peopled with novelty and delight.
      —William Hazlitt, "On Going a Journey"

. . . may my hands rot off,
And never brandish more revengeful steel.
      —*Richard II* 4.1.49–50

. . . altar, sword, and pen,
Fireside, the heroic wealth of hall and bower,
Have forfeited their ancient English dower
Of inward happiness.
      —William Wordsworth, "London, 1802"

If an effect is signified by a remote cause, the figure is called metalepsis, a kind of metonymy.

EXAMPLE: Metalepsis

Thy hyacinth hair, thy classic face,
Thy Naiad airs have brought me home
To the glory that was Greece
And the grandeur that was Rome.
      —Edgar Allan Poe, "To Helen"

Trope Based on Division: Synecdoche

Synecdoche is a trope based on division. It substitutes the part for the whole, the whole for the part, species for genus, or genus for species.

EXAMPLES: Synecdoche

The news that Daisy Miller was surrounded by a half dozen wonderful mustaches checked Winterbourne's impulses to go straight-way to see her.

—Henry James, *Daisy Miller*

She gave a helping hand to the cause.

Give us this day our daily bread.

—Luke 11:3

Like to a pair of lions smeared with prey.

—*The Two Noble Kinsmen* 1.4.18

Trope Based on Contraries: Irony

Irony is a trope based on contraries. By naming one contrary it intends another.

EXAMPLE: Irony

But at my back I always hear
Time's winged chariot hurrying near;
And yonder all before us lie
Deserts of vast eternity.
Thy beauty shall no more be found,
Nor, in thy marble vault, shall sound
My echoing song; then worms shall try
That long-preserved virginity,
And your quaint honor turn to dust,
And into ashes all my lust;
The grave's a fine and private place,
But none, I think, do there embrace.
—Andrew Marvell, "To His Coy Mistress"[11]

Gloucester [*to himself*]. Simple, plain Clarence! I do love thee so
That I will shortly send thy soul to heaven.

—*Richard III* 1.1.118–119

Ineffective Figures of Speech

1   Mixed figures—blending two or more comparisons—for example: The flower of our youth is the foundation on which we will build until our light will shine out to all the world.

2   Clichés—trite, stereotyped figures of speech—for example: brave as lions, cunning as foxes, raven tresses, lily hands, alabaster neck.

POETRY AND VERSIFICATION

Poetry may be divided into narrative, didactic, and lyric poetry. Narrative poetry includes drama, epic, ballad, and romance; what has been said of plotted narrative applies to these species in so far as they are plotted. Didactic poetry is not poetic in Aristotle's sense of imitating action; rather, it is expository. It merits the name poetry if it has the requisite qualities of thought, style, and rhythm, which will be discussed presently. Outstanding examples are Lucretius' *"De Rerum Natura"*[12] and Pope's "Essay on Criticism." Lyric poetry includes the song, hymn, sonnet, ode, rondeau, and many other special verse forms. It expresses the poet's feelings, impressions, and reflections rather than an objective incident, although an incident may occasion the reflections. Drama developed from lyric poetry, and there are many songs and lyric passages in plays, particularly in Greek and Renaissance plays. When people think of poetry, they primarily think of lyric poetry.

Aristotle distinguishes poetry from other modes of imitation according to the means employed. Music employs rhythm and harmony; dancing, rhythm alone; and poetry, rhythm and language. Meters in language are species of rhythms.

The classical and neoclassical ideal is that poetry should be objective, should appeal to the intellect, and should achieve beauty through forms which perfectly order matter that has intrinsic dignity and elevation. The romantic ideal is that poetry should be subjective, should appeal to the feelings, and should achieve beauty through the free and spontaneous play of imagination and fancy on material that may be either picturesquely strange or homely and commonplace.

Although the conceptions of poetry vary considerably, it is generally agreed that poetry is a communication of experience, of emotion as well as thought, which embraces the universal under the particular.

Poetry may be defined as the expression in apt, rhythmical language of the thought, imagination, and emotion of the poet, reflecting some aspect of beauty and truth, and capable of arousing a response in the imagination and feelings of the reader or listener.

The language of poetry is distinguished by an enhanced rhythm, although, according to Aristotle as well as Wordsworth, meter is not essential. It is further distinguished by exceptional energy, vividness, imagery, penetration, and compression, whereby much meaning is packed into few words. While achieving these qualities, great poets have as their primary mark, so far as form is concerned, the capacity to arrange words in eloquent, inevitable, and unimprovable order and beauty; so far as matter is concerned, they must have a deep perception of truth and beauty in nature, man, and God.

Poetry communicates experience that cannot be expressed in any other way. The poet sees and feels with a depth and intensity beyond that of the ordinary person; the poet communicates not thought only but this experience. To read poetry is to share the experience of the poet.

The form of poetry is of its essence to such a degree that the form is felt to be inevitable; that is, it is felt to be the only form in which that matter could be satisfactorily communicated. Hence matter and form are united in poetry more intimately than in merely logical communication. It is true that what one person considers to be poetry another may not. Poetry depends greatly on the psychological dimension of language, which is less objective than the logical dimension; the subjective varies from person to person. There is, however, much poetry capable of evoking poetic response in so many readers through the years that it is universally judged to be truly poetry.

The subjective character of a poetic impression is the theme of the following poem:

The Solitary Reaper

Behold her, single in the field,
Yon solitary, Highland lass!
Reaping and singing by herself;
Stop here, or gently pass!
Alone she cuts and binds the grain,
And sings a melancholy strain;
O listen! For the vale profound
Is overflowing with the sound.

No nightingale did ever chaunt
More welcome notes to weary bands
Of travelers in some shady haunt
Among Arabian sands.
A voice so thrilling ne'er was heard
In springtime from the cuckoo-bird,
Breaking the silence of the seas
Among the farthest Hebrides.

Will no one tell me what she sings? —
Perhaps the plaintive numbers flow

For old, unhappy, far-off things,
And battles long ago.
Or is it some more humble lay,
Familiar matter of today?
Some natural sorrow, loss, or pain
That has been, and may be again?

What'er the theme, the maiden sang
As if her song could have no ending;
I saw her singing at her work,
And o'er the sickle bending—
I listened, motionless and still;
And, as I mounted up the hill,
The music in my heart I bore
Long after it was heard no more.
                    —William Wordsworth

Unlike the popular idea that the opposite of poetry is prose, the true opposite of poetry is matter-of-fact, as Wordsworth insists in his "Preface to the Lyrical Ballads." The opposite of prose is verse; both have rhythm, but verse has meter, and prose has not.

Consequently, poetry should not be identified with verse: poetic passages occur in novels and other prose writings; some verse is distinctly, often dully, matter-of-fact and anything but poetic. The following bits of verse are decidedly not poetry:

Thirty days hath September,
April, June, and November.

Early to bed and early to rise
Makes men healthy, wealthy, and wise.

ELEMENTS OF FORM

RHYTHM

The emphasized rhythm essential to poetry may be achieved by various means.

Parallelism

Parallelism is the chief rhythmical device of Hebrew poetry. Parallelism has been called thought-rhyme because the commonest form is a repetition of thought in different words. If a psalm is read with the repeated parts omitted, one perceives at once that it is prosaic.

There are three main types of parallelism. The following examples are from the Psalms.

> *Repetitive parallelism* (thought repeated):
> For my life is wasted with grief; and my years in sighs. (31:11)

> *Antithetical parallelism* (thought contrasted):
> For divine anger lasts but a moment;
> Divine favor lasts a lifetime. (30:6)

> *Additive or synthetic parallelism* (thought repeated and amplified):
> Such are the people who love the Lord
> that seek the face of the God of Jacob. (24:6)

Caesura

Caesura is a pause in a line of poetry usually in or near the middle. The Anglo-Saxon poets developed the alliterative line, which used the caesura with alliteration to create a strong and distinctive rhythm. Usually, two words in the first half of the line connected alliteratively with one or two words in the second half of the line.

> We twain had talked, in time of youth
> and made our boast, — we were merely boys,
> striplings still, — to stake our lives
> far at sea: and so we performed it.
> —*Beowulf* (Gummere's translation)

Cadence

Cadence relies on the natural rise and fall of the speaking voice. Free verse or *vers libre* uses the inherent cadence of language rather than a set metrical pattern. Brought to modern attention by the French symbolist poets of the late nineteenth century, free verse can be found in much modern poetry as well as in the Bible, particularly in the Psalms and the Song of Solomon.

Had I the choice

Had I the choice to tally greatest bards,
To limn their portraits, stately, beautiful, and emulate at will,
Homer with all his wars and warriors—Hector, Achilles, Ajax,

Or Shakespeare's woe-entangled Hamlet, Lear, Othello—
    Tennyson's fair ladies,
Meter or wit the best, or choice conceit to wield in perfect rhyme,
    delight of singers;
These, these, O sea, all these I'd gladly barter,
Would you the undulation of one wave, its trick to me transfer,
Or breathe one breath of yours upon my verse,
And leave its odor there.

                                  —Walt Whitman

Meter

Meter is measured rhythm which conforms to a predetermined regular pattern of stressed and unstressed syllables. It is the chief rhythmical device of the great body of English poetry.

THE METRICAL UNIT

The foot is the metrical unit; it is made up of one stressed syllable and one or more unstressed syllables. A metrical foot may be

1   Disyllabic

Iambus   unstressed, stressed (ca-rouse')
Trochee   stressed, unstressed (un'-der)

2   Trisyllabic

Dactyl   stressed, unstressed, unstressed (si'-lent-ly)
Anapest   unstressed, unstressed, stressed (in-ter-fere')
Amphibrach   unstressed, stressed, unstressed (in-sis'-ted)

SCANSION

Scansion is the marking off, orally or in writing, of the feet in verse so as to make explicit the metrical structure. In English verse, an ictus is more proper than a macron to mark stressed syllables, but the macron, proper to Latin and Greek verse, may be more convenient to use.[13]

    To name the meter of a poem is to state the kind of feet, the number of feet in one verse, and any irregularities. According to the number of feet, the verse is called monometer (one foot), dimeter (two feet), trimeter (three feet), tetrameter (four feet), pentameter (five feet), hexameter (six feet), heptameter (seven feet), octameter (eight feet), etc.

VARIATIONS

1 *Catalexis*: the omission of one or two unstressed syllables at the end of a verse.

2 *Feminine ending*: the addition of one or two unstressed syllables at the end of a verse.

3 *Anacrusis*: the addition of one or two unstressed syllables at the beginning of a verse.

4 *Truncation*: the omission of one or two unstressed syllables at the beginning of a verse.

5 *Spondee*: a foot consisting of two stressed syllables; it is usually a substitute for a dactyl and is relatively infrequent in English.

6 *Pyrrhic*: a foot consisting of two unstressed syllables.

Note that the catalexis and feminine ending often belong to the pattern. Anacrusis and truncation never do. They are only means of adapting irregular lines to the prevailing pattern; for example, there are six anacrustic lines out of twenty-four lines in Blake's "The Tiger." The anacrustic lines are marked with asterisks.

The Tiger

Tiger! Tiger! burning bright
In the forest of the night,*
What immortal hand or eye
Could frame thy fearful symmetry?

In what distant deeps or skies*
Burnt the fire of thine eyes?
On what wings dare he aspire?*
What the hand dare seize the fire?

And what shoulder, and what art,
Could twist the sinews of thy heart?
And when thy heart began to beat,
What dread hand forged thy dread feet?

What the hammer? what the chain?
In what furnace was thy brain?*
What the anvil? what dread grasp
Dare its deadly terrors clasp?

When the stars threw down their spears,
And watered heaven with their tears,*
Did he smile his work to see?
Did he who made the lamb make thee?

Tiger! Tiger! burning bright
In the forests of the night,*
What immortal hand or eye
Dare frame thy fearful symmetry?
—William Blake

RHYTHM OR VERSE PHRASING

Rhythm, or verse phrasing, is not identical with meter. Poems of the same meter may be dissimilar in rhythm, for the thought pattern may not coincide with the metrical pattern, although it fits into it. Compare the rhythm in the following excerpts from Pope's "An Essay On Criticism" and Browning's "My Last Duchess," both written in the same meter, iambic pentameter rhymed in couplets.

A little learning is a dang'rous Thing;
Drink deep, or taste not the *Pierian* Spring:
There *shallow Draughts* intoxicate the brain,
And drinking largely sobers us again.
—Alexander Pope, "An Essay on Criticism"

That's my last Duchess painted on the wall,
Looking as if she were alive. I call
That piece a wonder, now; Fra Pandolf's hands
Worked busily a day, and there she stands.
—Robert Browning, "My Last Duchess"

Pope's use of end-stopped rhyme emphasizes the meter while Browning's use of run-on lines makes it more subtle. Each poet is making a choice that suits the purpose of the work.

Poor verse, unpoetic, deserving to be called doggerel, results when the rhythm coincides too exactly with the meter. In good verse, the rhythm seldom corresponds exactly with the meter, although it harmonizes with it and may be metrically perfect. The variety within order which thus characterizes good verse is achieved not by violating the metrical pattern but by using more subtle, artistic devices: by shifting the caesura, by using run-on lines as well as end-stopped lines, phrases of light and of heavy syllables, words of varying number of syllables—in a word, by setting the thought pattern in harmony with, but not in identity with, the metrical pattern. Good verse can be regular in meter but must have a varied rhythm. Both Pope and Browning write verse in which the rhythm is artistically varied.

RHYME

Rhyme is identity of sounds at the end of two or more words, with a difference at the beginning. The rhyming must begin on stressed syllables.

Kinds of Rhyme

1 *Masculine*: words having one final stressed syllable rhyming, for example: reign, gain; hate, debate.

2 *Feminine*: words having two or more syllables rhyming (the first of which must be stressed), for example: unruly, truly; towering, flowering.

Note that feminine rhyme is not identical with feminine line-ending, which is the addition of one or two unstressed syllables at the end of a line of verse.

EXAMPLES: Masculine and feminine rhyme

With rue my heart is laden
For golden friends I had,
For many a rose-lipt maiden
And many a lightfoot lad.
　—A. E. Housman, "With rue my heart is laden"

This illustrates masculine rhyme in the second and fourth lines, and feminine rhyme in the first and third lines.

Our lives would grow together
In sad or singing weather.
　—Algernon Swinburne, "A Match"

This illustrates feminine rhyme and feminine ending.

Variations of Rhyme

Imperfect rhyme or slant rhyme refers to words that are not identical in rhyming sounds, for example: heaven and even, geese and bees. (But geese and fleece are perfect rhymes; so are bees and ease.)

Eye rhyme is a name given to the imperfect rhyme of words that look alike but do not sound exactly alike, for example: seven and even, love and prove.

Position of the Rhyming Words

End rhyme is the rhyming of a word at the end of one line with a word at the end of another line. This is the most usual form.

Internal rhyme is the rhyming of a word in the middle of a line with another in the same line, usually at the end of it.

EXAMPLES: End rhyme and internal rhyme

Who will go drive with Fergus now,
And pierce the deep wood's woven shade,
And dance upon the level shore?
Young man, lift up your russet brow,
And lift your tender eyelids, maid,
And brood on hope and fear no more
—William Butler Yeats, "Who Goes with Fergus?"

Yeats' poem illustrates end rhyme in lines one and four, two and five, and three and six.

The splendor falls on castle walls
And snowy summits old in story;
The long light shakes across the lakes,
And the wild cataract leaps in glory.
Blow, bugle, blow, set the wild echoes flying,
Blow, bugle: answer, echoes, dying, dying, dying.
—Alfred Lord Tennyson, "The splendor falls on castle walls"

Tennyson's poem illustrates end rhyme (lines two and four, five and six) and internal rhyme ("falls" and "walls" in line one, and "shakes" and "lakes" in line three).

OTHER POETIC ELEMENTS

Assonance

Assonance is identity of vowel sound in the middle of two or more words in the same line, with a difference at the beginning and end. An example is Tennyson's line: "A hand that can be clasped no more."

Alliteration

Alliteration is identity of sound at the beginning of two or more words in the same line. An example is Poe's line: "What a tale of terror now their turbulency tells." The following do not alliterate: *s* and *sh*; *t* and *th*.

Onomatopoeia

Onomatopoeia refers to words imitating sounds, for example, boom, swish.

The Stanza

The stanza is the unit of metrical discourse somewhat as the paragraph is the unit of prose discourse; poets may, however, let their sentences run from one stanza to another, as Tennyson does here:

from In Memoriam A. H. H.

Dark house, by which once more I stand
    Here in this long unlovely street,
    Doors, where my heart was used to beat
So quickly, waiting for a hand,

A hand that can be clasped no more—
    Behold me, for I cannot sleep,
    And like a guilty thing I creep
At earliest morning to the door.

He is not here; but far away
    The noise of life begins again,
    And ghastly through the drizzling rain
On the bald street breaks the blank day.
        —Alfred Lord Tennyson

Verse is metrical discourse. A verse is one line of metrical discourse. A stanza is a group of verses, that is, of lines, constituting a typical, recurrent unit of a poem; the stanza is usually characterized by a combined metrical and rhyme pattern.

A stanza is described by stating the rhyme pattern and the meter of the verses composing the stanza. It is an important means of variation and of originality in poetic form. Metrical discourse may or may not employ rhyme, assonance, alliteration, etc. When adopted, rhyme usually becomes a part of the pattern of the poem.

Forms of Metrical Discourse

BLANK VERSE

Blank verse is unrhymed iambic pentameter. Iambic pentameter is the most important meter in English. Iambic meter is best adapted to the English language; and pentameter, neither too long nor too short, is least monotonous. Moving the caesura creates a pleasing variety of effect since the caesura does not divide the line into halves. William

Shakespeare and other Renaissance dramatists followed the lead of Christopher Marlowe and used blank verse in their plays. The following excerpt from *Hamlet* is written in blank verse.

> O that this too too sallied flesh would melt,
> Thaw and resolve itself into a dew!
> Or that the Everlasting had not fix'd
> His canon 'gainst self-slaughter! O God, God,
> How weary, stale, flat, and unprofitable
> Seem to me all the uses of this world!
> Fie on 't, ah fie! An unweeded garden
> That grows to seed, thing rank and gross in nature
> Possess it merely.
> —*Hamlet* 1.2.129–137

HEROIC COUPLET
A heroic couplet is iambic pentameter in rhymed couplets. It was a popular verse form in the eighteenth century as it suited the expression of both moral axioms and witticisms.

An Essay on Man: Epistle II

Know then thyself, presume not God to scan;
The proper study of Mankind is Man.
> —Alexander Pope

HEROIC QUATRAIN
A heroic quatrain is iambic pentameter, rhyming abab. In the following poem by Edwin Arlington Robinson, the heroic quatrain adds to the irony in the poem by setting up the expectation of a "happy ending." Robinson effectively uses this form to underline the difference between appearance and reality.

Richard Cory

Whenever Richard Cory went down town,
We people on the pavement looked at him:
He was a gentleman from sole to crown,
Clean favored, and imperially slim.

And he was always quietly arrayed,
And he was always human when he talked;

But still he fluttered pulses when he said,
"Good-morning," and he glittered when he walked.

And he was rich—yes, richer than a king—
And admirably schooled in every grace:
In fine, we thought that he was everything
To make us wish that we were in his place.

So on we worked, and waited for the light,
And went without the meat, and cursed the bread;
And Richard Cory, one calm summer night,
Went home and put a bullet through his head.
                              —Edward Arlington Robinson

ITALIAN SONNET
The Italian or Petrarchan sonnet is written in iambic pentameter. All
sonnets are fourteen lines. In an Italian sonnet, the poem divides into
an octave and sestet, rhyming abbaabba cdecde. The sestet may vary
from this somewhat, for example, cdcdcd, or cdcdee. The form is
named for Francesco Petrarch (1304–1374), who wrote a series of sonnets to a woman named Laura. John Milton used the more classical
form of the sonnet in contrast to earlier English Renaissance writers,
who used an adaptation.

On His Blindness

When I consider how my light is spent
Ere half my days in this dark world and wide
And that one talent which is death to hide,
Lodged with me useless, though my soul more bent
To serve therewith my Maker, and present
My true account, lest he returning chide;
Doth God exact day-labour, light denied?
I fondly ask; but Patience to prevent
That murmur, soon replies, God does not need
Either man's work or his own gifts; who best
Bear his mild yoke, they serve him best. His state
Is kingly. Thousands at his bidding speed
And post o'er land and ocean without rest;
They also serve who only stand and wait.
                              —John Milton

ENGLISH SONNET

The English or Shakespearean sonnet is written in iambic pentameter. It is composed of three heroic quatrains followed by a rhymed couplet. The pattern is abab cdcd efef gg. Shakespeare did not create this adaptation of the sonnet, but he was the most famous writer who used the form.

Sonnet 18

Shall I compare thee to a summer's day?
Thou art more lovely and more temperate.
Rough winds do shake the darling buds of May,
And summer's lease hath all too short a date.
Sometime too hot the eye of heaven shines,
And often is his gold complexion dimmed
And every fair from fair sometimes declines,
By chance or nature's changing course untrimmed;
But thy eternal summer shall not fade
Nor lose possession of the fair thou ow'st,
Nor shall Death brag thou wander'st in his shade,
When in eternal lines to time thou grow'st.
As long as men can breathe and eyes can see,
So long lives this and this gives life to thee.
　　　　　　　　　—William Shakespeare

SPENSERIAN STANZA

The Spenserian stanza has nine lines rhyming ababbcbcc; the first eight lines are of iambic pentameter, but the last is an alexandrine, which is iambic hexameter. The form is named for Edmund Spenser (1552?–1599), who devised it for his epic, *The Faerie Queene*. In the nineteenth century Lord Byron used the form in his long narrative poem, *Childe Harold's Pilgrimage*.

from Childe Harold's Pilgrimage Canto IV, Stanza 1

I stood in Venice, on the Bridge of Sighs,
A palace and a prison on each hand:
I saw from out the wave her structures rise
As from the stroke of the enchanter's wand:
A thousand years their cloudy wings expand
Around me, and a dying Glory smiles
O'er the far times, when many a subject land

Looked to the winged Lion's marble piles,
Where Venice sate in state, throned on her hundred isles!
                                        —George Gordon, Lord Byron

RONDEAU

The rondeau is a lyric poem of fifteen lines divided into three stanzas of no determined length. It rhymes aabba aabR aabbaR (R means refrain). The refrain usually picks up a word, a phrase, or a clause from the opening line of the poem.

In Flanders Fields

In Flanders fields the poppies blow
Between the crosses row on row,
        That mark our place; and in the sky
        The larks, still bravely singing, fly
Scarce heard amid the guns below.

We are the Dead. Short days ago
We lived, felt dawn, saw sunset glow,
        Loved and were loved, and now we lie
        In Flanders fields.

Take up our quarrel with the foe:
To you from failing hands we throw
        The torch; be yours to hold it high.
        If ye break faith with us who die
We shall not sleep, though poppies grow
        In Flanders fields.
                                        —John McCrae

TRIOLET

The triolet rhymes ABaAabAB. (The capital letters stand for lines repeated.) Usually the lines are short, but they may vary in length and rhythm.

Serenade Triolet

Why is the moon
        Awake when thou sleepest?
To the nightingale's tune
Why is the moon
Making a noon

> When night is the deepest?
> Why is the moon
>   Awake when thou sleepest?
>   —George Macdonald

LIMERICK

The limerick is the only indigenous English verse form. It is five lines long, and the dominant foot is the anapest.

Untitled

A diner while dining at Crewe,
Found a rather large mouse in his stew.
Said the waiter, "Don't shout
And wave it about,
Or the rest will be wanting one too."
                —Anonymous

CINQUAIN

The cinquain is a free verse form of twenty-two syllables arranged in five lines. It is modeled on the Japanese *hokku* and *tanka* and was devised by Adelaide Crapsey.

Triad

These be
Three silent things:
The falling snow . . . the hour
Before the dawn . . . the mouth of one
Just dead.
                —Adelaide Crapsey

THE ESSAY

Definition and a Brief History

The essay is difficult to define because it encompasses a wide range of writing. An essay can be broadly defined as a short prose work on a single topic. Michel Eyquem de Montaigne first used the word as a literary term with the publication of his *Essais* in 1650. The French word *essais* means "attempts" and suggests that the works offered by Montaigne were more informal and personal than an academic, philosophical work on the same subject. Francis Bacon, the first English writer to use the term, published a collection of aphorisms on a specific topic but later expanded the concept into longer works that were more developed in length and more personal in tone.

The invention of the periodical in the seventeenth century gave the essay a broad audience. Joseph Addison and Richard Steele wrote lively essays on the manners and quirks of their day and published them in the *Tatler* and the *Spectator*. The names of the periodicals suggest the mode of the writing. Addison and Steele observed and commented in a colloquial manner that invited the reader in as a fellow observer. The American writer Washington Irving wrote a similar type of essay. During the Romantic movement in the early nineteenth century, the essay developed a familiar and informal tone. Writers often used autobiographical material and made it interesting through the use of whimsy, wit, and sentiment. Charles Lamb, William Hazlitt, James Leigh Hunt, and Thomas DeQuincey are the most famous writers of the personal essay of this era.

The American Romantics, Ralph Waldo Emerson and Henry David Thoreau, did not adopt the whimsical tone of the English essayists. Thoreau's nature writing uses autobiography, but the writing is less self-consciously literary. Both Emerson and Thoreau wrote formal essays elucidating their beliefs.

In the Victorian Age, the formal essay was more popular. Long book reviews and essays on historical, scientific, religious, and educational topics were written by Victorian writers including Thomas Carlyle, John Ruskin, Walter Pater, Thomas Huxley, Matthew Arnold, and John Henry Newman.

The difficulty of labeling or defining the essay becomes more apparent when one thinks of Pope's "Essay on Criticism" and "Essay on Man," both of which are poetry. Also, the linear history from Montaigne to the Victorian writers ignores works like Aristotle's *Poetics*, which fit the concept of the essay.

The Familiar Essay

The familiar essay aims to please rather than to inform the reader. It stands between story and exposition, and, like the lyric, it is a subjective communication of thought and feeling colored by the personality and mood of the author. A commonplace, even trivial, subject is made charming, amusing, or piquant when discussed in a chatty, casual, informal manner by a person who is delightfully whimsical, fanciful, belligerent, or even pompous. The style of the familiar essay is an essential element and should have a quality similar to that of a story, full of feeling, imagination, and vivid detail.

The Formal Essay

The style of the formal essay varies depending on the theme, purpose, and audience. It would include philosophical, scientific, religious, and historical writing.

The literary critical essay may, like Aristotle's *Poetics* or Dryden's "Essay of Dramatic Poesy," expound critical principles with a few illustrations for clarity; or it may apply critical principles in evaluating a particular work, as in a book review or a critical study such as a dissertation or a research paper.

A BRIEF GUIDE TO COMPOSITION

Expository writing has as its primary aim to inform, to communicate ideas from writer to reader directly through words, not indirectly through character and situation.[14] Clear expository composition is needed in all walks of life. It is the indispensable tool both of teaching and of being taught. Textbooks, class explanations, lectures, recitations, examinations are expository. So also are such practical matters as describing a process, writing directions, summaries, reports, business letters, social letters. Other, more literary forms of expression include the essay which defines a term or elaborates a general proposition, literary criticism, dramatic and art criticism, the formal and the familiar essay.

Before you begin to write, carefully think through your purpose and the means to gain and hold the interest of the particular readers you address. Find a common ground with them. Begin perhaps with a question or an unexpected statement. Do not write what is obvious, trite, or insipid to *them*—what anyone can see on the run. Penetrate into your subject. Divide[15] and conquer. For example, the ordinary observer sees a drop of blood as a mere blob of red, and he has little to say about it. The expert looking through a microscope sees it divided into plasma and red and white corpuscles that indicate health or disease; she has much to say about it that is enlightening and valuable, pointing to remedies.

To discover the parts of the whole, their relation to each other and to the whole, is a prime means to advance in knowledge and a measure of intellectual power. Discover differences, contrasts. Distinguish meanings. Penetrate likenesses; use comparison, analogy, metaphor, examples. Use other topics of invention, especially definition, cause and effect. The four causes equivalent in rhetoric to *who, what, how, why* help to open up a subject.

Divide, first to penetrate into your subject matter, then to analyze it into its parts, and finally to organize it into a whole having unity, coherence, and emphasis. These three principles should govern the construction of the sentence, the paragraph, and the whole work.

Outline your comparison, determine which topics are coordinate, which subordinate. Every division results in at least two parts. The subordinate topics should add up to the main topic which they divide, and the main topics to the whole composition. What sequence of topics will most effectively promote coherence and emphasis? The position of greatest emphasis is at the end; the next greatest, at the beginning; the least, in the middle. You can also emphasize an idea by repeating it in different words, or in the same words skillfully placed, and by giving it a greater proportion of space. Announce your plan early in your paper and keep your reader reminded of it by clear transitions from one topic to the next.

Clarity is the first requisite of style in expository writing. (Grammatical correctness is a prerequisite.) Help your reader to understand the abstract by providing concrete examples from which the reader can make the abstraction and so comprehend it thoroughly. The intellect is normally reached through the imagination, and therefore, even in workaday prose, figurative language is an effective means to promote both clarity and interest. The writer must achieve clarity and hold interest by avoiding monotony.

Variety is a cardinal principle of effective style. There should be variety in diction through the use of synonyms, in sentence length, in grammatical structure, and in rhythm. Variety in grammatical structure and rhythm are secured through omitting or adding conjunctions, through differences in word order, in sentence beginnings, in the use of simple, compound, and complex sentences, of prepositional and participial phrases, of clauses, of loose and periodic structure, of parallel structure. These structures may be clarified and emphasized by the effective repetition of words.

In the following passage from Washington Irving, the repeated *he must* emphasizes parallel structure, while each verb following it is varied, as is also the length of the clauses. Conjunctions are omitted in one clause and an extra one is added in another. This paragraph is developed by division.

> The stranger who would form a correct opinion of the English character . . . must go forth into the country; he must sojourn in villages and hamlets; he must visit castles, villas, farmhouses, cottages; he must wander through parks and gardens; along hedges and green lanes; he must loiter about country churches; attend wakes and fairs and other rural festivals; and cope with the people in all their conditions and all their habits and humors.

In a periodic sentence the meaning is held in suspense until the end, as in this sentence from Thomas Carlyle's *Sartor Resartus*:

> Considering our present advanced state of culture, and how the Torch of Science has now been brandished and borne about, with more or less effect, for five-thousand years and upwards; how in these times especially, not only the Torch still burns, and perhaps more fiercely than ever, but innumerable Rush-lights, and Sulphur-matches, kindled thereat, are also glancing in every direction, so that not the smallest cranny or doghole in Nature or Art can remain unilluminated—it might strike the reflective mind with some surprise that hitherto little or nothing of a fundamental character, whether in the way of Philosophy or History, has been written on the subject of Clothes.[16]

In the following passage from Stewart Edward White's "On Making Camp," the rhythm reflects the boy's unorganized and scattered efforts.

> Dick was anxiously mixing batter for the cakes, attempting to stir a pot of rice often enough to prevent it from burning, and trying to rustle sufficient dry wood to keep the fire going. . . . At each instant he had to desert his flour sack to rescue the coffee pot, or to shift the kettle, or to dab hastily at the rice, or to stamp out the small brush, or to pile on more dry twigs.

Condense your sentences. Pack much meaning into few words. Use words that are fresh, accurate, vivid, specific—like *torrent, strode, sauntered*. Vivid diction and imagery, effective combinations of words, especially of nouns and verbs, arresting phrases, metaphors, and allusions contribute to compression of style. Verbs, above all, are the key to a vigorous style.

To give your writing life and movement, use vivid verbs in the active voice. Put the verb idea into the verb rather than into an abstract noun with an empty verb like *occur*. Cut out deadwood—needless words that dilute your thought and make your style insipid, dull, wordy. Prefer the specific expression to the general, the positive to the negative, the definite to the indefinite.

NOTES

1 THE LIBERAL ARTS

1. *Trivium* means the juncture of three branches or roads and has the connotation of a "cross-roads" open to all (*Catholic Encyclopedia*, vol. 1, s.v., "the seven liberal arts"). *Quadrivium* means the juncture of four branches or roads.

2. "Endymion," John Keats (1795–1821). "A thing of beauty is a joy forever: / Its loveliness increases: it will never / Pass into nothingness."

3. Excerpts from the Bible are quoted from *The New American Bible* (World Catholic Press, 1987).

4. This motto appears on the seal of the New Program and was first used in 1938. It is still used on printed materials from Saint John's College. The original (1793) and official seal of the college bears the motto "*Est nulla via invia virtuti.*" "No way is impassible to virtue."

5. The expression, "small Latine and lesse Greeke," comes from Ben Jonson's poem, "To the Memory of My Beloved, the Author, Mr. William Shakespeare." Other famous lines from the poem include "Marlowe's mighty line" referring to Christopher Marlowe's use of blank verse in drama, which Shakespeare adopted, and "He [Shakespeare] was not of an age, but for all time!" Ben Jonson (1572–1637) was a colleague and a friend of Shakespeare.

6. Elements of Dionysius Thrax's outline of grammar are still basic components in a language arts curriculum: figures of speech, use of allusion, etymology, analogies, and literary analysis.

7. John Henry Newman (1801–1890), author of *The Idea of a University Defined* and *Apologia pro Vita Sua.*

8. Matthew Arnold (1822–1888), English poet, essayist, and critic. The expression, "sweetness and light," comes from his essay, "Culture and Anarchy."

9. Matthew Arnold, "To a Friend."

10. Aristotle's *Metaphysics* followed his work on physics. In Greek *meta* means "after" or "beyond." In the *Metaphysics* Aristotle defined first principles in understanding reality. Ontology is a branch of metaphysics and deals with the nature of being.

11. The reality of the planet Pluto, whether anyone knew it existed or not, belongs to the realm of metaphysics. Its human discovery brings it into the realm of logic, grammar, and rhetoric.

12. To call rhetoric "the master art of the trivium" is a reminder of the ambivalence associated with the term. During the research for the third edition of the *American Heritage Dictionary*, the editors asked a usage panel if the phrase *empty rhetoric* was redundant. A third of the panel judged the term *empty rhetoric* redundant, and the majority still accepted the traditional meaning of the term. In his work on rhetoric,

Aristotle gives this definition: "Rhetoric may be defined as the faculty of observing in any given case the available means of persuasion" (1.2). However, even in the *Rhetoric*, Aristotle must defend its use. He argues that the use of a good thing for a bad end does not negate the goodness of the thing itself. "And it might be objected that one who uses such power of speech unjustly might do great harm, that is a charge which may be made in common against all good things except virtue, and above all against the things that are most useful, as strength, health, wealth, generalship" (1.1). Aristotle, *The Rhetoric and the Poetics of Aristotle*, trans. W. Rhys Robert [*Rhetoric*] and Ingram Bywater [*Poetics*] (New York: The Modern Library, 1984).

13. John Milton, *Artis Logicae*, trans. Allan H. Gilbert, vol. 2, *The Works of John Milton* (New York: Columbia University Press, 1935), 17.

14. *The Trivium* offers a precision in thinking that is frequently reflected in the use of categories. In this regard Sister Miriam Joseph follows Aristotle, whose writings inform *The Trivium*. *Categories* is among Aristotle's works that present his theory of logic.

2   THE NATURE AND FUNCTION OF LANGUAGE

1. Sister Miriam Joseph's contention that human beings are the only animals to have developed language is compatible with contemporary scientific thought. In "The Gift of Gab," *Discover* 19 (1998): 56–64, Matt Cartmill notes, "The birds and beasts can use their signals to attract, threaten, or alert each other, but they can't ask questions, strike bargains, tell stories or lay out a plan of action." Cartmill's article explores the physiological adaptations that made language possible for *Homo sapiens*. The search implies that the ability to create language made higher-order thinking possible.

2. When an angel chooses to use language, he might sound like Gabriel in Milton's *Paradise Lost*. Here, Gabriel is addressing Satan, who has escaped from hell to find Adam and Eve. Gabriel taunts Satan by suggesting that he deserted his followers because he is too weak to endure the consequences of defying God.

But wherefore thou alone? Wherefore with thee
Came not all hell broke loose? Is pain to them
Less pain, less to be fled? Or thou than they
Less hardy to endure? Courageous chief,
The first in flight from pain, hadst thou alleged
To thy deserted host this cause of flight
Thou surely hadst not come sole fugitive.
　　　—*The Works of John Milton*
　　　(New York: Columbia University Press, 1931), book 4, lines 917–923.

3. Both "temporary" and "permanent" are relative terms in regard to symbols. Usually a larger group of people accept the convention of a permanent symbol. Moreover, permanent symbols, such as chemical formulas or numbers, are incorporated into standardized bodies of knowledge.

4. The answer is DCCCCXXXX, which could be shortened to CMXL. The Roman numerals translate to Arabic numerals as follows: $235 \times 4 = 940$.

5. Esperanto still exists. Basic English does not. Klingon could be included among attempts to create an artificial language. (Todd Moody, Professor of Philosophy at Saint

Joseph's University in Philadelphia; henceforth referred to as *TM*. All other notes were written by the editor.)

6. Although Latin was used in the liturgies of the Catholic Church for centuries, after Vatican II (1962), congregations began using the local language. However, the Vatican still writes in Latin on matters of doctrine. Scientific nomenclature also uses Latin.

7. The metaphysical concepts of matter and form are central to the view of the trivium presented in this book. The concepts become easier to understand as they are woven throughout the text.

8. The International Phonetic Alphabet can be found in most dictionaries.

9. The word *class* means any type of grouping that recognizes those characteristics which the individuals in the group have in common. As used in *The Trivium*, class refers to both species and genus.

10. Designations of species and genus are relative in language, unlike in science. For example, tulip, grass, elm could be designated as a species in that they are all growing things. Tulip could be grouped with daffodil and hyacinth and considered as the species spring bulbs. Spring bulbs could then be labeled in the genus perennial. Annual flowers, perennial flowers, and vegetables could be labeled as the species nonevergreens and then be included in the genus plants, along with evergreens and other nonevergreens. In binomial nomenclature, the system of biological classification invented by Carolus Linnaeus, each species belongs to a genus and then a family, an order, a class, a phylum, and a kingdom. The species is known by the two names (binomial) that designate species and genus, and they do not change unless the scientific thinking on the species changes. A dog is always *Canis familiaris*.

11. One might argue that some animals are capable of some degree of abstraction. For example, if a dog has been hit with one sort of a broom, it will know enough to cower from another kind of broom. At some level the dog has abstracted the concept of "broomness." *TM*

12. Thomas More (1478–1535) was an English statesman, writer, and humanist. He refused to sign the Act of Supremacy, which declared that Henry VIII rather than the Pope was head of the church, and he was beheaded for treason. He is a saint in the Roman Catholic Church.

13. More is defending the Catholic Church's use of statues and pictures in response to the suspicion expressed about them from Protestant writers. More's argument builds on the premise that words are images also and can be less effective than visual images.

14. *The Confutation of Tyndale's Answers*, vol. 8 of *Complete Works of Saint Thomas More*, Louis A. Schuster, Richard C. Morris, James P. Lusardi, and Richard J. Schoeck, eds. (New Haven: Yale University Press, 1973). William Tyndale was a follower of the philosophy of John Wycliffe. He translated part of the scriptures into English, and More, in a letter to Erasmus (June 14, 1532), attacked the translation as "containing mistranslations, worse, misinterpretations of Scriptures." Elizabeth Frances Rogers, ed. *Saint Thomas More: Selected Letters* (New Haven: Yale University Press, 1961), 176.

15. *Praedicamenta* means those characteristics that can be asserted about a subject.

16. To predicate means to state that something is a characteristic of the subject.

17. Thomas Aquinas (1224?–1274) was one of the founders of the medieval intel-

lectual movement known as Scholasticism. A Dominican monk, he reconciled the Christian perspective with the works of Aristotle. The *Summa Theologica* presents an overview or a "summary" of Christian theology.

18. Words used in second intention are not italicized.

19. Extension refers to all the items which a word denotes. For instance, in the sentence "Deciduous trees lose their leaves in autumn," the phrase *deciduous trees* includes all deciduous trees that have existed or will exist.

20. The word *intension* means the sum of attributes contained in a word. *Intention* means the way in which a word is used. In the sentence "Roses lined the walkway of the cottage garden," *roses* is used in first intention because it symbolizes the reality of the flower. Its intension (or meaning) is a flower with prickly stems, pinnately compound leaves, and variously colored petals.

21. The plays and sonnets of William Shakespeare are quoted from *The Riverside Shakespeare* (Boston: Houghton Mifflin, 1974).

22. In the stanza from Gray's "Elegy," *awaits* is the third person, singular form of the verb *await*, so it must have a singular subject. *Hour* is the subject of *awaits*. In normal English word order, the sentence would read, "The inevitable hour awaits the boast of heraldry, the pomp of power, and all that beauty, all that wealth e'er gave."

3   GENERAL GRAMMAR

1. Chapter Three presents grammatical concepts that can be applied to all languages—those that exist now, those no longer used, those not yet invented. General grammar describes the relationship between language and reality. General grammar poses the question: How does the intellect use language to translate reality?

2. Syntactical refers to the arrangement of words into sentences.

3. Ten categories of being which are introduced in Chapter Two are substance and the nine accidents: quantity, quality, relation, action, passion, *when*, *where*, posture, and habiliment.

4. The word *accident* comes from the Latin *accidere*, to happen. Normally, accidents refer to those events that cannot be predicted. In the ten categories of being, however, accidents are those elements that cannot exist alone. Accidents exist in substance. Some accidents are essential to the substance, in the sense of making it what it is, and some accidents are nonessential. Consider the sentence "A person thinks." *Person* is a substance and as such is a reality designated by a noun. *Thinks* is an action (one of the nine accidents within the categories of being) and as such is a reality designated by a verb. The ability to think is an essential quality of human nature, but it is not a quality that exists outside the person.

5. Words such as *anger*, *love*, and *happiness* express emotion, but the intellect abstracts those emotional qualities from experience. The process of abstracting ideas from reality differs from the emotion expressed by an interjection, which expresses an emotion that has not been processed by the mind.

6. Recall that accident refers to those elements that can only exist within substance. By conceiving of the accident as an abstract quality, the thinking being makes the quality into a substantive or noun. The word *love* expresses a reality which can only exist within a being who experiences emotion. The mind's ability to abstract, to conceive of

qualities apart from the reality within which they exist, creates the necessity for abstract nouns.

7. The categories referred to are quantity, quality, relation, action, passion, posture, and habiliment.

8. *The Story of English* written by Robert McCrum, William Cran, and Robert MacNeil (New York: Viking Press, 1986) provides an interesting note on the introduction of abstract substantives into English. "The importance of this cultural revolution [the introduction of Christianity into England by the Benedictine monk Saint Augustine in 597] in the story of the English language is not merely that it strengthened and enriched Old English with new words, more than 400 of which survive to this day, but also that it gave English the capacity to express abstract thought. Before the coming of Saint Augustine, it was easy to express the common experience of life — sun and moon, hand and heart, sea and land, heat and cold — in Old English, but much harder to express more subtle ideas" (55 and 56).

9. Substantives, as defined in general grammar, include phrases as well as single words.

10. Consider the sentence, "Sophia is the girl whom I know from school." In the clause — whom I know from school — *whom* is in the accusative case because it receives the action of *know. Whom* refers to *girl*, which is in the nominative case, but the case of *whom* is determined by its use in the clause.

11. The distinction between *term* and *word* is explained in Chapter Four. Briefly, a term is a word used to communicate a concept.

12. In English grammar words in the dative case are called indirect objects. In the sentence, "Shakespeare gave the world *A Midsummer's Night Dream," world* is an indirect object (dative case) and *A Midsummer's Night Dream* is the direct object (accusative). The dative case follows verbs like *give, tell, deliver*, etc. which predicate a receiver and something to be received. "The quarterback threw Dan the football." The quarterback did not throw Dan; he threw the football, so the football receives the action.

13. *Puero* is the dative singular of *puer* and means "to the boy." *Noctis* is the genitive singular of *nox* and means "of night."

14. A gerund is the *ing* form of a verb used as a noun. Swimming requires strength. Climbing dangerous mountain peaks involves skills, training, and courage. *Swimming, training*, and *climbing* are gerunds.

15. A participle is a word formed from a verb that acts as an adjective. A present participle ends in *ing* and a past participle ends in *d, ed, n, en, t*. If a word ends in *ing*, it needs an auxiliary verb to function as the verb in a sentence: He <u>was riding</u> the waves. *Was* is the auxiliary verb. If an *ing* word modifies a noun, it is a participle. If an *ing* word acts as a noun, it is a gerund. The riding cowboy entertained the crowd (participle). Riding a wave in Hawaii was her dream (gerund). A gerund or a participle still retains some qualities of a verb and so can take an object or be modified by an adverb.

16. This sentence illustrates the importance of correct punctuation. If the sentence were punctuated the following way, "Jane, my uncle's law partner, considers that man to be a scoundrel," then *Jane* would be the subject and *partner* an appositive.

17. The concept of the copula will be explained fully in this chapter.

18. The infinitive form is the word *to* plus the singular, first person, present tense

of the verb, for example, to sing, to joust, to read. The infinitive can be used as a noun, an adjective, or an adverb. In the sentence, "Jane, my uncle's law partner considers that man to be a scoundrel," *to be* is used as an adjective *modifying man*. What kind of man? A (to be a scoundrel) man.

19. Indirect discourse refers to the statements of a speaker which are summarized rather than reported verbatim and enclosed in quotation marks.

20. The predicate is that which is asserted (predicated) of the subject.

21. The Decalogue refers to the Ten Commandments.

22. The nicety of addressing inferiors in the imperative and superiors in the optative is less followed today.

23. Optative refers to wishing, and hortatory, to persuading.

24. The verb *turns*, when it means to change, is another example of an intransitive verb which requires a complement. "He turned angry when he heard the news."

25. An intransitive verb never requires a direct object because a direct object receives the action of the verb, and an intransitive verb does not pass the action along to a complement. An intransitive verb, like *to become* or *to turn*, takes a subjective complement.

26. Under the category of attributives, verbals are considered along with verbs. The other primary attributive is the adjective.

27. Because of its length and because it contains a dependent clause, the following phrase could be mistaken for a sentence, but it is, of course, a fragment. "Swimming so far that she reached the outer limits of the bay and could look back and see the coastline." It could not even be labeled as a gerund phrase or a participial phrase unless it were part of a sentence.

28. In English an infinitive can also perform the function of an adjective (The play to see is *Hamlet*) or of an adverb (Robert joined the health club to lose weight).

29. The gerund has the same form as the present participle.

30. James Harris (1709–1780), author of *Hermes or a Philosophical Inquiry Concerning Language and Universal Grammar.*

31. The punctuation rules in this chapter apply to English grammar.

32. In grammar the word *restrictive* means to limit, define (therefore restrict) meaning. Some grammar books discuss restrictive elements as essential and nonrestrictive as nonessential. In other words, if the modifying clause limits the meaning so that without the clause the sentence does not communicate the correct information, the clause is essential.

33. The statement that substances do not coalesce in nature seems to be contradicted by the chemical elements, which combine to create different substances. Perhaps the distinction that Sister Miriam Joseph intends is based on exactly that point: when substances coalesce in nature, they change and become a new substance.

34. A construct is a composite concept. Frequently, a word symbolizes a concept which combines both natural species with qualifications that are only accidental. Bending is not germane to the species tree.

35. A verbal auxiliary combines with another verb. The words *have* and *has* act as verbal auxiliaries in creating the perfect tenses.

36. When a sentence is converted from active voice to passive voice, the direct object should become the subject. In a sentence with a retained object, the object is "re-

tained" in the position of direct object even though logically it should be the subject. Such an anomaly occurs when the active voice sentence has an indirect object which then becomes the subject of the passive voice sentence.

37. Germanic is the branch of the Indo-European family of languages that contains German and English.

38. *Them* refers to *ends*.

39. Separating the sentence into phrases helps in understanding the meaning. That "that is" is that "that is not" is not.

40. Looking at the grammatical function of the *that's* helps in understanding the meaning. He said that (introduces noun clause) that (a pronominal) *that* (should be italicized because in this case *that* is used in second imposition) that (introduces adjective clause) that (a pronominal) sentence contains is a definitive.

41. The sentence could be read, The boy, said his father, was to blame. Also the sentence could be read, The boy said [that] his father was to blame.

4   TERMS AND THEIR GRAMMATICAL EQUIVALENTS

1. The famous Mrs. Malaprop from *The Rivals* by Richard Brinsley Sheridan would thwart a logician's view of coming to terms. A famous example of her misuse of words is a description of her niece Lydia "as headstrong as an allegory on the banks of the Nile." She calls another character "the very pineapple of politeness." She bristles when someone criticizes her use of language, saying he cast "an aspersion upon my parts of speech." Shakespeare's characters also misuse words either wittingly as when Feste in the role of Sir Topas says, "Out hyperbolical fiend" (*Twelfth Night* 4.2.29), or unwittingly as when Abraham Slender says, "I will marry her, sir, at your request; but if there be not great love in the beginning, yet heaven may decrease it upon your better acquaintance. If you say, 'Marry Her,' I will marry her that I am freely dissolved and dissolutely" (*The Merry Wives of Windsor* 1.1.243–251).

2. In *The Odyssey*, Odysseus often speaks with "winged words" as in the following excerpts. When Odysseus is leaving the Phoenicians, he places a libation cup in Queen Arete's hand and "uttering his voice spake to her winged words. 'Fare thee well, O queen, all the days of thy life, till old age come and death, that visit all mankind'" (Book XIII). When Odysseus returns to Ithaca, he plans the demise of the suitors. "Now the goodly Odysseus was left behind in the hall, devising with Athene's aid the slaying of the wooers, and straightway he spake winged words to Telemachus. 'Telemachus, we must needs lay by the weapons of war, within, every one'" (Book XX). *The Odyssey of Homer*, trans. Richard Lattimore (New York: Harper and Row, 1967). The concept of "winged words" would seem to be the poetic equivalent of "coming to terms." The one addressed correctly understands the reality symbolized by the speaker's language.

3. In considering whether a term is general or empirical, ask whether the term refers to the entire category of beings (general) or to an individual or individuals within that category (empirical). *TM*

4. The reference is to Aristotle's categories of being.

5. The earlier example of the teacher and the pupil used in the section, Absolute and Relative Terms, illustrates that terms that are categorically different can coexist in

the same substance. The term *teacher* includes the categories of substance, quality, relation, and action. In fact, most terms include several categories.

6. This important concept is revisited and becomes clearer in the chapter on syllogisms.

7. The intension of a term is the set of necessary and sufficient conditions for applying the term. *TM*

8. This concept would not apply to mathematical objects. For example, the term prime number is more narrowly specified than the term integer, but both refer to an infinite number of objects. Also, animals with kidneys and hearts is more intensionally specified than animals with hearts, but the two terms are at least empirically coextensive. *TM*

9. Porphyry (232?–305?) was a Neo-Platonic philosopher who tried to bring together the philosophies of Aristotle and of Plato. He wrote an influential book on Aristotle's *Categories*.

10. *Res* means the thing itself, and *aliquid* means the other. The concept is the "whatness" of a reality as opposed to "other" reality.

11. Other philosophers would agree with Sister Miriam Joseph that transcendental concepts elude logical definition, but the attempt to define them has preoccupied philosophers for centuries. The different "theories of truth" are based on different definitions of these concepts. *TM*

12. Efficient cause is the agent and the instruments. Material cause refers to what was used to make something. Formal cause is what kind of thing is being made. Final cause is the purpose that motivated the agent. The four metaphysical causes as defined by Aristotle are treated more fully in Chapter Ten.

13. One might question whether rhetorical definition is definition in a real sense. Explication, exegesis, and textual clarification are better terms than rhetorical definition for the process described. *TM*

14. The examples of virtual or functional division demonstrate that some realities can be thought of as having parts but cannot be actually divided. Also, the unifying principle of the reality exists within each part but not to the same degree.

15. Thomas Aquinas, *Summa Theologica* I, question 76, article 8.

16. Chemists have identified all the naturally occurring elements, but the possibility of synthesizing new elements is open-ended.

17. Positive division is based on empirical investigation and, therefore, is always open to revision. Declaring positive division inferior from a logical point of view reflects a bias against empirical reasoning that goes all the way back to Plato. *TM*

18. The six methods of classifying terms are by the kind of reality signified, by contradictory terms, by concrete and abstract terms, by absolute and relative terms, by collective and distributive terms, by the ten logical categories of terms.

5   PROPOSITIONS AND THEIR GRAMMATICAL EXPRESSION

1. The concepts in this paragraph—a proposition expressing a relation of terms and a proposition consisting of subject, copula, and predicate—refer to the most common type of simple propositions. Compound propositions are introduced later in the book. *TM*

2. Mode refers to the way that terms in a proposition are related. Categorical propositions merely state that this is the way reality is. A modal proposition which is necessary states that this is the way reality must be. A modal proposition which is contingent states that this is the way that reality could be.

3. Obeying a red light implies that one keeps the promises one makes. In applying for a driver's license, one promises to obey the rules that regulate motorists. *TM*

4. Post-classical logic challenges the Aristotelian contention that "a simple proposition is one that asserts the relation of two terms and only two." It is possible to have a simple proposition with more than two terms. Baltimore is between Philadelphia and Washington is a simple proposition, but it has three terms. *TM* (A solution to the problem *TM* poses might lie in re-formulating the proposition thus: "Baltimore is a city located between Philadelphia and Washington." Manipulating the terms this way might not always work, however.)

5. Conversion is the reversal of the subject and the predicate.

6. Leonhard Euler (1707–1783) was a Swiss mathematician.

7. The reference is to the Aristotelian ten categories of being: substance and the nine accidents. In the categories of being, accident includes concepts which would be categorized differently in the predicables. Among the predicables, accident would not include characteristics germane to a species, but within the ten categories of being, accidents do include characteristics germane to a species.

8. Richard McKeon, ed., *The Basic Works of Aristotle* (New York: Random House, 1941).

9. Ibid.

6   RELATIONS OF SIMPLE PROPOSITIONS

1. Dante Alighieri, *The Divine Comedy: The Inferno*, trans. Charles S. Singleton (Princeton: Princeton University Press, 1970).

2. *Rhetoric*, trans. W. Rhys Robert.

3. The place of subalterns relates to the issue that a proposition must refer to something "in fact or fiction." In modern logic, this is called the problem of *existential import*. If I say that "All students who plagiarize are guilty of an offense against their peers," I do not imply that any students are, in fact, plagiarizing. If I assert the subaltern of this, namely the statement "Some students who plagiarize are guilty of an offense against their peers," I do imply that at least one such student really exists. That is, I statements carry a kind of existence commitment that A statements lack. So in cases such as these many would claim that the truth of the I proposition doesn't follow from the truth of the A proposition. *TM*

4. Note that in the example, nonstarchy-food, there is a hyphen between *starchy* and *food*, unlike the first example. The hyphen makes the expression one part of speech and a true contradictory term. Nonstarchy-food is equivalent in meaning to anything that is not starchy food.

5. In this example, the word *low* is used in two different meanings or intensions resulting in the material fallacy of equivocation, which is fully explained in Chapter Nine.

7   THE SIMPLE SYLLOGISM

1. Modern logic recognizes that there is valid deductive reasoning that cannot be captured by syllogisms. *TM*

2. Sister Miriam Joseph explains later in the chapter why she chooses this order: the minor premise, the major premise, the conclusion. Many logic texts use the order: the major premise, the minor premise, the conclusion. Either is correct.

3. Sister Miriam Joseph is making the distinction here between the formal aspects of a syllogism or enthymeme and the material aspects. If a syllogism or enthymeme follows the rules of logic, a valid syllogism or enthymeme results. Validity is a relationship between premises and conclusions such that if the premises are true, the conclusion cannot be false. Analyzing a syllogism formally does not involve analyzing the truth or falsity of the premises. It is possible to have a valid syllogism with false premises and a true conclusion, or with false premises and a false conclusion, but never with true premises and a false conclusion. *TM*

4. Thomas Huxley, "A Liberal Education and Where to Find It," *Autobiography and Essays* (New York: Gregg Publishing Co., 1919), 181–210.

5. Although the epicheirema in this example has stood the test of time as a logical argument, one might question if the nutritional advice has stood the test of time as well. Recall the "ice cream is nourishing food" example from Chapter One.

6. Marcus Tullius Cicero (106–43 B.C.), Roman statesman, orator, and philosopher.

7. John Stuart Mill (1806–1873) advanced this argument in *System of Logic*, published in 1843.

8. Nathaniel Hawthorne (1804–1864), author of *The House of the Seven Gables*, *The Scarlet Letter*, and other novels. Famous short stories include "Young Goodman Brown" and "My Kinsman Major Molineux."

9. Charles Dickens (1812–1870), author of *A Tale of Two Cities*, *David Copperfield*, *Hard Times*, *A Christmas Carol*, and many other famous novels.

10. Although in other parts of this book, the number of valid moods is noted as eleven, this list of nineteen includes duplicates of moods that are valid in more than one figure.

11. In Dorothy L. Sayers's mystery novel, *Strong Poison*, Lord Peter Wimsey quotes this mnemonic to Harriet Vane. He sees it as a proof of his diligence as a lover since he learned it to honor a woman named Barbara, who had spurned him.

12. Thomas Fuller, "The General Artist," *The Holy State and the Profane State*, ed. Maximilian Walter (New York: A. M. S. Press, 1966), 73.

8   RELATIONS OF HYPOTHETICAL AND DISJUNCTIVE PROPOSITIONS

1. In modern logic, this type of disjunctive proposition is called the exclusive disjunctive. Modern logic allows for the inclusive disjunctive, also, in which the disjunction is true if at least one disjunct is true. For example, "You can buy either sheets or towels in that store" would still be true if you could buy both. The exclusive disjunctive, on the other hand, requires that the choices be mutually exclusive. *TM*

2. *Rhetoric*, trans. W. Rhys Roberts.

3. In modern logic a *sine qua non* hypothetical proposition can also be represented as an "if and only if" proposition, which is called a biconditional. Thus, "if and only if a substance turns blue litmus paper red is it an acid." *TM*

4. *The Confutation of Tyndale's Answers*, vol 8 of *Complete Works of Saint Thomas More*, eds. Louis A. Schuster, Richard C. Marius, James P. Lusardi, and Richard Schoeck (New Haven: Yale University Press, 1973).

5. The first rule is called *modus ponens*, meaning "way of affirmation." The second rule is called *modus tollens*, "way of negation." *TM*

6. *Ponendo tollens. Ponendo*, from *ponere*, to posit, and *tollens*, from *tollere*, to remove. The meaning is "to posit the negative." *Tollendo ponens* means "to negate the positive."

7. *To hale* means "to force to go." The expression "hauled into court" is also correct since *to haul* means "to drag forcibly."

8. Empson was an employee of Bishop Morton, who was a mentor of Thomas More. This type of dilemma in which the accused is guilty no matter how the dilemma is resolved is also called Morton's Fork. Bishop Morton probably wrote the biography of Richard III, often credited to Thomas More, which vilifies Richard and is the source for Shakespeare's portrait.

9   FALLACIES

1. Plato, *Gorgias*, in *Plato: Complete Works*, trans. Daniel J. Zeyl, ed. John M. Cooper (Indianapolis: Hackett Publishing, 1997), 791–869.

2. Surely, this explanation of the "feed a cold" conundrum solves one of life's minor mysteries.

3. Thomas Wilson (1528?–1582), author of *The Rule of Reason*.

4. If this sentence were punctuated correctly, light would be written as *light*, and the italics would serve as the clue that the word is not being used as a symbol for reality. Quotation marks can also serve this function.

5. In "Man is rational," all the terms are used in first imposition, and in first intention. In "Rational is a differentia," *rational* is used in second intention. In "*Differentia* is a polysyllable," *differentia* is used in zero imposition. In "*Polysyllable* is a noun," *polysyllable* is used in second imposition. In "Therefore, *man* is a noun," *man* is used in second imposition.

6. This is an important point, and it extends to the fact that one cannot disprove a conclusion by showing that an argument is invalid; it may be supported by other, valid arguments. *TM*

7. A variation on this fallacy is the "straw man fallacy." This is committed when one refutes a position that is not the same as the one the other disputant has advanced but some weaker substitute for it. *TM*

8. Some logicians distinguish between abusive *ad hominem*, which deals with attacks on the character and conduct of persons, and circumstantial *ad hominem*, which attempts to refute an argument by pointing out the identity or interests of the people who hold it. For instance, "This study is worthless because it was funded by a special interest group." *TM*

9. The form of this fallacy is: There is no proof of *p*, therefore *not-p*. For example, money does not bring happiness; therefore poverty does. *TM*

10   A BRIEF SUMMARY OF INDUCTION

1. Psychology and the philosophy of mind both deal with how we obtain concepts and judgments from the real world, but they do so in different ways. Sister Miriam Joseph's approach leans toward the philosophical. *TM*

2. Sister Miriam Joseph's statement that "there is no correct formula of inference by which a general proposition can be derived as a conclusion from empirical premises" means that there is no deductive way to draw a general conclusion from empirical data. Her solution, by calling induction an intuition, comes down to the notion that induction is a form of direct, noninferential knowledge. *TM*

3. Most logicians say that induction *is* a form of inference, different from deduction, but there is ongoing, scholarly deliberation on the nature of induction. The following proposition illustrates the problem: All unsupported objects fall toward the center of the earth. How do we know that proposition is true? Strictly speaking, the most we can say is that all unsupported objects *observed so far* fall toward the center of the earth. The second statement says less than the first. There is no valid deductive inference from "All unsupported objects observed so far fall" to "All unsupported objects fall." That is the problem of induction. *TM*

4. Modern logicians would question whether "enumerative" induction qualifies as induction. *TM*

5. In scientific reasoning, the only one of Aristotle's four causes that is still considered is efficient cause. *TM*

6. William Stanley Jevons, *Elementary Lessons in Logic* (New York: Macmillan, 1914), 241.

7. In Chapter Seven the explanation of analogical inference relates to the method of elimination in scientific reasoning. There must be selection achieved through other scientific methods for the process to be effective.

8. One reason that mere elimination provides no certitude is that there is generally no certitude that all the relevant disjuncts have been discovered. *TM*

9. Sister Miriam Joseph's complaint against logical positivism has some justice in it. Logical positivism is now generally regarded as defunct. *TM*

10. Modern logic still deals with propositions that are true or false. Furthermore, syllogisms, conversion, obversion, and the like have not vanished from modern logic. Rather, they are subsumed under more general forms and principles as special cases. *TM*

11   COMPOSITION AND READING

1. Sister Miriam Joseph is referring to Aristotle's and Cicero's topics of invention which include cause and effect. We analyze the plot, the organizational structure of a story, by investigating the workings of cause and effect in the story. The topics of invention are in Chapter Six.

2. Sister Miriam Joseph's view of literature as a moral guide follows from the classical sources she is following as well as her own worldview. Plato attacked poetry on four points: poets use inspiration, not reason; poetry teaches the wrong things; poetry because it is imitation is two steps removed from reality; poetry encourages the emotions of the audience. Aristotle addresses the moral benefits of poetry in response to Plato's view.

3. Quintilian (first century A.D.) is the author of *Institutio Oratoria*, which outlines the education of an orator.

4. Obversion, the logical equivalent to litotes, is explained in Chapter Six. In obversion the predicate changes in quality from negative to affirmative or affirmative to negative. The predicate changes to the contradictory of the original. For example, the A proposition "Jane is known for her brilliance" could be obverted to "Jane is not unknown for her brilliance."

5. An enthymeme is a syllogism logically abridged by the omission of one proposition. It contains three terms and can be logically expanded into a full syllogism. For example, "You are talking during the film, and you should be removed from the theater." The missing proposition is "People who talk during films should be removed from the theater." It is the major premise of the syllogism.

6. A disjunctive syllogism asserts that of two propositions, one must be true. For example, "Either Mary is lying or she committed the murder." A hypothetical syllogism asserts the dependence of one proposition on another. For example, "If the environment is protected, water quality will be good."

7. A dilemma is a syllogism which has for its minor premise a disjunctive proposition, for its major premise a compound, hypothetical proposition, and for its conclusion either a simple or a disjunctive proposition. For example, "Either death is a state of nothingness and utter unconsciousness, or it is a migration of the soul from this world to another. If you suppose that there is no consciousness, death will be an unspeakable gain, for eternity is then only a single night and it like to the sleep of him who is undisturbed even by dreams, and not only a private man but even a great king will judge that better than other days and nights. If death is the journey to another place where all the dead are, where the pilgrim is delivered from the professors of justice in this world to find true judges there, where a man may converse with Orpheus, Hesiod, Homer, Ajax, Odysseus, and numberless others, death will be a gain. Therefore there is great reason to hope that death is a good." —Socrates in Plato's *Apology*

8. The topics of invention are definition, division, genus, species, adjuncts, contraries, contradictories, similarity, dissimilarity, comparison, cause, effect, antecedent, consequent, notation, conjugates, testimony.

9. Epithet is a descriptive word or phrase used to characterize a person, place, or thing. In a literary work, the phrase becomes so associated with what is described that it is often used as a substitute. Epics provide many examples of this practice.

10. The efficient cause is the agent and the instruments; the final cause, the purpose which motivated the agent; the material cause, the substance used; and the formal cause, the kind of thing made.

11. Andrew Marvell (1621–1678) constructs "To His Coy Mistress" as a mixed hypothetical syllogism. The first stanza poetically presents the following view of reality: If courtship should take ages, it means that time is endless. The second stanza, presented

here, sublates the consequent by poetically stating that time is finite. The third stanza presents the conclusion: Courtship cannot take ages. Part of the final stanza is used to illustrate the simile.

12. Lucretius (96?–55? B.C.) was a Roman philosopher whose *"De Rerum Natura"* (On the nature of things) presents a scientific view of the universe.

13. An ictus is slanted, like a backslash, and a macron is a straight horizontal line. Either an ictus or a macron is placed over the stressed syllable.

14. Earlier in the chapter, Sister Miriam Joseph explains Aristotle's premise that expository writing is immediate and that poetics is mediate, that is, communication occurs through characters and situations.

15. Chapter Four explains division as a tool and lists the categories of division: logical, quantitative, physical, virtual, metaphysical, and verbal.

16. Thomas Carlyle, *Sartor Resartus* (Berkeley: University of California Press, 2000), 3.

Sister Miriam Joseph (1898–1982)

by John Pauley

Sister Miriam Joseph, C.S.C., seemed destined to be involved in the arts of discourse from her earliest days. She was born Agnes Lenore Rauh in Glandorf, Ohio, on December 17, 1898. Her father, Henry Francis Rauh, known as the "Professor," was a church organist, founder of a building and loan company, superintendent of schools, journalist, and publisher and owner of a newspaper. Perhaps influenced by her father's vocation, but definitely inspired by a lecture delivered by A. P. Sandles, editor of the *Putnam County Sentinel*, during her senior year in high school, Agnes decided to study journalism at Saint Mary's College.

When she arrived at Saint Mary's in the fall of 1916, Agnes found that she could not take a journalism class that semester; in fact, there were no journalism courses scheduled for that term. Disappointed but not deterred, Agnes lobbied the administration, and two weeks into the semester her determination paid off. She gladly transferred from astronomy into a newly created journalism course. Agnes passionately believed that journalism and American society would benefit from the presence of more women. In her essay "Women and Journalism" (1919), she wrote, "[The profession of journalism] long ago recognized that women have minds, perhaps in several aspects different from men's minds but of equal merit and that their ideas and works are not to be despised. Moreover, women have special aptitudes peculiar to themselves, whereby they fill a definite need in certain spheres of thought and endeavor." Sounding the alarm for women to become involved in journalism she warned, "[O]ne cannot estimate the danger, the harm, that comes from insidious propaganda, which, under the cloak of high-sounding new movements, threatens to undermine the most fundamental principles of social and family life." Women must take up the pen, for, "[I]f this propaganda succeeds in winning the support of the women of our country, it has secured the stronghold because an entire people derives its ideals from the mothers." The battle must be waged and the "most effectual means to combat this danger is to turn the enemies' own weapons against them: to fill the magazines with articles based on the right principles." She concluded the essay with a call for "Catholic writers, especially those who have had efficient technical training in colleges of Journalism, along with the study of modern problems in economics, politics, ethics, and sociology, from a Catholic and Christian point of view," arguing that such writers were best suited to stem the tide of societal ill.

The desire for advocacy journalism was not the only passion that burned in Agnes' soul. Sensing the call of God, she entered the novitiate of the Sisters of the Holy Cross at Saint Mary's in September 1919. The following August she was received as a novice, and within a year was teaching in a middle school. Sister Miriam Joseph was taking steps to fulfill the call she herself had issued in 1919. She would be directly involved in the process of training writers who would articulate "the right principles." Teaching during the school year (St. Joseph's School, Pocatello, Idaho, 1921-1923; St. Joseph's Academy, South Bend, 1923-1927) and being a student herself in the summer, Sister completed her course work at Saint Mary's and graduated with a Ph.B. in Journalism in 1923; in 1927, she was awarded an M.A. in English from the University of Notre Dame. Miriam Joseph solidified her commitment to the Sisters of the Holy Cross and to their ministry by making her first profession of vows in 1922 and her final profession in 1925.

Continuing in a now-familiar pattern, Sister spent the next few years teaching during the school year (Saint-Mary-of-the-Wasatch Academy and College, Salt Lake City, Utah, 1927-1930; Saint Angela's Academy, Morris, Illinois, 1930-1931) and continuing her own studies in the summers at Notre Dame. Sister Miriam Joseph returned to her alma mater in 1931 and assumed the position of Assistant Professor in the English Department. She had traveled full circle: the call she had issued in 1919 for well-trained Catholic writers would now be her charge. In 1931, Miriam Joseph was assigned five sections of freshman English: "College Rhetoric." During the next four years, she continued teaching Rhetoric and courses in "General Literature," "Grammar and Composition," and "Composition and Rhetoric."

In the spring of 1935, Sister Miriam Joseph's life and teaching career took a momentous turn. On Friday, March 8, Dr. Mortimer Adler, from the University of Chicago, delivered a lecture at Saint Mary's entitled "The Metaphysical Basis of the Liberal Arts." According to the campus newspaper, *The Static*, Adler contended that college students of the day "know little or nothing about . . . the liberal arts." Adler "centered his discussion on the three arts of language, pointing out that whereas among the Greeks and the Medievalists their integral unity and harmony was always recognized and preserved, since the fifteenth century specialization

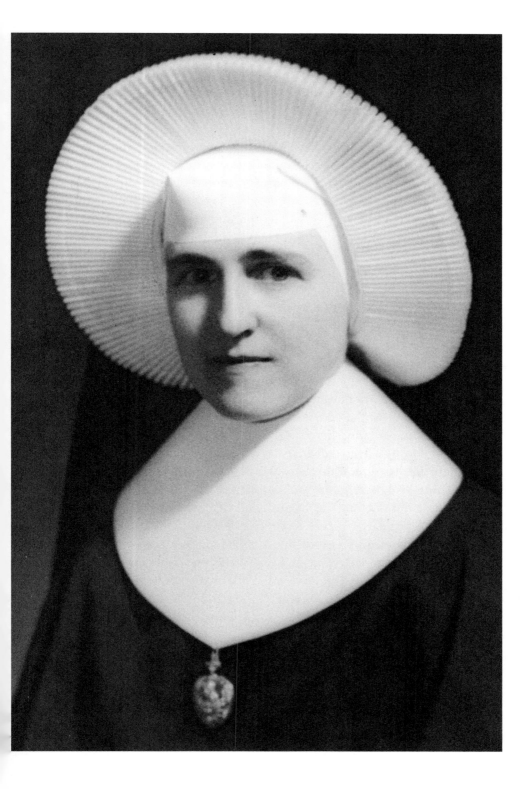

has contrived to separate them to the consequent deterioration and even the ruination of their educative function — to develop the power of the individual to read, write, and speak — in other words, to acquire mastery over the tools of learning." Following the lecture, Father William Cunningham, C.S.C., Professor of Education at Notre Dame, asked Adler if it would be feasible to revive the united Trivium again in the freshman English class. Years later, Sister Miriam Joseph wrote that when the question was asked "[m]any in the audience turned and looked at me." Whether Sister Madeleva, President of Saint Mary's, turned to see Sister Miriam Joseph's reaction to the query, we do not know. What we do know is that Sisters Madeleva, Miriam Joseph, and Maria Theresa (then teaching at Bishop Noll High School, Hammond, Indiana) spent Saturdays in April and May of that year studying with Adler in Chicago. Traveling to Columbia University in New York, Miriam Joseph and Maria Theresa continued their studies with Adler through the summer.

In the fall of 1935, Sister Miriam Joseph returned to Saint Mary's to teach for the first time a course that was to become a college institution, "The Trivium." Required of all freshmen, the course met five days a week for two semesters. As Sister Miriam Joseph saw it, the course was designed to train students how to think correctly, read with intelligence, and speak and write clearly and effectively. Since no existing textbook was adequate for the course Sister wrote her own. *The Trivium in College Composition and Reading* was first published in 1937.

For the next twenty-five years, all freshmen at Saint Mary's were taught the trivium with Sister Miriam Joseph bearing much of the teaching load herself. She was absent from campus from 1941 to 1945, pursuing her doctorate in English and Comparative Literature at Columbia University. She was awarded a Ph.D. in 1945, and her dissertation, "Shakespeare's Use of the Arts of Language," was published in 1947 by Columbia University Press. Sister's teaching and research all pointed in the same direction. In the first chapter of her dissertation she wrote, "The extraordinary power, vitality, and richness of Shakespeare's language are due in part to his genius, in part to the fact the unsettled linguistic forms of his age promoted to an unusual degree the spirit of free creativeness, and in part to the theory of composition then prevailing." She continued, "It is this last which accounts for those characteristics of Shakespeare's language which differentiate it most from the language of today . . . The difference in habits of thought and in methods of developing thought results in a corresponding difference in expression principally because the Renaissance theory of composition, derived from the ancient tradition, was permeated with formal logic and rhetoric, while ours is not." Shakespeare had the benefit of being trained in the trivial arts — modern students did not. Sister Miriam Joseph was attempting to correct that error.

Remaining active on all fronts of academic life, Sister Miriam Joseph became chair of the English Department at Saint Mary's in 1947, a position she held until 1960. She was a regular participant in regional and national conventions of learned societies and published a number of articles including, "The Trivium in Freshman English" *The Catholic Educational Review* (35, 1937); "Why Study Old English?" *College English* (3, 1942); "The Trivium in College" *The CEA Critic* (10, 1949); "Orthodoxy in *Paradise Lost*" *Laval Théologique et Philosophique* (8, 1952); Discerning the Ghost in *Hamlet*" PMLA (76, 1961); "A 'Trivial' Reading of *Hamlet*" *Laval Théologique et Philosophique* (15, 1962); and "*Hamlet*, a Christian Tragedy" I (54, 2, Pt. 1, 1962). While publishing almost thirty book reviews and lecturing on other college campuses, she continued to teach and teach with passion. Sister Miriam Joseph retired from teaching at Saint Mary's in 1965, was granted emeritus status in 1968, and was awarded an honorary doctorate in 1969 when Saint Mary's celebrated its 125th anniversary.

Sister Miriam Joseph Rauh died on November 11, 1982. In a letter to the Saint Mary's faculty after her death, Vice President and Dean of Faculty William Hickey wrote that Sister was "perhaps the most distinguished scholar to be identified with the College in this century." But perhaps the greatest tribute came from Mary Frances Schaff Meekison (SMC '40), who wrote in the Saint Mary's *Courier*, "In class her brilliance and zeal in teaching were quite apparent." Sister "Mickey Jo" was a "taskmistress and a perfectionist," inspiring "even the most reluctant student to stretch her intellect and to strive toward perfection." Meekison concluded her letter to the *Courier* by writing, "Though I was only an average student, Sister believed that I could stretch not only my intellect, but also my writing ability. Because of her faith, I have been lucky enough to find my by-line in print many times over. I am certain there are hundreds of alumnae out there who could make even stronger testimonials than mine." So, Agnes Lenore Rauh, Sister Miriam Joseph, C.S.C., aspiring journalist turned teacher and Shakespeare scholar, accomplished her goal. She influenced a generation of women to think carefully, to read thoughtfully, and to write and speak "the right principles" eloquently.

Index